CATHOLIC
APOLOGETICS
TODAY

CATHOLIC APOLOGETICS TODAY

Answers to Modern Critics

Does It Make Sense to Believe?

By
Father William G. Most

*"Let your speech be always in grace
seasoned with salt: that you may know
how you ought to answer every man."*
—Colossians 4:5-6

TAN BOOKS AND PUBLISHERS, INC.
Rockford, Illinois 61105

TAN BOOKS AND PUBLISHERS, INC.
P.O. Box 424
Rockford, Illinois 61105
1986

"Always be ready to give a defense to anyone who asks of you a reason for the hope that is in you."

—1 Peter 3:15

CONTENTS

Chapter 1

FOR OPENERS

How do some people come to have faith? Do they just decide to believe without any reason for believing, as if they took a leap and jumped up onto a cloud? If so, then their faith would have as solid a foundation as a cloud! That method is not for a rational person. It is for such unreasonable and unreasoning ones as Kierkegaard, the Danish Existentialist, who says faith is precisely a leap;[1] or Bultmann, grandfather of Form Criticism, who thinks it even *sinful* to want to have any basis for faith. Rather, says Bultmann, the man of faith, "has nothing in his hand on which to base his faith. He is suspended in mid-air."[2]

The Catholic Church does not ask for or even permit such unreasonable thinking. Vatican Council I, quoting *Romans* 12:1, taught that our faith should be a "reasonable service of God," not an irrational leap.[3] The First Epistle of St. Peter says the same. "Always be ready to give a defense to anyone who asks of you a reason for the hope that is in you."(*1 Peter* 3:15).

So we are going to start out on a search. There will be two stages: first reason, then faith. That is, before anyone can or should believe, he should go through a process of discovery based on reason, not on faith. We will face all problems squarely, including the fact that some today deny God, deny miracles, and even—believe it or not—deny the very possibility of writing any reliable history. Only after these necessary preliminaries will we look for the rational foundations for faith.

1

After this basic work, we will consider the claims of other religions including Protestantism, Judaism, and non-Christian religions.

Finally, in the appendices, we will answer objections about specific teachings of the Church.

Chapter 2

CAUSES OF TEENAGE DOUBT

Although written for the young, others will find this chapter valuable for their own information or to use the data to help a young person who does not have an opportunity to read this.

A strange phenomenon appears in most young people sometime near the end of high school. It starts then, and lasts varying lengths of time—sometimes for years—and is of varying severity.

The symptoms? The young person finds his formerly solid religious beliefs beginning to wobble. He is no longer sure of them; and he is hesitant to ask an older person, for he is definitely inclined not to trust the opinions of any older person. So he is forced to be miserable all by himself, unless of course he talks to others of the same age and finds them in the same quandary, but equally without any way to get out.

We said the length of time this trouble lasts is varying; some never fully emerge from it. That brings us to see the first of the reasons for the problem. When we were children, we simply believed what older people told us. Really, that is all that could be done at an early age. But then as we grow up, we begin to want to know for ourselves, to be able to give a *reason* for what we believe.

This process is not only quite normal, it can even be a good thing, *provided that* it is carried all the way to its conclusion. If not, a person may lack stability indefinitely, perhaps for the rest of his life. This process is, then, the normal changeover from the child to the adult pattern of beliefs. It is proper, because adults should not act like children and should be able to give a reason for their beliefs.

No one can be quite comfortable between the shore of childhood belief and the shore of solidly grounded adult faith. For, there one is neither fish nor fowl. He lacks both kinds of security and so he flounders. Eventually he may just give up trying, but yet never achieve the solidity he reasonably wants. Worse, if some great test of faith comes, he may not have the solid basis on which to endure.

Obviously, the rational thing for a young—or even older—person to do in such a quandary is to ask for help from those who are able to give it. Sadly, this is not so often done. First, the young persons are disinclined to think older persons could possibly know anything; second, many older persons never completed the rational process themselves, and are really in no position to help.

There is a second very potent reason for this "at-sea" condition. Young people are apt to have their *somatic resonance* in a state of flux. Somatic resonance is a common term in psychology. It is not hard to understand. A major psychologist of our times, T. V. Moore, told in his last book of a case he met when he was a practicing psychiatrist in Washington, D.C.[4] A patient came in for help who suffered from manic-depressive psychosis. He told Dr. Moore he was losing his faith. Moore reports that the man really was not losing his faith; instead, the process of the disease was interfering with his somatic resonance to faith.

Here is the way it works. We are, of course, made up of body and soul, matter and spirit. These elements are so closely joined as to add up to one person. As a result of that union if we have a condition on either side, body or soul, then for smooth running (not for mere survival of the condition) we ought to have a parallel condition on the other side. That parallel is called a *resonance.* When the resonance is on the side of the body—the more common combination—then it is called *somatic* resonance, from a Greek word meaning "bodily."

So, then, faith is obviously on the side of the spirit. But faith needs—not for mere survival, but for normal function—a resonance on the bodily side. The process (probably bad biochemistry) of the disease in Moore's patient interfered with the somatic resonance to faith. [The result was that faith was not rejected, but neither could it function normally.] Hence, the poor man thought he was losing his faith.

Now, young people can have a parallel problem. They enter a time of life when there are great bodily changes in the glandular system, especially at the start of sexual functioning. They have not yet had time to learn to live with these changes, to come to terms with them. As a result, their somatic resonance to many things is in a state of flux, so that faith lacks its normal resonance. No wonder faith tends to wobble, to seem to have no foundation.

Obviously, if a young person could only realize what is going on inside him and see that he is being hit by a dramatic changing process, he would be very relieved. We do not say he would quickly find everything easy. But he could step outside himself and see himself objectively. Then at least he would not be so mystified by what he cannot help feeling.

The two conditions we have just explained are clearly part of the process of growing up. As such, they have *always* affected people, not just in our day. But *today,* young and old alike are affected by still a third influence: the immense upheaval in the Church and the many claims that everything has changed. It is no wonder many are uncomfortable with their Faith.

So we are going to set out upon a search—to prove that there is help, there is a solid, rational basis for faith.

Chapter 3

WONDERS NEVER CEASE

"It is impossible to use electric light and wireless . . . and at the same time to believe in the New Testament world of spirits and miracles."[5] The writer is one we have met before, R. Bultmann, founder of New Testament Form Criticism. Modern man is so sophisticated and smart, according to Bultmann, that he can no longer accept miracles.

He explains, "A miracle—i.e. an act of God—is not visible or ascertainable like worldly events."[6] In fact, "The conception of miracles as ascertainable processes . . . makes belief in miracles (or rather *superstition*) susceptible to the *justifiable* criticisms of science."[7] Yet, on the other hand, he insists, "When worldly happenings are viewed as a closed series . . . there is certainly no room for any act of God. But this is just the paradox of faith: it understands an ascertainable event in its context in nature and history as the act of God . . . This is the only genuine faith in miracles."[8]

If the reader finds the above somewhat confusing, he is probably grasping Bultmann correctly. What Bultmann really says is that modern man is too smart to accept miracles. If *science* cannot explain something, it would be *superstition* to call it a miracle. But something science *can* explain can be a miracle.

It is impossible to be more perverse. Really, Bultmann is showing the kind of faith we rejected in our opening chapter, a faith based on nothing at all, a faith as solid as a cloud.

But we, on the other hand, insist on being rational. When we begin our study of the Gospels, we will find accounts of miracles, so it is good right now to ask: Can we believe in miracles?

The answer is: No. For we do not have to *believe* in miracles—rather, we see and accept as a miracle something that has no other conceivable explanation but the hand of God.

Did such things ever happen? The easiest way to find the answer is to ask: Do they still happen? Let us proceed, therefore, and see.

Madame Biré, a French woman, became blind in February 1908. Medical examination showed blindness was due to atrophy of the papilla; in other words, the optic nerve was withered at the point where it enters the eye. Obviously, there was organic reason for her blindness. No one can see with a withered optic nerve. She was taken to Lourdes, the great shrine at which it is reported the Blessed Virgin appeared in 1858. On August 5, 1908, Madame Biré received Holy Communion at the Grotto of Lourdes. At 10:15 a.m., the priest who was carrying the Blessed Sacrament in procession passed beside her. Madame Biré at once saw the statue of the Blessed Virgin.

She was taken at once to the permanent Medical Bureau at Lourdes where doctors are always available. In fact, any doctor, even an atheist, is permitted to go there and examine cases to his heart's content. (One of these, Dr. Alexis Carrel, came to scoff, but left a convert.[9]) Dr. Lainey, an oculist, examined her. What he found was even more astonishing than a miraculous cure: She could read even the smallest letters of a newspaper, *but the optic nerve was still withered!* A month later another eye examination by three specialists found that the nerve had been restored.[10] No possible suggestion nor any natural means can make a dead, withered optic nerve functional!

In passing, we note that a case such as this is not only a miracle, it also proves the presence of Christ in the Blessed Sacrament, for it was when the Host passed her that she was cured instantly. It also proves the claims of the Church with regard to the Eucharist, that It is the real Presence of Christ—His Body, Blood, Soul and Divinity.

We often hear claims of cures by faith healers and similar persons. There is no careful checking on these; but some fakes have been detected. The supposed cures are generally of maladies open to the power of suggestion. The mind can do some remarkable things. But no one would dare to claim suggestion could restore a withered nerve.

Some have proposed that Jesus in His earthly life worked miracles by suggestion, or even, that He had found some marvelous natural means not known to others. The claims are false. First, He said He did things by the power of God. If it were merely by natural means, He would have been a liar and a fake. But His whole life, His lofty moral tone and His teaching contradict that. And this cure of Madame Biré— worked by His presence in the Blessed Sacrament— could not have been accomplished by natural means of any kind. For no natural process can make a nerve operative while still withered. Our next cases, too, are far beyond any natural process, as we shall see.

Around 700 A.D., in the church of St. Legonziano in Lanciano, Italy, a priest was celebrating Mass. He began to doubt the Presence of Jesus in the Host and chalice. Then it happened. Most of the Host changed to flesh (the center kept the appearance of bread), and the Liquid in the chalice became five clots of blood. The treasure was guarded over the centuries by monks.

Finally, in November 1970, the authorities of the Church gave permission for a study. A team of biological and medical scientists gathered. They took small samples of the flesh and the blood and put them through a full battery of tests. They found that the flesh really was human flesh, a part of the heart, and the clots were human blood. The proteins in the blood were the normal ratio contained in fresh blood. Other features of the chemistry were normal. The type of the blood in the clots was the same as the blood in the flesh. Yet, no trace of any preservative or embalming agent was found. Obviously, flesh and blood would ordinarily begin to decay in a day or two—yet after so many centuries, and right up to today, they have not decayed.[12]

So now we ask Bultmann: What natural law can change bread and wine into human flesh and blood and keep them without decay, without preservatives, for centuries, so that every scientific test can verify they really are human flesh and blood?

Here is one more case. On December 9, 1531, an Aztec Indian, Juan Diego, claimed he had seen the Virgin Mary in the countryside near Mexico City. He told his Bishop, who was quite properly skeptical. The Bishop told him that if it happened again to ask the Blessed Virgin for a sign. On December 12 she came again, and Juan did ask for a sign. She told him to pick some roses growing nearby, which ordinarily would not be found there in December. He put them into his cloak and went to see the Bishop. But the Bishop did not look at the flowers; he kept staring at the cloak. Juan had not noticed, but the cloak now held a large, full-color image of the apparition Juan had seen.

On November 14, 1921 a powerful bomb hidden in a vase of flowers was placed before the image. The bomb exploded and did extensive damage, heavily twisting a large metal crucifix (which I myself have seen), but it did not harm the image or the glass in front of it!

In 1929, Alfonso Marcue Gonzales was studying the image, and to his surprise he saw a picture inside of the eyes. In 1956, two ophthalmologists, Dr. Javier Toroello-Bueno and Dr. Rafael Torija-Lavoignet confirmed that there is indeed an image in the eyes. This image follows the pattern of the Purkinje-Sanson Law: there should be a threefold reflection in a normal eye, two right side up, one upside down. More recently, Dr. Jose Aste-Tonsmann, using computer-enhanced images, found that at least four figures can be seen, one seeming to be an Indian peasant with hands lifted in prayer. Dr. Aste believes it is Juan Diego. The image shows also a bearded Spaniard.

Further, extensive studies made by infrared and ultraviolet photography and by microchemical analysis of fibers and pigments prove that some trimmings have been added to the picture by human hands, but that the basic picture is totally inexplicable by science; e.g., no brush marks, no sizing on the cloth, no cracking of pigments, etc. The cloth itself should have decayed in 25 to 30 years from the time of the apparition.[13]

As we said, we could quite rationally claim that these events, which we do not *believe* but rather *see* for ourselves, not only prove the existence of a God, but prove the truth of the Catholic Church, which alone proclaims the Real Presence in the Eucharist and the dignity of the Blessed Virgin Mary.

However, without in any way denying that these marvels do prove these things, we are going to put them aside, and show still another way of establishing the solid ground for faith.

Chapter 4

IS THERE A GOD?

Is there a God? The scientifically checked miracles of Chapter 3 really answer this question, for as we have seen, God has made Himself known by these miracles—has shown His hand, as it were. Even so, it is worthwhile to look at a different kind of proof of His existence. First will come some preliminary proofs, then the "clincher."

There is a story—it may not be true, but it is a good illustration even so—that an atheist came to call on an astronomer friend. While waiting, he admired a clever mechanical model of the solar system. He pushed a button, and each planet, made to scale, revolved at the right proportional rate. When the astronomer came in, the atheist asked, "This is clever; who made it?" The astronomer replied, "No one." "But you are kidding." "No. You think the real thing made itself. Why not this little model?"

Again, a good mathematician could calculate the chances of one perfect human ear being formed merely by chance. The odds against it are astronomical. Consider then the chance of two ears developing at the same time? And, with other working parts of a human too, such as the human brain? Before birth, the brain develops hundreds of thousands of neurons each minute.[14] Each neuron makes from 1,000 to 10,000 synapses (connections) to a total of about 100 trillion synapses, and about 100 billion neurons. Yet, no two neurons are identical in form. But they all do develop and all make the right connections, to form one working human brain. Could they do it all on their own, without the help of a higher power?

In addition, as we said, there are really solid proofs of God's existence. We are going to examine the best form of proof twice: first, in technical philosophical form, in which it has maximum power, but is less easy to follow. Later we will repeat it in a looser but easier form and in popular language.

The great Greek philosopher, Aristotle, made some remarkable discoveries. One of them was this—and it is so simple: If I am here and want to go to there I must first have the *capacity*—then next I must *actually* go. He named the first of these principles *potency* or potentiality; the second, *act* or actualization or perfection (they all mean the same).

This truth is quite obvious. Perhaps we even would have seen it without his help. But now we need to notice something further. Not only when I travel from place to place, but also any time something moves or changes in any way, the same set of conditions must exist, namely: first the *capacity* or *potency* for the move or change; second, the *fulfillment* or *act*.

We notice, too, that whenever there is a rise from potency to act, new, higher perfection or being appears. Before, there was only a possibility or capacity or potency—afterwards, when that possibility or potency got its fulfillment, there is an improvement—there is new being or higher being, as a result.

But I cannot give myself what I do not have. If I do not have $1,000 I cannot give myself $1,000. I must get it from elsewhere. Therefore, when this rise takes place, from potency to act, where does the extra come from? It might, in some cases, come from a different part of me (if I am the one in which the rise takes place). But if so, where did the other part get the added perfection, or how did it get up from potency to act? It had to come from somewhere; and at least eventually, that means from some being outside me.

As you will see, we have not solved the problem yet for we must still ask another question. Where did that outside being get the perfection; how did it move from potency to act?

Will the problem go away if we suppose there is a long chain of beings, each moving the other from potency to act? No, the problem is *still with us, as long as we have beings that need help to get from potency to act. It is only when we come to a being that does not need help that we get an answer.* That being is what Aristotle calls the First Cause, or God. And the First Cause is *pure Act,* with *no potency or potentiality mixed in.*

Let us use a comparison—no comparison is perfect and neither is this one, but it will help. Suppose we take a playing card and try to stand it on its edge or on a slant on the top of a table. Of course it needs support. So we put another card behind it at the same angle, as a prop. But then that too needs a prop . . . and so on and on. No matter how many cards we put there in the same way, there is no solution to the problem. Instead, the problem gets worse: there are more cards to support. It is only when finally we put in a solid prop (not just a card) that can stand on its own that the whole chain stands.

Similarly, beings that cannot supply their own perfection cannot really explain things. For that we need a being that needs nothing else: the First Cause.

Now let us try a comparison from astronomy. Most astronomers today favor the Big Bang theory of the origin of our universe. There are still some difficulties with it, yet most astronomers favor it. For certain, it will give us an illustration. This theory says that at first there was one great ball of matter. Then it exploded. As the parts flew farther and farther out, some matter joined to form stars, planets, and galaxies.

Is there good evidence for this theory? If we only had a time machine that would let us look back in time for 1 million years first, then for 5 million, then for 10 million, and so on, to observe the state of the universe at these various points, then we could visually check to see if things were as supposed in this theory.

Of course, we do not have a time machine. But, believe it or not, without one we can still look back in time. Think for example of the nearest galaxy to ours, Andromeda. Its distance from us is about 2.2 million light years. Now we know that light races at a speed just over 186,000 miles per second. So when we say Andromeda is 2.2 million light years away, we are really saying it is so far out that even at that staggering speed of over 186,000 miles per second, its light takes 2.2 million years to reach our eyes.

Further, let us notice this: If the light takes that long to reach us, then the way Andromeda looks to us now is not the way it really *is* now—we are seeing Andromeda the way it *was* 2.2 million years ago. So we can really look back in time. Of course, then, we can also look at other objects in space, and see in each case the state of things many million years back.

Let us come back to the start of the theory. There was a giant ball of matter, and it exploded. What brought that ball of matter into existence? It could not just make itself. What made it "explode"? That could not happen without cause. Therefore the cause that brought it into existence and made it "explode" into a great universe is what we call God.

But it is time to go farther than what even Aristotle could see. When the universe was made out of nothing, how great a rise on the scale of being did that require? If we think of a rise from, let us say, three degrees to seven degrees, we seem to be able to measure that—it seems to be a limited rise. But how great is the rise from utter nothing to something—and moreover to something good? Such a rise is actually infinite. What kind of power does it take to cause an infinite rise? Obviously, infinite power. So, God must be infinite. (Aristotle would have really enjoyed this added step in this reasoning process.)

There is still another train of reasoning that brings us face to face again with infinity. Aristotle saw that potency is *capacity*—but he did not notice that it is also a *limit.* Think of an eight-ounce and a twelve-ounce glass. Each has a capacity for eight or twelve ounces. But each also has a *limit:* each can take *no more* than eight or twelve ounces.

Now we saw above that the First Cause must have no potency—it must be only pure act. (If it had a potency, it would have the problem of getting up from potency to act). Now act without potency is the same as act without limit, for potency is limit. Therefore act without limit is infinite. And, since act is the same as perfection, God is Infinite Perfection.

We can see too that God must be unchangeable. For before anything can change, it must have potency, or capacity for change. But He has no potency—so He cannot change.

We can also see that He must be beyond and outside of time, for time is a restless succession of changes. What was future a moment ago changes to present, and then to past. But He is incapable of change, so He is beyond time. Hence His life is called eternity, in the strict sense: all is *present* to Him—no past, no future. When someone dies, we say in a *loose sense* that he goes to eternity. But we really mean that he goes outside of time. Yet he certainly still has had a past, and will also have a future. So the word "eternity" is used loosely about a departed one. In the strict sense, the word *eternity* applies only to God. Yet, we do say: God *made* the world—an expression about the past. And Christ *will* return at the end—an expression about the future. But to the Infinite Mind, these are all present, with no past or future. With these observations, we can begin to suspect the limited capability of our minds compared to the Eternal.

Now that we have expressed these things in somewhat technical language, we can reiterate in common terms. Basically, if anything changes, it must first have the *capacity*—followed by the *fulfillment.* And we can see that when something higher appears as a result of an action or when something comes into existence, there must be a higher power behind it. Now, where does the "extra" come from? It might be a part of the one that changes—but that only postpones the reckoning, for that other part also has to get the "extra" from somewhere—which means from some being outside itself. But that outside being has the same problem—and so on and so on, until we get to a Being with no such problem. That being is the First Cause, the source of all being, or God.

Again, when the *first* things came into existence, they came from nothing: otherwise they would not be the first. But that ascent from nothing to something is an infinite rise. To cause it takes infinite power. So God has to be infinite.

The "chariots of the gods" theory held by Von Danniken and others now seems silly in comparison. They suggest that perhaps long ago astronauts visited our earth, and awed the simple earthlings. Now, we cannot deny that such a thing could have happened—if the spacemen could overcome the problem of staying alive long enough to come from even the nearest heavenly bodies at the speed of light—or could even exceed what seems to be the speed limit in the universe. But even if we could grant the possibility of such visitors, we would still have to ask: Who made the astronauts? Who made their world? Who made ours? So our proofs hold, even if there could have been such space visitors.

Chapter 5

A GOOD GOD VS. GREAT EVILS

Some people, in spite of all evidence, say there cannot be a God because there are so many evils in the world. This is not a rational position because emotion is its foundation. For, once we have solid proof of something, such as the existence of God, objections, even unanswered ones, cannot destroy what is once solidly proved.

But we can begin studying this objection now, even though the full answer must wait until we have established by reason that we can and should believe Scripture.

We begin by noticing that there are two kinds of evil: physical and moral. Physical evils include such things as illness, poverty, and losses. Moral evils include all types of sins, i.e., evils purposely done by human beings.

It will be helpful to look at the unusual and inaccurate ideas some people have had about physical evils. In ancient times, the Zoroastrians and the Manichees believed errors which we call *dualistic*. They reasoned this way: There are good things in the world; therefore, there must be a good God who made them. But there are also evils in the world; therefore, there must be some other powerful being (not necessarily a god) who made the evils. Thus, in dualism there are two principles: one good, one evil.

Not only in ancient times, but also today, people continue to be fooled by the concept of dualism. To see the flaws in this theory, we must ask the question, "What is evil?" There are three possible answers. First, evil must be either positive or negative; that is, it must be *a thing,* or the *absence of a thing.* If evil is negative, if it is the absence of a thing, there are two further possibilities: it could be a *simple,* or a *privative* lack. A simple negative is the lack of something that is not really called for, like wings on a cat (the birds are relieved at this!). A privative negative is the lack of something that is called for, such as paws on a cat.

Now if we thought, as did the Manichees and the Zoroastrians and some other unfortunate groups, that evils were positive, then we could literally get a suitable container, fill it up with 100% pure evil, and hang out a danger sign. But there is no thing that is by substance or nature evil: evil is the absence of something that is necessary. Clearly, therefore, is no god or other powerful being needed to make it, for it is a nothing, a mere *lack.*

God does *permit* such evils. But what would He have to do to stop them? Here we must distinguish between physical and moral evils.

A world without physical evils, if a material world, would have to be comprised of one miracle after another, simply because material things can go to pieces, can come apart, can slip, as common sense testifies. Now it is not really rational for God to work miracles *routinely,* for a miracle is extraordinary, and the extraordinary cannot become ordinary.

What of moral evils, i.e., those coming from free decisions of men? The question contains the answer: they *do* come from the *free* decisions of men. In other words, let us imagine God considering creating a human race. The very decision to make human beings, having intellect and free will, entails freedom, and that leaves open the possibility for moral evil. But then moral evil comes from men misusing their freedom, not from God.

Of course, God *permits* moral evil. But to stop it, He would have either to multiply miracles indefinitely, which would be irrational—making the extraordinary ordinary—or He would have to withhold or at least reduce free will. But then He would be contradicting Himself, for then He should not have made a human race at all, for a race that is not free is not human. He judged that there was a great good—and there is—in making a race that is free. So He did, in fact create a human race.

Of course there is much, much more to say on this topic. But without the aid of Scripture to back up specific points, we can only speculate. You can see at this point in our discussion we have not proved, however, that one may and should accept Scripture.

Let us suppose for a moment, without help from Scripture, that this short life on earth is followed by an unending, happy life in Heaven—that the evil which we encounter in this earthly existence can be turned into pure gold for the future life, into happiness beyond our greatest dreams. Such a speculation would make a lot of sense. Now, further on, with the help of Scripture we will prove it is true!

Chapter 6

THE HEART OF THE MATTER

We have spent much time on preliminaries, but they were all worthwhile, even necessary, for many readers. Now it is time to examine the positive, reasonable proof that we can—in fact, intellectually cannot help but—believe the Catholic Church.

How shall we start? There are many approaches, but we will use the best one—the Gospels—to establish the validity of the Church. Immediately someone will argue, "You say we should believe the Church because the Gospels say so; and we should believe the Gospels because the Church says so—this is a vicious circle, like a dog chasing his tail. You will never prove things that way!"

We agree and hasten to assure readers that we have no such intention. We will start with the Gospels, yes, but we will *not* consider them as sacred, inspired, or any such thing. We will look at them merely as documents from ancient times. We will treat them the same way we treat other ancient documents, e.g., those from Caesar, Livy, Tacitus and others, and then see if we can arrive at some facts from them. Only after establishing the claims of the Church, do we take up the question of whether the Gospels are sacred or inspired.

But before we even start our work, we meet with two loud objections that seem very formidable today: historicism, and the claim that even eyewitnesses cannot be trusted.

Historicism is the claim that every person and every

event is so unique that we have too little in common
with the past to be confident of understanding the past.
The consequences are devastating. History of any kind
is thereby put under much doubt; the Gospels cannot
be trusted; even the sense of past doctrinal statements
of the Church cannot be known with certainty. And
therefore, "Contemporary philosophy of history relativ-
izes the past and thus neutralizes it . . . we are freed
from the past . . . if the past imposes no pattern upon
us, we are free to try to create the future."

Obviously, before we can try to get any facts from
the Gospels, we must meet this threat to all history.

To start, it is very helpful to go back to almost the
beginning of history writing. Herodotus, the early fifth
century Greek author of a History of the Persian Wars,
who is often called "The Father of History," wrote,
" . . . my duty is to report all that is said, but I am not
obliged to believe it all alike—a remark which may be
understood to apply to my whole history."[16] Later in
the same century, Thucydides wrote about the Pelopon-
nesian War, in which he himself had been a general:
"Of the events of the war I have not ventured to speak
from any chance information, nor according to any notion of my own: I have described nothing but what I
either saw myself, or learned from others, from whom I
made the most careful and particular inquiry";[17] and
again, "I took great pains to make out the exact
truth."[18]

We could easily fill many pages with similar statements. What we need to notice is that these early writers intended *to report facts.* Their critical ability and
techniques were somewhat less developed than those of
modern historians. Yet they did strive to report facts,
and did so remarkably well. A later Roman historian,
Tacitus, is judged by most scholars to be almost the
equal of a modern writer in reporting facts.[19]

Besides reporting facts, these Greek and Roman writers added *interpretations*.

Can we tell fact from interpretation? Historians have no doubt or problem about that in general. We mention this point since, oddly, some Scripture scholars today say we cannot distinguish the same two elements in the Gospels. Let us take two examples to show concretely how we *can* distinguish fact from inference.

Tacitus writes in his *Annals*, "He [Tiberius, right after the death of Augustus, when Tiberius was to become Emperor] only showed signs of hesitation when he addressed the senate. This was chiefly because of Germanicus who was extremely popular . . . Tiberius was afraid Germanicus might prefer the throne to the prospect of it."[20]

Notice the hesitant manner of speaking and acting which Tiberius used at the time. This manner was a *physical fact,* readily visible to countless witnesses. We can assume that Tiberius feared to speak too fast for fear of provoking Germanicus to make a move for the throne. This is of course an *interpretation.* It tries to read the mind of Tiberius. If Tiberius had explicitly *said* such was his motive, it would have been a physically observable fact—but he clearly did not. Tacitus was just trying to infer this. The inference may or may not have been correct.

In *Luke* 10:30-37, we have the story of the man who went from Jerusalem to Jericho, was beaten and left half dead by the road. Again, we distinguish two components, 1) the simple physical fact that he was found half dead at the roadside after having been beaten; 2) the interpretation: What was the motive? Robbery? Senseless violence? Revenge? The Gospel tells us he was robbed. Had it not provided that information we might not have been sure of the *interpretation* of the beating.

As we see, we can easily distinguish between the two kinds of materials. We have stressed this because historicists seem to forget it, and so they focus their attention entirely on the second item, interpretation—forgetting the first, the simple physical facts. It is true that it is often difficult to determine the interpretation of a past event, especially if it involves customs, beliefs or attitudes of a culture different from ours. We may find it hard to reconstruct the picture with certainty—though often enough it can be done. Thus, for example, it is possible by careful detective work to recapture the almost lost ancient concept of *hesed* in the Old Covenant.[21]

With regard to physical facts, anyone, no matter what his cultural background, customs or beliefs, can observe them.

So the historicists have made a serious mistake at the outset in forgetting this obvious distinction.

Historicism developed as an "equal and opposite" pendulum reaction. J. Bossuet in his *Discourse on Universal History* (1681) claimed that Divine Providence is so all-pervasive in the course of history that it directs events even to *goals in this world.* Now of course, there is a measure of truth in this. Providence does affect events. But Bossuet exaggerated much.

Next, the men of the so-called Enlightenment and the Positivists, chiefly in the 18th century, had similar beliefs. They did not appeal to Divine Providence, but they thought there was so much *pattern* in the course of history that we could treat history like the experimental sciences, that is, find laws, make hypotheses, and thus be able to predict many things and even have much control over events. This was another great exaggeration.

In about 1810, G.F.W. Hegel, a philosopher, introduced the theory that all history could be found to be in clusters of three stages: thesis, antithesis, synthesis. That is: Someone takes a position, someone else takes an opposite stand; the interaction leads to a third position. Again, there is much truth in this, but not everything fits so tightly.

As we said, the equal and opposite reaction had to come. Historicists began to deny all pattern[22] and thus to contend that each person and each event is so unique that we have not enough in common to understand them in relationship to each other. Again, they had a measure of truth; but they failed to distinguish mere physical events from interpretations. Culture, customs and beliefs do not affect one's perception of simple physical events—though they do, as we said, create difficulties of varying degrees in making interpretations.

But, for our purpose, to lay the groundwork for faith, we need only physical facts from the Gospels—and very few of them, very simple ones, as we shall see. Hence, the worries of the historicists do not affect us. In fact, at the conclusion of our work, we will find it very simple to make an end-run around the claims of historicists.

Further, the historicists are wrong in refusing to recognize that there are many patterns in people's lives and in events. Anthropologists tell us primitive people have much the same moral codes as we have, though how well they keep them can be another question. Their codes are similar to our Ten Commandments. Medical doctors describe standard reactions among their patients. So too do psychologists. Ascetical and mystical theologians likewise can point to large general patterns in the way people grow in the spiritual life. And even the old schools of biology, that said there are four kinds of temperaments in people, though based on inaccurate biology, turn out to give a fine description of basic groups of tendencies in behavior. Sociologists too can give us large groupings of attitudes and conduct. And even in the everyday simple matters of what kind of exercise one likes, or what kinds of food one prefers, or one's taste in the fine arts—there are large groupings among people. So, while there are many individual differences, there are also extensive and numerous patterns which help us much, even in the *interpretation* of things.

So the historicists have not proved anything that would prevent us from using the few simple physical facts we need from the Gospels for a basis of faith.

Of course, we still have a lot of things to work out before we ask the Gospels for even those. But we can use them, and we will use them.

We said that doubts have been raised today even about the validity of eyewitnesses. Experiments done on eyewitnesses have raised some questions about how much we can depend on even them to report facts. In one experiment,[23] students were shown a film of a multiple car accident, then given 22 questions to answer. There were divergences on the answers to the question, "Did you see a broken headlight?" In another experiment, a news magazine printed several copies of pennies, each slightly different, and people were asked to pick out the one that matched the actual penny.

Of course there were differences in the answers in both experiments. But the experimenters forgot to make necessary distinctions, the usual root of errors in solving such problems. They did not notice two factors that affect the outcome: motive and opportunity. In both cases, there was little motive for the witnesses to remember. Surely, we do not pay attention to the precise wording on pennies, and other similar details about them. There is no point in doing so. As to the car accident: Accidents happen so suddenly, and usually when the witnesses are not looking, or, if looking, are not paying attention. The opportunity to see is very brief, very sudden. So it was easy for them to fail to note things such as whether or not a headlight was broken. Plus, they had small motive to watch carefully.

But consider a case in which there is high motivation and high opportunity. Suppose, to take a wild example, a space ship really landed in the parking lot of a large shopping center. People would not only hear it coming down, but would also be unable to take their eyes off it as the door opened and some odd little people emerged. Yes, their emotions might make some *details* confused even then, but the big basic fact—that a space ship landed and odd people came out—no one could possibly fail to get that right.

Similarly with the Gospel miracles: If a man says to a leper, "Be made clean" and instantly he is cured; or if he ordered a blind man to see; the onlookers could not forget those basic facts, though they might disagree on unimportant details. They had ample opportunity, and strong motive to remember.

What about the man himself who was healed? Would he not get it straight, and other things about Jesus too? Of course. He could not help it. But now—and this is really remarkable—we happen to have an early writer, Quadratus, writing about 123 A.D., who tells us that in his time, people healed by Christ, and even raised from the dead by Him were still around. What powerful witnesses such people make! (We will quote Quadratus at the end of Chapter 10).

For the time being, we are not trying positively to prove that the Gospels are reliable. We are just doing preliminary work, clearing away possible obstacles or objections that would say we cannot trust any history, or any eyewitnesses.

Chapter 7

A FAITHFUL TEXT?

Let us imagine St. Luke sitting down to write, or to dictate, his Gospel. Do we have the copy he wrote? Definitely not. There is no ancient work whatsoever for which we have the original copy or the autograph. How close are we? In the case of pagan works, a gap of nine to ten centuries between the autograph and our oldest manuscript is not unusual. For example, the oldest manuscript of Caesar's work on the Civil War, written in the middle of the first century B.C., comes from the tenth century A.D.

But in the case of the Gospels, we can do far better.[34] The oldest complete copies we possess of the New Testament are the Vatican and the Sinai Codices, each dating from around 350 A.D. Far closer than the spread that exists for Caesar's work. We have also the Alexandrian Codex, and the Codex Bezae, from the early 400's A.D. But we can do something to narrow even this small gap. We have papyri[35] giving parts of the New Testament. Thus, the papyrus called P[46], the Chester Beatty Papyrus II, comes from the early 200's A.D. It includes most of the Epistles of St. Paul. Then there are the several Bodmer Papyri: P[75] comes from around 200 A.D., and has parts of Luke and John; P[66], from the same time, has parts of John; P[72] has the Epistle of Jude, and the two Epistles of Peter. Oldest of all is the P[52], the Rylands Papyrus 457, which has only four verses from John 18, but dates from 135 A.D.

We also have other checks on the state of the text,

from the old translations. The Old Syriac and the Old Latin versions are earlier than the papyri in general, coming from the late 100's A.D. The Coptic and Sahidic translations date from the early 200's A.D. Thus, we can examine the state of the text that early.

Besides, the Fathers of the Church in the early centuries often quoted Scripture, and so we can see what their copies were like. Of course, they sometimes quoted from memory, not precisely word for word. But even then, the substance is surely correct.

Really, no scholar at all worries about whether our text of the Gospels is accurate or not. For with extremely few exceptions, the differences between one manuscript and the others are trifling. Even those differences that are larger have no bearing on the *essential* facts we will need to build the foundation for faith. So we do not, strictly speaking, have to take up this subject at all. Yet, for the sake of completeness and thoroughness, we want to continue in this vein.

There is a whole science that deals with the question of the faithful transmission of texts. It is called Textual Criticism. We will not go through every aspect of it here; we will examine only some major points.

Let us again picture a Scriptural author writing or dictating his Gospel. Printing was centuries away, of course, so copies had to be made by hand from that autograph. We do not know how many were made off that first copy. Let us imagine, for the sake of illustration, that three copies were made. Now when we copy even our own compositions, it is not unusual for us to make small mistakes in copying. So it is likely that the first scribes did that too. Further, it is not likely that the identical errors would be found in each of the three copies.

From each of the three copies, others were made by hand—let us imagine a half dozen from each. These further copies would be apt to reproduce the slips of the copies from which they were made, or to add slips of their own; and so on into further copies from copies.

The result is that there must have been, as it were, a family tree of manuscripts. The trunk represents the autograph; from the trunk come the three great branches; from the three come smaller branches; and so on.

From what we said at the start of this chapter, we can gather that there must be a "water line." In other words we could draw a line, perhaps horizontal, through this tree. We do have all manuscripts above the line; we have none of those below the line.

Then we try to figure out which manuscripts belong to which larger branches. For if two or three merely copy one previous manuscript, their testimony in this respect carries no more weight than the single branch from which they come. Therefore, to judge the correct reading, we cannot merely count manuscripts. We must try to reconstruct the family tree, and to see which manuscripts carry the greater weight, or seem more reliable. In doing this, of course, we look for small mistakes that are common to different manuscripts and for other types of common characteristics, so as to find the family traits.

Scholars today think the text found in the Vatican and Sinai manuscripts is, on the whole, the best.

After selecting the best family of manuscripts, we need to pick between the variations within them. There are many principles used for that. Let us mention just two that are especially important.

Suppose we have three variant readings at one spot and must pick. Clearly, if one of the three can more readily provide a ground or common base from which the others could have been derived, that one is more likely to be the original reading.

Secondly, we do well to pick that reading which best agrees with the known habits and tendencies of the author.

We could go into greater detail, but as we said, there is no need to work further here. All scholars agree that nearly all the variations we find in the Gospels are so tiny and insignificant that it is agreed that a good 90% of the text is above suspicion, and does accurately give the sense of the original. Those parts that do leave doubt are such that they are not needed for our work of building the foundation of faith. As we shall soon see, for that we need only a half-dozen very simple facts, physical facts, which are completely unaffected by the variants.

Chapter 8

WHAT DID THE AUTHOR WANT TO SAY?

Imagine an archaeologist three or four thousand years from today, digging in the ruins of our civilization. He makes a great discovery! A complete book on the Civil War in the United States turns up! Excitedly, he pores over it. He finds details hitherto unknown, including word-for-word conversations between President Lincoln and several important persons!

So far into the future, our imaginary archeologist will probably belong to a culture very different from ours. But we hope and pray he will show a basic piece of common sense in recognizing that the ancient authors of 20th-century America did not necessarily write in the same literary patterns or *genres* as the people of his age. After all, it would be a coincidence, a matter of chance, if they did, since the cultures would be so different.

You see, what our imaginary archaeologist found was really an historical novel. Now we, being natives of this culture, know perfectly well what credence to give to historical novels. We know they are a mixture of history and fictional fill-ins. The main thrust is historical, the background scenes fit the period (during the U.S. Civil War there were steam trains and telegraphs, but no planes or TV). Yet we, as natives, know the author of this novel would make fill-ins, which are fictional, such as the word-for-word conversations of Lincoln with important people. The author may capture the general sense of the discussion, but we cannot be sure. He may not have even that; we *expect* him to fill in.

Suppose our imaginary future archaeologist would not realize this point, that he would try to take those conversations as being fully historical. It would be a sad and silly error because he should know better than just to assume all cultures did the same things his would do.

Now these patterns of writing are commonly called *genres*.

Of course, we have more than one genre in English. We picked the historical novel to illustrate our point because it is a specially clear example. We have inherited our literary genres for the most part from Greece and Rome, with very little change. As a result, if we do our reading anywhere in that culture stream, our almost instinctive reactions—knowing how it was meant, and how to take it—serve us well.

But, if we start to read something from a different culture, then it would be foolishness—really, tragic foolishness—for us to assume that the other culture did everything the same way 20th-century Americans do.

Scripture obviously comes from a different culture; it was ancient; it was Semitic. Therefore, for us to assume that the writers of Scripture wrote in our patterns would be very foolish. Yet, many today do that. They are called Fundamentalists. They reach such regrettable conclusions as insisting that the first chapters of Genesis teach that God made the world in six periods of 24 hours each. In so interpreting the Bible they think they are exercising great faith. Really, they are *not* being faithful, for *they are not asking what the Scriptural writer intended to assert via his genre; they are instead imposing their own ideas upon Scripture.*

We hope it is clear why we have spent this time on literary genres. We want to make clear that before we read any part of Scripture, our first duty is to see what the genre was, the pattern the Scriptural writer intended to use, so we may know the "rules" by which it was to be understood, rules which were common both to the Scriptural writer and to his original readers.

We may, of course, find overlaps with our patterns. But we cannot assume anything in advance. We must check carefully.

Therefore, since we intend to use the Gospels as ancient documents in which we want to find a few *facts* as a basis for faith, we must ask, even before we start to look at the Gospels, "What is the genre in which the Gospels were written? What did the Gospel writers intend to *assert?* What medium did they choose for it?"

We are going to study only the first three Gospels writers: Matthew, Mark and Luke. It is not that we reject John, but we think it at least likely, even from a cursory reading, that the genre of John is somewhat different from that of the first three. The first three are often called Synoptics, a convenient name to use instead of repeating three names.

At first sight we get the impression that the Synoptics intend, among other things, to give us some facts about the man called Jesus. But that is just our preliminary impression. We must work carefully to see if that is true, and what qualifications need to be added to it.

We begin by examining the Hebrew concept of the genre of history, for Christianity grew out of and completed Judaism. That concept can affect the genre of the Gospels.

The Greeks and Romans, not all, but many of them, were given to the *cyclic* theory of history, the view that history is not developing forward, as it were, but instead, that the course of events turns back on itself and keeps repeating itself. For example, Plato taught a cycle of rebirths for every individual (though a good philosopher might eventually escape).[26] Still earlier, the Greek philosopher Anaximander (c. 610-545 B.C.)

taught an unending cycle of destructions and restorations of the world. Aristotle[26a] tells us Empedocles and Heraclitus held such a theory. The influential Stoics had similar views, as we learn from the work of Diogenes Laertius on Zeno.[27] Aristotle himself, speaking of certain features of culture in Egypt and Crete said, "These and many other things have been invented several times over in the course of ages, or rather, times without number."[28] Most primitive peoples seem to have held similar cyclic ideas, as we see in detail in the important study by Mircea Eliade, *The Myth of the Eternal Return.*

All these cyclic views, which think that the world is going nowhere—is only repeating itself—differ sharply from the Hebrew concept of history. As Mircea Eliade tells us, "The Hebrews were the first to discover the meaning of history as the epiphany [manifestation] of God, and this concept, as we should expect, was taken up and amplified by Christianity ... For Christianity, time is real because it has a meaning—the Redemption ... The development of history is thus governed and oriented by a unique fact, a fact that stands entirely alone."[29]

As Eliade pointed out, the Christian current rather naturally continues the Hebrew current, for Christianity is the fulfillment of Judaism. Eliade adds, "The destiny of all mankind, together with the individual destiny of each one of us, are both likewise played out once, once for all [in contrast to unending recurring cycles] in a concrete and irreplaceable time, which is that of history and life."[30]

Really, this is most natural and is what we would expect. Once a person comes to *believe*—or rather, for the first Christians to *see*—that there was a unique event that was the turning point of all history, that is, the coming of Christ, and to see that that event is the key to the personal fate, and the eternal fate of each man, then no mere fancies or imaginings to the contrary will suffice or even be of any interest to him. The great question for each man will be, *"What really happened? How does it affect me for eternity?"* He will spare nothing to get the facts, and once he has them, he will hold on to them in spite of everything.

This is precisely what the first Christians did. We find it already in St. Paul, writing to the Corinthians (*Cor.* 15:1-19) in 57 A.D., "And if Christ be not risen again, then is our preaching vain, and your faith is also vain . . . If in this life only we have hope in Christ, we are of all men most miserable." Miserable, yes, for by the hundreds and the thousands the early Christians died rather than say the facts were not facts, rather than deny Christ, on whom they understood their eternity to depend.

A brilliant example comes in the letter to the Romans of St. Ignatius, Bishop of Antioch. He died, eaten by the wild beasts in the Arena at Rome about the year 107 A.D. He wrote to the Christians at Rome, "May I enjoy the beasts prepared for me, and I pray they may be prompt. I will even entice them to eat me promptly, so they will not refrain from touching me, as they have for some, out of fear . . . Understand me, brothers, do not hinder me from living eternally [by dying for Christ]. Do not wish me to die [to have to stay in this life]."[31]

Let someone today take this letter and read it in front of the lion cage in the zoo. He will understand that the man who wrote it was concerned with facts, the facts of Christ, His death, and his own likeness to Christ by dying for Christ. St. Ignatius even added a plea to the Christians at Rome that they should not use their influence to free him, in case some Christian might have such influence. He *wanted* to die to testify to Christ.

The case of St. Ignatius is but one sample. Christians all over the Mediterranean world, well before 100

A.D., were so absolutely insistent on the factuality of Christ that they all held basically the same beliefs— even though scattered all over the Mediterranean. If they had been dealing in fancies, in unsupported claims, there could not have been such an agreement. Facts are necessary to give consistency to any story— especially where numerous people are involved.

By now it is quite obvious what the Synoptic writers intended to do: *they meant to give facts,* and took great care with those facts, for their eternity depended on that. Therefore, that is the chief feature of the genre of the Gospels. Obviously, *they also would give interpretations.* In Chapter 6 of this book, we saw that the Greek and Roman writers also tried to give these two things: facts plus interpretations. We noticed too that some Scripture scholars, foolishly, think we cannot tell facts from interpretations! We showed by concrete examples that we can make this distinction, and do so quite easily.

In spite of the above knowledge, some have still suggested that the Gospels were really only of a loose genre, like some ancient biographies, and not interested in facts.

But the Gospels are not like that, and for several reasons. First, some—not all—of the pagan biographers could not readily get at the facts; some probably did not try hard to do so. But some ancient biographies are very concerned with facts, e.g., Suetonius' *Lives of the Twelve Caesars.* Michael Grant, a noted classicist, in his introduction to the Penguin edition of *Suetonius,* credits Suetonius with a "relatively high degree of objectivity" and adds that he "gathers together, and lavishly inserts, information both for and against them [the Emperors] usually without adding any personal judgement in one direction or the other, and above all without introducing . . . moralizations."

The chief example of a loose ancient biography that

is often suggested for comparison to the Gospels is the life of Apollonius of Tyana by Philostratus. It is actually strange that anyone should seriously suggest the comparison, since an actual reading of Philostratus points out so many extensive, major differences.

First, Philostratus wrote long after the events. The Synoptic Gospels were probably written before 70 A.D., less than 40 years after the death of Jesus. Even if they were written as late as 80-90 A.D., as some propose, they would still be far closer than the account of Philostratus to the person portrayed. And, as we will see in Chapter 10, there were still persons alive who had been cured or raised from the dead by Jesus in 90 A.D.

Further, Apollonius is really just a Pythagorean philosopher, not one who claimed to be sent by God to bring eternal salvation by His own suffering. Philostratus and Apollonius believed in many pagan gods. The Egyptian god Proteus appears to the pregnant mother of Apollonius. It seems Apollonius is a reincarnation of Proteus.

Philostratus enters into a very large number of philosophical discussions. There are even some contrived scenes, some poor imitations of Platonic dialogues, and even some glib moralism. We find a discussion on the intelligence and breeds of elephants (2:11-16). Some discussions reported were enormously long. At Olympia, for instance, all of Greece assembled before Apollonius (8:15-19), as he holds no less than forty days of philosophical discussions and debates. Yet, in spite of such philosophical pretenses, we find Apollonius playing up unabashedly to Vespasian's desire for imperial power (5:28-30). Of course, there are no mere philosophical discussions in the Synoptic Gospels, and all presentations are brief.

Philostratus also introduces very large quantities of mere travelogue material. Many people then never went far from home, and therefore liked to hear about "far-away places with strange-sounding names." In India, Apollonius sees dragons some sixty feet long (3:7). Their eyes contained mystic gems; and it is explained how to get those gems. Gems in India are described as so large that if hollowed out, they hold enough drink for four men (3:27). In one place, there are robot tripods that serve meals (3:27). Apollonius seeks and finds the source of the Nile: a place of giant geysers in a dense mountainous region (6:26). He fears permanent deafness from the roar, and is apprehensive of the fact that all the demons of the world used the area for a gathering place. By contrast, our Gospels never sound like a tabloid equivalent of *National Geographic!*

Miracles in this book are much different from those of the Gospels. They are never done in the sort of framework needed to prove the wonderworker is a messenger from God (conditions will be explained in Chapter 12). In one place Apollonius finds a satyr annoying women; he quiets the satyr with wine (6:27). He also meets a woman who has a son possessed by a demon. It turns out that the demon is really the ghost of a man who fell in battle; he had been much attached to his wife, and so when she married three days after his death, he became disgusted with women. After death he became homosexual over the 16-year-old boy he was possessing. Apollonius gives the woman a letter containing threats to the ghost (3:38). When he met a woman who had suffered in labor seven times, he told her husband that whenever his wife was about to bring forth the next child, he should go into her room carrying in his bosom a live rabbit. He should walk around the wife once, and then release the rabbit, and drive it out of the room, otherwise the womb would be expelled together with the child. (3:39).

In the final episodes, Apollonius proclaims it is fitting for the wise to die for philosophy. Yet he says he cannot be hurt when he has to appear before the emperor. Finally, he disappears from the courtroom. Here there is nothing parallel to Jesus, who voluntarily accepted suffering as a means of the redemption of mankind.

But the most critical difference between such things and our Gospels is motive. The loose pagan biographies were not dealing with things on which eternity depended; the Gospels were. No one was going to die in torment to vouch for the factuality of the tales about Apollonius.

Finally, we can easily judge for ourselves in this whole matter. For there really were some loose compositions written about Jesus, e.g., the Gospel of James. But even a cursory reading shows the lack of concern for factuality in that gospel, as compared with the real Gospels. Hence the Church and the first Christians never accepted such things as parts of Scripture. They wanted facts, not fancies, on which to stake their own eternity.

To sum up, the genre of the Synoptic Gospels is one that attempts to give facts plus interpretations. The first Christians' tremendous insistence on factuality, since their eternity depended on it, assures us that the interpretations will not falsify or distort the facts, and that the facts themselves will be reliable.[32]

Some object that Form and Redaction Criticism have shown that the Gospels cannot be trusted. Fortunately, one of the chief proponents of this position, Norman Perrin, gives us what he considers the strongest instance in which Form Criticism shows the Gospels unhistorical. He dares to say that he once trusted the Gospels, but, "The gospel materials themselves have forced us to change our mind."

The prize instance which "forced" Perrin is *Mark* 9:1, "There are some standing here who will not taste death before they see the kindgom of God come with power." *Matthew* 16:28 reiterates this idea, except it says they will see "the Son of man coming in his kingdom." *Luke* 9:27 says they will see "the kingdom of God."

Perrin thinks that Matthew and Mark refer to the End of the World, but Luke has given up on hope for an early end.

Are we, therefore, *forced* to understand the passage with Perrin's interpretation? Hardly. First, all three Synoptics put this line just before The Transfiguration of Christ. What they describe could be the thing they were about to see. But, more probably, since "with power" refers to displays of the power of God (miracles) and since it is admitted[34] by many that the kingdom of God stands for the Church, in this world and in the next, we can say that Mark means that some will see the kingdom, the Church, being established with displays of divine power or miracles after the first Pentecost. That, of course, has happened.

As to the reading in Matthew, the "Son of Man" is of course Christ. "Coming" can refer to the Hebrew concept of *paqad,* a "visitation." And so the meaning is that they will see Christ coming, visiting the world in His kingdom, His Church—not in His return at the end. Luke merely says they will see the kingdom, that is, the Church established. Dr. Perrin's theory does not hold up under our scrutiny, as you can see.

Form and Redaction Criticism correctly suppose that our Gospels developed in three stages: 1) the deeds and words of Jesus, adapted in presentation to His audience; 2) the way the Apostles and first generation preached these things with adaptation to the audience again; 3) that some individuals, moved by the Spirit, wrote down *some part* of this original preaching—and that is the Gospel. Therefore, *the Church has something more basic than the Gospels, its own ongoing preaching.*

After noting that there are these three stages, the critics then try to find out at which of the three stages any given part of the Gospel reached its present form. For the Church may reasonably have adapted the wording to the needs of the people present at that time.

We fully agree with scholars in wanting to find out answers to these questions. But we must point out that the evidence from these studies never *proves* anything because it is too *subjective.* Even the more sanguine Form Critics now admit this, and many are relying less and less on this approach.[35]

However, even if they could prove solidly at which stage something took its present form, that would mean nothing against the reliability of the facts given. As we have said, the Apostles and others in the early Church—and we too—know eternity itself depends on getting the facts right! So their rewording, if, in fact, they did this, would still convey the same facts.

We will be seeing, in the next chapters, how to *construct a bypass* around all such worries of the form critics. We need to establish only six very easy points about Jesus, things not at all difficult to understand, things not affected by the claims of the form critics. With these six points, we will know that there is a body or group of people, commissioned to teach as a messenger sent by God and promised divine protection for their teaching. This group, then, can assure us of other things we want to know about Jesus.

A full study of form and redaction criticism can be found in W. Most, *Free from All Error* (Prow Press, 1985) pp. 121-149. Cf. also idem, *The Consciousness of Christ,* pp. 174-228 and pp. 8-38.[36]

Chapter 9

EXTRA! EXTRA!
GREEK DOCTOR WRITES GOSPEL!

We are imagining how the *Antioch Times*—had there been such a publication—might have headlined it. It would have been true that Luke, a doctor from Antioch did write a Gospel. Yes, there are counter claims saying it was not Luke, and that Luke was not a doctor. We will take up those questions in the next chapter. However, for our purposes now, we need only know that he, and the other Synoptic writers, did intend to give us facts, plus interpretations. We now acknowledge that their intense concern for their own eternity would make them careful. We still have to ask to what extent they were in a position to get the facts. We will do that in the next chapter.

We want to stress, before beginning, that this chapter really is an "extra," and in a very real sense different from that of newspaper extras. It is "extra" in the sense that we do not need it at all. It is just a confirmation of what we saw in the last chapter. This chapter is not strictly conclusive, but it does give us impressive evidence, from entirely new research,[37] that the author of Luke's Gospel was deeply concerned with accuracy.

Luke is the only Scriptural writer who was not a Semite. He was a Greek, an educated Greek, a doctor. For that reason, we need to recall Greek and Roman ideas on history writing.

We said previously that many Greeks and Romans held cyclic theories that contended that history is not

43

going anywhere, that things just repeat themselves in cycles. That did not prevent them from writing up the history of certain stretches of those cycles as known to them. In Chapter 6 we saw some small part of the evidence that the Greek and Roman historians did intend to write facts plus interpretations, and that many of them did surprisingly well with their facts, though they lacked some of our techniques.

We should add that the ancient historians had another characteristic which we do not share. They would insert speeches in their histories at suitable points, e.g., the speech of Hannibal to his men before crossing the Alps. When it was obtainable, they would get at least the substance of what was said in these important speeches. Unfortunately, when the information was unavailable, they would make it up.

We should expect, then, that Luke, an educated Greek, would follow the Greek and Roman pattern of giving facts, carefully researched, plus interpretations. He is likely also to give speeches. In doing so, we should expect him to follow the Greek and Roman practice of trying to get at least the substance of the speeches. Could he do so? In the next chapter we will show that the answer is very definitely yes. But here we want to show that in doing his work, he used extraordinary, really meticulous care.

All scholars know and admit that the Greek of Luke's Gospel shows far more Semitisms than do the Gospels written by Semites. A Semitism consists in bringing some features of Semitic speech or structure into Greek, where it does not really belong. For example, in the parable of the wicked husbandmen, Mark's Gospel is content to merely say that after the first servant was mistreated, the master "sent another," and later again, "he sent another." But *Luke* 20:9-12 reads oddly, "And he *added* to send another servant"; and later, "he *added* to send a third." The language sounds stilted in English, and so did it in Greek. The reason is evident. Hebrew, in such a sentence, would use the root *ysf,* to *add.* So we can see Luke, who is not a Semite, is taking care to reproduce the precise structure of his source, a Hebrew source, although Mark, who was a Semite, did not do it. We notice in passing that many scholars think Luke copied much from Mark. This example proves he did not do it all the time, if ever.

But the most fascinating results come from studying what Luke does with a very odd Hebrew (not Aramaic[38]) construction called apodotic *wau* (which becomes apodotic *kai* in Greek, if used). Here is an example from *Luke* 5:1:[39] "It happened, when the crowd pressed on Him to hear the word of God, AND He stood by the lake." We are struck by that odd *and.* It is surely out of place in English to use an *and* to connect the opening subordinate clause with the main clause. It is similarly out of place in Greek. It was not found in normal Aramaic either (except when they were tightly translating a Hebrew text, in the Targums[40]). But it is quite normal in Classical Hebrew.

Why did Luke insist on reproducing this bizarre Hebraism? The almost unanimous answer has been that he was deliberately imitating the Septuagint to give a Biblical flavor (the Septuagint is the old Greek translation of the Hebrew Old Testament). It is similar to injecting *thee, thou,* etc. etc. in English for the same purpose.

But we can prove statistically that Luke did not want to imitate the Septuagint.

First, we must check to find out if the Septuagint usually carried over into the Greek that Hebrew structure when it was found in the Old Testament. We are fortunate to have a very thorough study by M. Johannessohn on precisely this point.[41] Johannessohn, by actual count, tells us the Septuagint for the most part does reproduce this Hebrew structure in Greek wherever it finds it.

So, if Luke really is imitating the Septuagint, we should expect him to use this structure most of the time too. If he does it only a small part of the time, it is as unlikely as if someone added *thee, thou,* etc., but did it only a small part of the time.

To reach some conclusion, I made two counts to see what Luke actually did. First, a count of how often Luke really does have the apodotic *kai;* second, a count of how many places he *could have* used it, were he really following the Septuagint practice of copying the Hebrew structure, but yet did not. The results of the two counts are surprising. Luke uses that Hebraism only one-fourth to one-fifth of the time!

Now imagine, again, someone injecting *thee, thou,* etc. to give a Biblical flavor in English, but doing it only one-fourth of the time. He would be inconsistent and odd. No intelligent person would do that—surely a doctor would not.

Still further, if we recall that sample passage of *Luke* 5:1 quoted earlier, we can notice there are three elements in the sentence: "1) And it happened; 2) when the crowd pressed on Him . . . 3) AND He stood by the lake." Let us focus on the second item. It is an expression of time. Such time expressions commonly come ahead of this odd "and" structure in Hebrew. For the time expression, the Hebrew uses an odd bit of language—a preposition, "be," plus an infinitive—a construction which does not exist at all in English. But Greek did have a parallel structure, yet the Septuagint usually chose *not* to use that parallel Greek structure. Luke usually did choose to use it. So we see, again, Luke is *not* following the Septuagint, but is being tightly faithful to Hebrew structure.

What should we conclude? First, it is entirely obvious that the common view, that Luke used Semitisms to give a biblical flavor, like the Septuagint, is wrong. So then, what was his reason? Let's take seriously what

Luke himself tells us in the opening lines of his Gospel. He says that he knows many have tried to compile a narrative of the things about Christ using eyewitnesses. He will write an orderly, careful account using such sources.

Now if Luke used sources, oral and written, he could easily have met sources in three languages—for there were three native languages for Jews in Palestine at that time, Aramaic, Hebrew and Greek.

Where he was using Greek sources, it would not, of course, affect his Greek. Greek on Greek does not show: Aramaic might show, but efforts of scholars to trace it have so far led to little general agreement.

But we have seen that in some places (20 to 25 per-cent of the time) he is following a Hebrew source. We would not expect him to use only Hebrew sources—he would be apt to use others, too. But the fact that he so carefully, even slavishly, imports strictly Hebrew (not Aramaic) structures into his Greek in this apodotic *kai* reveals his extreme care for accuracy. This slavish sort of Scriptural translation is known elsewhere, in some of the Old Latin translations, which bring Greek struc-tures into Latin. We know too that the Latin translators did that out of extreme reverence for the sacred text, and extreme care to reproduce everything with utmost fidelity.

So then it is clear what Luke was doing. He did use sources, as he said; and he used them with such great care for fidelity that he even—not very suitably—brought Hebrew structures into Greek. We can con-clude, therefore, that Luke must have taken meticulous care for accuracy.

Chapter 10

DID LUKE WRITE LUKE?

The opening question sounds silly, yet it is serious. Many today say that what we call the Gospel according to St. Luke was not written by St. Luke, but by someone else, whose name is unknown. Today we sometimes use pen names. In ancient times they often did that too, but the name they used was apt to be that of a famous person, a thing we would not think quite proper. So it happens that the same question is asked about all the writers of the Gospels, not just St. Luke. Therefore, we need to address it.

At the outset, let us say that precisely because they usually picked the name of a famous person for a pen name, Luke and Mark were unlikely to be chosen, though it could have happened to Matthew and John.

But let us take things in the right order. We saw that the writers of the Synoptics surely intended to give facts plus interpretations. We saw an added bit of evidence on the meticulous care Luke took for accuracy. But the next logical question is this, did these writers have a good chance to get to know the facts? Under that heading we ask two things: *Who* wrote them? (to see if they were eyewitnesses or got information from eyewitnesses); and *when* did they write them? (to see if information would still be available then). We will take up each question separately. First, the question of authorship.

There are two kinds of evidence to consider on authorship: external and internal evidence. External evidence means the testimony of witnesses, i.e., ancient

48

writers who can tell us who wrote what. Internal evidence looks inside the writings themselves for indications. We must note that courts of law commonly accept witnesses if properly qualified, but that internal evidence by nature seldom can prove anything at all.

What ancient witnesses have we on the authorship of the Synoptics? Quite a few. Earliest of all is Papias, Bishop of Hierapolis, who, around 140 A.D., wrote *Exegesis of the Lord's Sayings.* This work is lost, but fortunately, Eusebius, the first Church historian, preserved several quotations from it, as well as quotations from many other works now lost. Papias tells us he inquired from those who had heard the Apostles and disciples of the Lord. St. Irenaeus, writing sometime before 200 A.D., in his *Against Heresies,* adds that Papias was a companion of St. Polycarp, who had known St. John the Apostle personally.[42]

Papias tells us this about Mark: "Mark became the interpreter of Peter, and wrote accurately the doings and sayings of the Lord, not in sequence, but all that he remembered. For he [Mark] had not heard the Lord, or followed Him, but, as I said, followed Peter later on, who, as needed, gave teaching, but did not make an arrangement of the sayings of the Lord ... He gave attention to one thing, to leave out nothing of what he had heard, and to make no false statements about them."[43] Papias says this about Matthew: "Matthew collected the sayings in the Hebrew language, and each interpreted them as he could."[44]

We also learn from Eusebius that Papias here was quoting the Presbyter John. He is clearly not the Apostle John, but seems to have lived about the time of the Apostle. Hence, we really have a testimony reaching back into the first century itself.

We notice too that Mark wrote down the preaching of St. Peter himself, the prime eyewitness, and that he took care, "to make no false statements." Matthew collected these things in Hebrew. Some think Papias really means Aramaic, not Hebrew. However, whichever language it may have been, that text is now lost. What we have is a Greek translation, made also very early. Some suspect it was made by Matthew himself.[45]

Here we must mention an objection raised by some. Eusebius[46] also spoke of Papias as "a man of very small intelligence."

The objection is astounding. Those who make it do not seem to notice *in what respect* Eusebius makes this comment. He actually says that Papias showed small intelligence *in holding a millennium theory,* because he misunderstood *Revelation* 20:4-6, which says there will be a first resurrection after which the just "will reign with him [Christ] for a thousand years on earth." Now it is true that Papias did misunderstand that text, and led some others to do the same. But is it really a sign of poor intelligence to take that text at its seeming face value? It is a difficult, obscure text. So, to misunderstand may be erroneous, but hardly stupid.

Further, even granting Papias should not have made that mistake—does that prove he was incapable of correctly repeating the testimony of earlier witnesses on who wrote what Gospel? Hardly. As a result, at a colloquium on the relationships among the Gospels at Trinity University at San Antonio in 1977, George A. Kennedy, Paddison Professor of Classics at the University of North Carolina, in replying to a question about his use of Papias as a credible source, said, "He had studied carefully the second-century evidence for the tradition that Mark's Gospel reflects directly reminiscences of Peter, and had concluded that he would be thoroughly delighted to find such solid evidence for some other ancient historical tradition."[47] Kennedy is a classicist. Classicists went through an unfortunate period of misjudging evidence in the 19th century, but are well over it now; Scripture men are at present still suffering from a parallel fault.

Kennedy is clearly right. And Papias is confirmed by other early evidence. Thus, the Anti-Marcion Prologues to the Gospels, dating probably from 160-180 A.D., tell us, "Mark, who was called stumpfingered, was the interpreter of Peter. After the departure of Peter, he wrote a Gospel in Italy . . . Luke of Antioch in Syria, a physician, having become a disciple of the Apostles, and later followed Paul until his martyrdom . . . after the Gospels had been written—by Matthew in Judea, by Mark in Italy—moved by the Holy Spirit, wrote this Gospel in Achaia . . . with great care, for gentile believers."[48]

The odd detail that Mark was "stumpfingered" is intriguing. A later forger would be unlikely to know such an uncomplimentary detail about an Evangelist, nor is anyone likely to have just invented so odd and unusual a point. So we have an indication of the early date of those Prologues and of their accuracy.

St. Irenaeus, Bishop of Lyons, who seems to have died as a martyr around 200 A.D., gives us a precious testimony: "Matthew among the Hebrews brought forth in their own language, a written Gospel, while Peter and Paul at Rome were preaching and laying the foundations of the Church. After their death, Mark, the disciple and interpreter of Peter, himself handed down in writing the things preached by Peter. And Luke, the follower of Paul, set down in a book the Gospel preached by him."[49]

As we said, the testimony of St. Irenaeus is precious. He mentions the work of Papias, without quoting from it, and yet gives several facts not found in Papias. But more importantly, St. Irenaeus tells us that he, when a youth, had listened to St. Polycarp of Smyrna telling what he personally had heard from St. John the Apostle;[50] further, we know St. Irenaeus at least once went on a mission to Rome. Hence he had two likely sources of information in addition to Papias; and his report does coincide nicely with what we get from Papias and with the Anti-Marcion Prologues.

There are many other reports too which agree, e.g., Tertullian, writing around 207 A.D., says, "Of the Apostles, John and Matthew instill the faith in us; of apostolic men, Luke and Mark renew it."[51] Origen, writing after 244 A.D., also agrees with the others.[52]

Some have tried to discredit these witnesses saying Papias was unreliable, and all others copied from him or made legendary additions.[53] As to the charge of unreliability, we have already answered it above. As to the claim that all copied from one, there is no proof. On the contrary, the Anti-Marcionite Prologue has facts on Luke—Papias has nothing at all on him. The AntiMarcionite Prologue has an odd detail on Mark, that he was stumpfingered—but Papias lacks it. And as we have said, it is not the sort of thing someone would be apt just to invent, for it is uncomplimentary. St. Irenaeus too has facts not found in Papias. For instance, that Matthew wrote while Peter and Paul were preaching in Rome. Further, as we said before, St. Irenaeus had listened to St. Polycarp, who knew the Apostle St. John personally; and St. Irenaeus had visited Rome at least once, where he could easily have gathered information, especially on Mark recording Peter's preaching there.

So what do we have? We have a unanimous tradition, reaching back to around 100 A.D., that Mark wrote a Gospel based on the preaching of Peter with whom he worked in Italy; that Luke was a physician from Antioch, who traveled often with St. Paul, and based his Gospel on the preaching of St. Paul. St. Paul in turn insists vehemently in the first chapter of Galatians that he received his knowledge of Christ directly from Christ in the Damascus road vision, while adding that in Jerusalem he also compared notes with the other Apostles, who fully agreed with him.[54]

As to St. Matthew, the witnesses we quoted refer to the original Aramaic or Hebrew Matthew. What of our Greek? Some have even thought it could be a new composition because of the smoothness of the language and plays on words possible in Greek but not in Hebrew. But a good translator can make his work smooth, and it is not unknown for a translator to inject plays on words in the new language, which were not in the original. We have an instance in the Latin of *Hosea* 13:14, a play on *mors* and *morsus,* which is not possible in the original.

But, whether it is a new effort by St. Matthew himself (which it could easily be) or a translation, still we can depend on it as authentic: 1) The content is nearly all the same as Luke, or Luke and Mark together; 2) the author shows concern for his own eternity, which depended on getting things right and factual and would prevent fakery and carelessness; 3) the fact that Matthew, who so regularly likes to show the fulfillment of prophecies about Christ, does not mention the fulfillment of Jesus' prophecy of the fall of Jerusalem in 70 A.D., points strongly to a date before 70, when so many eyewitnesses of Jesus would still be alive.

In all, we have testimony that any historian would be glad to have to support the claims that the Synoptics knew their facts either from Peter and Paul or, in the case of St. Matthew, from his own personal experience.

In contrast, let us look at what kind of evidence those offer who think that the Gospels are later and written by those without personal knowledge of the facts. As we said at the start of this chapter, there are two kinds of evidence for authorship: external (witnesses, such as we have quoted) and internal (evidence within the Gospels). We noted too that internal evidence by its very nature hardly ever can prove anything. It could at times prove a date, when a document, for example, mentions as near, something which is readily datable, such as an eclipse of the sun.

First, the objectors point to the Gospel prophecies about the fall of Jerusalem. Many are inclined to think *Mark* 13 was written before 70 A.D., because of things that are unclear to us (chiefly *Mark* 13:14), and probably would have been unclear to people before 70 A.D., though clear afterwards. But then, being convinced that Matthew and Luke depend on Mark, these objectors say both must have been written after 70 A.D. Of course, they have no real proof that Matthew and Luke depend on Mark. In Appendix I.6.c, we list the modern authors who no longer believe Mark wrote first. Further, the objectors notice how clear the language of Luke is about the fall of Jerusalem, especially concerning the besieging army. That objection presupposes that Luke could have faked a prophecy, which is impossible. In contrast, many commentators note that the language Luke uses at this point is taken directly from the Old Testament, and so need not be faked.

Also, is it even imaginable that all three Evangelists would not mention the fulfillment of this major prophecy if they had written after 70? This is especially the case with Matthew who, over and over again, loves to point to fulfillments.

Another argument that is given for the late writing of these Gospels, especially of Matthew's, is that Matthew shows no knowledge of the debate in which St. Paul became so involved over the law. So the controversy must have been settled by the time Matthew wrote. St. Paul had insisted that we are free from the law; but Matthew reports that Jesus said the law will never pass away (*Matthew* 5:17): "Do not think that I am come to destroy the law, or the prophets. I am not come to destroy, but to fulfill."

This argument does not hold. St. Matthew had a different purpose in writing which was to give a basic account of the life and teachings of Jesus. The scripture "I came not to destroy but to fulfill" did not clash with the teaching of St. Paul. The objectors seem to presuppose there was a conflict in doctrine, not just a difference in expression. St. Paul really means that our keeping the law does not *earn* salvation (cf. Chapters 18 & 19). Jesus implies that too, in saying we are children of the Father and children do not *earn* their inheritance. St. Paul also insists many times that if we violate the law, we will earn punishment (*1 Cor.* 6:9-10; *Gal.* 5:19-21; *Eph.* 5:5; *Rom.* 3:31). He sums up this theme in *Rom.* 6:23, "For the wages of sin is death. But the gift of God is life everlasting, in Christ Jesus our Lord."

Further attempts to make Luke a later writing depend on making the *Acts of Apostles* also a later writing and therefore unreliable (with a presupposition that the author did not know Paul), for the Gospel of Luke was clearly written before *Acts*. These arguments are very vague, and the objections can be answered. Really, we could turn the argument around by saying that *Acts* ends with St. Paul in his first Roman imprisonment, probably 61-63 A.D. So the Gospel of Luke must come before that period.

But, to show the emptiness of the objections and to give you the complete picture, here are the chief reasons given for charging *Acts* with unreliability.

First, objectors notice that the decree of the Council of Jerusalem in *Acts* 15:28-29, while freeing the Gentile converts from the Mosaic law in general, prescribed a few little rules, among them, "That you abstain from things sacrificed to idols, and from blood, and from things strangled, and from fornication." The last item, of course, is just basic morality, but the first three are not. Yet, St. Paul in chapter 8 of *1 Cor.* does not flatly prohibit eating food sacrificed to idols, unless part of pagan ritual, or when scandal would be given.

Also in contrast, says the objector, St. Paul describes that council in *Gal.* 2:1-10 and does not mention these reservations, but says that the Apostles "added nothing to me." (*Gal.* 2:6).

The most basic refutation of these objections is so simple and obvious that it is strange it has not been noticed. If the Vatican today sends a letter with instructions or orders to the U.S. or Canadian Episcopal Conference, *the orders apply only to the area to which they are sent—they are not general law.* So, *Acts* 15:23 says the letter of the Council was addressed, "to the brothers who are of the gentiles of Antioch and Syria and Cilicia." That would not include Corinth, or even Galatia. The three special additions we mentioned were obviously just a concession to the feeling of those who loved the Old Law. As to the account in *Galatians 2,* Paul is giving a *general summary,* focusing on the point that even though he did get his *information and mission* directly from Christ on the Damascus road, yet, for further reassurance to those who hesitated to believe him, he did check with the Apostles in Jerusalem, and they did not tell him to change. In writing to the Galatians, Paul would need to mention only the basic *doctrinal point,* valid *everywhere,* that the Mosaic Law did not bind. There was no need to say that *for tactical reasons* some places had been asked to observe three small items of the Mosaic Law.

Some also object that *Acts* ends with Paul still in house arrest in Rome and does not tell the outcome of his trial. But this proves nothing against Luke's authorship. Luke's purpose could have been to trace the work of Paul to Rome, the center of the world. Having done that, he had fulfilled his purpose. Or, he could have intended to write a second book of *Acts,* which, for any of various reasons, he never did complete.

We see, then, that far from being strong enough to overturn the weighty testimony of so many ancient witnesses on the authorship of the Synoptics, instead the internal evidence offered against the witnesses turns out to be worthless. We conclude that the Synoptics were written by 1) an Apostle, Matthew (at least for the Semitic text), and 2) Mark, who got information from Peter and 3) Luke, who received it from Paul.

But even if we were to suppose, just for the sake of argument, that the Gospels were not by these men, but were instead written as late as 80-90 A.D., as some wish to claim, we can still show that the Gospel writers had ample opportunity to get information about Jesus.

First, as we have noted, by that time Christianity had spread into many places around the Mediterranean. It was being accepted in spite of its high and difficult moral demands (compared to paganism) and with its risk of persecution and death. Men do not cling to mere fancies when facing lions, torture and death. Second, Christianity was being confirmed by miracles. Some, of course, say there were no miracles at that time. Their real objection comes from their rejection of miracles as possible at *any* time. But we saw in Chapter 3 that miracles still happen and are checked with scientific strictness. In addition, as St. Augustine shrewdly observed, if the uneducated and ignorant Apostles had been able to sell such a difficult and demanding doctrine to sophisticated Greeks and Romans, without any miracles, that fact itself would be a miracle.[55] Yes, St. Paul had the education of a Rabbi, but Greeks and Romans would call that silly superstition.

Finally, as we indicated briefly, Quadratus, earliest of the Greek apologists for Christianity, writing about 123 A.D., said, "The things done by the Savior remained present always, for they were true. Those cured, those who rose from the dead were not only seen when they were being cured and raised, but were constantly present, not only while the Savior was living, but also for some time after He had gone, so that *certain of them came down even to our own time.*"[56]

This is remarkable. Quadratus says that some who

were healed by Christ or even raised from the dead
lived until his own time. Of course, that would not have
to mean 123 A.D., but it would surely include 80-90
A.D., the latest date suggested for the Synoptics. Such
persons would really remember Jesus and His
message—they had powerful reason to do so. As to
their living so long, if some of them were perhaps 15 to
20 years old in 30 A.D., by 80 A.D., they would be 65
or 70, not a hard thing to believe.

Others too, such as Pope St. Clement I, who ruled
from 92-101 A.D., were of the same generation as Sts.
Peter and Paul, as he tells us in his letter to Corinth.[57]
St. Polycarp, too, was still alive until 155 or 156, and
he had listened to St. John the Apostle.

So, information was not at all hard to get, if one
wanted it. We know that those writing, with their eternity at stake, wanted it intensely.

Chapter 11

A MAN SENT FROM GOD

We have covered quite a bit of ground. So, before
going ahead, let us briefly recall what we have studied
so far. We saw that science itself, by rigid checks,
proves that miracles do happen today and could have
happened in the time of Jesus. Then we examined the
proofs that there is a God and answered the objection
that there could not be a good God when there are so
many evils in the world.

Next we began a study of the Gospels, but looked at
them just as ancient documents, rather than as inspired
writings. We noted that historicists consider no writing
reliable as historical accounts, including the Gospels.
We countered their attack by making some distinctions.
We acknowledge that the fears of the historicists have
some relevance in regard to *interpretations* of things
that are intertwined with ancient culture, but they have
no real bearing on observing simple physical facts. Simple physical facts are what we need from the Gospels.

We checked next to see what type of literature the
Gospels intended to be, for each type of literature has
its own rules for understanding. We found that the
Gospels *intend to give facts* (since the eternity of the
writers was at stake) plus interpretations of those facts.
We saw some fascinating new evidence of the
meticulous care for accuracy that St. Luke showed.

Finally, we asked whether the Gospel writers were
able to obtain the facts. That led to asking questions
about the writers themselves. We found the evidence

excellent, the objections without real basis.

So now we are in a position to ask the Gospels for a few very simple, physical facts (in contrast to interpretations). Actually, we will see that we need precisely six such simple facts to establish a basis for faith.

The first two are that there was a man named Jesus and that He claimed to be a messenger, a prophet sent by God. Later we will discuss whether He was or was not divine. Really, no one doubts that He was named Jesus and that He claimed to be a divine messenger. Yet it is interesting and not without worth to review the evidence.

Tacitus, an outstanding Roman historian, whose accuracy is admired by scholars today, comments in connection with Nero's persecution of Christians as scapegoats after the burning of Rome, "The author of that name, Christ, was executed during the reign of Tiberius, by the procurator Pontius Pilate."[58]

But we do not need outside testimonies to His existence because the Synoptics are full of things about Him.

Did He claim to be a messenger from God, a sort of prophet? Again, this is entirely obvious, but let us review some of the evidence. One of the most striking things He said in this regard was His claim of authority over the sacred law given by Moses. Not even the greatest of the prophets would have dared to say what He said repeatedly:

"You have heard that it was said to them of old: You shall not kill. And whosoever shall kill shall be in danger of the judgment. But I say to you, that whoever is angry with his brother, shall be in danger of the judgment . . . You have heard it said to them of old: You shall not commit adultery. But I say to you, that whoever looks at a woman to lust after her, has already committed adultery with her in his heart . . . And it has been said, whoever puts away his wife, let him give her a bill of divorce. But I say to you, that whoever puts away his wife, excepting for the cause of fornication, causes her to commit adultery: and he who marries her that is put away, commits adultery."(*Matt.* 5:21-44).

The Jews of His day were so respectful of the Sabbath that they measured precisely how far a man might walk on that day and debated whether one might lawfully eat an egg if the hen had been working on the Sabbath to produce it! Yet Jesus dared to say, "Therefore the Son of man is Lord of the Sabbath also." (*Mark* 2:28; *Matt.* 12:8).

People rightly revered the great ancient King Solomon and the prophet Jonah. Yet Jesus told them, "The men of Ninive shall rise in judgment with this generation, and shall condemn it: because they repented at the preaching of Jonah. And behold one greater than Jonah is here."

"The queen of the south shall rise in judgment with this generation and shall condemn it: because she came from the ends of the earth to hear the wisdom of Solomon, and behold one greater than Solomon is here." (*Matt.* 12:41-43).

Once John the Baptist sent some of his disciples to Jesus to ask, "Are you he who is to come, or should we look for another? And Jesus in reply said to them: Go and tell John what you have heard and seen. The blind see, and the lame walk, lepers are cleansed and the deaf hear, and the poor have the Gospel preached to them." (*Matt.* 11:3-5; *Luke* 7:20-22).

It was obvious that He was claiming that He fulfilled the prophecy of *Isaiah* 35:5-6, "Then shall the eyes of the blind be opened, and the ears of the deaf shall be unstopped. Then shall the lame man leap like a hart, and the tongue of the dumb will sing out of joy."

Similarly, St. Luke tells how He came to His home town of Nazareth and went to the synagogue on the sabbath: "And the book of Isaiah the prophet was given to him. And opening the book he found the place where it was written: The Spirit of the Lord is upon me and he anointed me to preach the Gospel to the poor; he has sent me to proclaim liberation to captives and sight to the blind, to set free those who are oppressed, and to announce an acceptable year of the Lord. And closing the book and giving it to the attendant, he sat down. And the eyes of all in the synagogue were attentive to him. He began to say to them: today this Scripture is fulfilled in your hearing ... And they said: Is not this the son of Joseph? .... and he said: Amen I say to you, no prophet is acceptable in his own country." (*Luke* 4:17-24; cf. *Matt.* 13:53-57; *Mark* 6:1-4).

Jesus read *Isaiah* 61:1-2 and declared that He fulfilled the prophecy. If so, He then is the Anointed One; and His comment at the end makes it clear that He is a prophet.

Finally, an especially clear claim, with deep implications, is shown in *Luke* 10:16 (cf. *Matt.* 10:40). Jesus tells His disciples as He sends them forth, "He that hears you, hears me; and he that rejects you, rejects me; and he that rejects me, rejects him that sent me." He makes it quite clear that He is sent, and sent by God.

Did He then claim to be a messenger from God, a sort of prophet? Obviously yes, and far more. He dared to revise the sacred law of the Jews; He claimed to be Lord of the Sabbath, greater than Jonas or Solomon; He declared He was the one foretold by Isaiah. He went so far as to affirm, "He who rejects you, rejects me, and the One who sent me."

Need we fear, with the historicists, that these texts are so affected by the culture of the time that we cannot be sure of understanding them? Hardly. The claim is so simple: He says God sent Him. Any nation, any culture can grasp the meaning of that statement with no difficulty.

Of course, the next question will be: Did He prove His claim? Our next chapter will take up that matter.

Chapter 12

SIGNS AND WONDERS
TO BELIEVE

The Roman Emperor Vespasian was sitting on a throne at Alexandria in Egypt before returning to Rome. There, reports the Roman historian Tacitus, "Many miracles happened."[59] He gives two instances: A blind man came and threw himself at the feet of Vespasian, and said the god Serapis had told him to come to have Vespasian heal his blindness. "He asked the prince to sprinkle his cheeks and eyes with his spittle."

A second petitioner had an ailing hand. At the insistence of the same god Serapis, "He begged that he be stepped on by the foot of Caesar." Vespasian at first laughed and refused; he feared a charge of vanity if he failed. But the two victims kept pleading, and his courtiers kept flattering. So Vespasian asked the doctors for an opinion: "The power of the eyes was not completely gone, and would return if obstacles were removed; for the other, the joint had slipped the wrong way, could be corrected if salutary force were applied." So Vespasian did as requested: "At once the hand became usable; the day returned for the blind man."

Many other marvels or miracles are reported in paganism. We chose this one because it is reported by Tacitus, a careful historian.

What should we think of them? Some cases are apt to be the result of suggestion, which has such great power that the Catholic Church will not take up a case for consideration as a miracle unless suggestion can be

63

ruled out. As we saw earlier at Lourdes, only those claims are examined for which there is a medical certificate *before,* to testify that there is an *incurable* condition, and of course, examination by several doctors *after* the alleged cure. Commonly there will be 25 to 50 doctors with the pilgrimages, sometimes even a hundred.[60] Even so, in the more than 100 years since Lourdes, the Church has accepted only about 50 miracles as authentic out of a far greater number claimed.

In the case Tacitus reports, we note that the afflictions according to doctors were naturally curable. But, may we or should we just reject all pagan claims of miracles? St. Thomas Aquinas thinks not. He observes that evil spirits have great powers, which are natural to them but marvelous to us. He even thinks God might at times work a miracle for some good pagan, and mentions especially the case of a Vestal Virgin in ancient Rome who was accused of unchastity. The penalty was that she was to be buried alive. She claimed innocence and was given a chance to prove it by bringing water from the river in a sieve. She did it.[61]

So we can see that merely working a miracle will not of itself prove anything. More is needed. *A special connection of miracle and claim is required.* For if a miracle is to be used to prove a false claim or a lie, God, who is Truth itself, cannot work a miracle or provide the power to do so, for then He would no longer be the Truth.[62]

Therefore, the mere fact that Jesus worked miracles is not enough to prove He was a messenger sent by God. We need, in addition, a tie or a connection made between the miracle and the claim.

It is just such a connection that was present many times in the miracles of Jesus. For example, in *Luke* 8:41-56 (cf. *Mark* 5:21-43), Jairus, a ruler of the synagogue, fell at the feet of Jesus and begged Him to come to his dying daughter. But a man came from the ruler's house and said, "Your daughter is dead, do not trouble him. And Jesus hearing this word, answered the father of the girl: Fear not; just believe and she will be well."

So they went into the house, "and Jesus took her by the hand and called out saying: Child, arise. And her spirit returned, and she got up at once."

The case of the centurion in *Matthew* 8:5-13 (cf. *Luke* 7:1-10) is even more striking. At Capernaum the centurion begged Him to help his sick servant. Jesus said He would come. "And the centurion answering said: Lord, I am not worthy that you should come under my roof but only say the word, and my servant will be healed." He said he knew the effect of a word from *one having authority*.

"When Jesus heard this he marveled, and said to those who followed him: Amen I say to you, I have not found such great faith in Israel . . . And Jesus said to the Centurion: Go, and be it done to you as you have believed. And the servant was healed at the same moment."

Again, *Matthew* 9:27-29 (cf. *Mark* 10:46-52; *Luke* 18:35-43) tells of two blind men asking for their sight. Jesus said, "Do you believe that I am able to do this? They said, Yes Lord. Then he touched their eyes saying: Be it done to you *according to your faith*. And their eyes were opened."

In *Luke* 11:14-20 (cf. *Matt.* 12:22-30) Jesus cast out a devil from a dumb man, and the dumb man became able to speak. But some charged, "He casts out devils by Beelzebul, prince of devils. Jesus replied, 'If I cast out devils by Beelzebul, by whom do your sons cast them out? Therefore they will be your judges. But if by the finger of God I cast out devils, then the Kingdom of God has come upon you.'"

There are, of course, many similar incidents in the Gospels. Let us take just one more case, an especially striking one, reported in all three Synoptics (*Mark*

2:1-12; *Luke* 5:17-26; *Matt.* 9:1-8). Jesus was in a crowd when some men came, carrying a paralytic on a stretcher. They could not get near Jesus, so they opened the roof over Him, and let the paralytic down before Jesus. According to Mark, "When Jesus saw their faith, he said to the paralytic, 'Son, your sins are forgiven': And some of the scribes were sitting there and thinking in their hearts: What does this man say? He blasphemes. Who is able to forgive sin, but God alone?..."

They had not learned to see that there could be delegated authority to forgive sins, so they understood the words of Jesus as a claim to divinity: "Jesus at once knowing in his spirit that they were thinking these things within themselves said to them: Why do you think these things in your hearts? What is easier: to say to the paralytic, your sins are forgiven, or to say: Get up and take your bed and walk? But that you may know that the Son of Man has power on earth to forgive sins, he said to the paralytic: Get up and take your bed and go to your house. And he got up at once and took his bed and went out before them all, so that all wondered and glorified God saying: We never saw the like."

Here is indeed a tremendous display! The scribes thought Jesus claimed divinity by forgiving sins. Yet Jesus, reading their hearts, asked which was easier to say: Your sins are forgiven; or, take up your bed. He meant, of course, that they could not check to see if sins were forgiven, but they could see if the man got up and walked. So, He would perform one act to prove He had done the other. And the man did get up and walked at once. So, Jesus proved He could forgive sins and thus also proved He is far more than just a messenger from God. In fact, we could make a claim to His divinity here, for in the minds of the onlookers, that was the claim that was being proved. But for our purpose we need only claim this shows He is a messenger from God, even though, of course, He actually is divine.

Therefore, we see that again and again Jesus worked miracles in order to establish a connection with a point He wished to make. He raised the dead on condition of belief in Him, at least, as a prophet or messenger from God. He healed the centurion's servant from a distance by a mere command when seeing the faith the centurion had that He was a messenger from God. Similarly with the blind man, and most dramatically of all in the case of the paralytic whose sins Jesus forgave and whom He healed as a visible proof that He really had forgiven sins.

As we said previously, there is no need here to consider the fancies of the historicists. Anyone, regardless of his culture or period of history, can see and report when a dead person comes back to life, when a sick man is healed by a mere command, when the blind suddenly see, and the paralyzed walk. And with equal ease they can hear that these things were done in connection with a statement of belief that He had special power. Anyone can understand the connection when He causes a paralytic to jump up as proof that He had forgiven the man's sins.

Someone may object: Are there not cures by suggestion? Yes, there are such cures, in ancient times and in our own. But we can be sure that at least some of the miracles and cures Jesus performed are not due to suggestion. No suggestion will multiply loaves and fishes to feed thousands; no suggestion will calm a storm at sea; no suggestion will cure a man *born* blind. Hysterical blindness might be cured by suggestion; but an organic failure in a man from birth is not the kind of defect open to suggestion. Leprosy cannot be cured by suggestion. Nor can suggestion bring a man out of the tomb who has been dead for four days.

Still further, would God, who *is* Truth, allow so monstrous a hoax on so large a scale to be used to prove a false teaching with such immense consequences for the entire world, for all later centuries? Hardly.

Further, the miracles of the Gospels are really in continuity with certain modern miracles, such as those of Lourdes, of which we read in Chapter 3. No suggestion could make a withered optic nerve operant—as happened in the case of Madam Bire. No suggestion could produce the host of Lanciano, or the image of Guadalupe. The miracles of Lourdes are normally worked precisely when the Blessed Sacrament passes, thereby confirming the Presence in that Sacrament of the same Divine Healer, and confirming the transmission over the centuries of the power of orders needed to confect that Sacrament.

Chapter 13

THE INNER CIRCLE

"And it happened in those days, that he went out into a mountain to pray, and passed the entire night in the prayer of God. And when day came, he called to himself his disciples, and those twelve of them, whom he also named Apostles: Simon, whom he named Peter, and Andrew his brother, James and John, Philip and Bartholomew, Matthew and Thomas, James the son of Alpheus, and Simon who is Zelotes, and Jude, the brother of James, and Judas Iscariot who became a traitor." (*Luke* 6:12-16).

Thus St. Luke tells of the choosing of the Twelve. Mark has a very similar account (3:13-19; cf. *Matt.* 10:1-4). We notice that the Twelve were chosen out of those who were already in a circle of disciples; they were to be more closely united with Him, to form His "inner circle," so to speak.

After this point in the Gospel narrative, we constantly hear about the Apostles' being with Him. The Gospels prove, and we would expect to find, an inner circle of some sort in the crowds that followed after Him. Also, we would expect that He would speak more to that inner circle and tell them things more fully than He would to the general crowd. That too is evident in the Gospels.

Specially significant, however, is the line in *Mark* 4:11 (See also *Matt.* 13:11 and *Luke* 8:10): "To you it is given to know the mystery of the kingdom of God: but to those outside all things are in parables." In the

69

arrangement St. Mark has made (we know the Evangelists did not always use chronological order), this passage comes right after the tragic incident in which He had cast out a devil, but the scribes commented (*Mark* 3:22), "He has Beelzebul, and by the prince of devils he casts out devils." This was, as Jesus Himself said, the unforgivable sin (*Mark* 3:28-29); not that God would refuse to forgive any repentant sinner any sin, but rather that such hardness is extremely unlikely ever to soften to the point of repentance. And without repentance, not even God, who is Mercy itself, will forgive. In fact, forgiveness is simply impossible without repentance, for the sinner who is unrepentant says, in effect, "I was right to sin and to offend You."

Consequently it was after this that, as St. Mark presents it, Jesus resorted to using parables as a teaching method. But for the Apostles He would still explain things, hence He added, "To you it is given to know the mystery of the kingdom of God: but to those outside, all things are in parables." And mysteriously He continued, "That seeing they may see, and not perceive; and hearing they may hear, and not understand: lest at any time they should be converted, and their sins should be forgiven them." (*Mark* 4:11).

Luke 8:10 has similar language, seeming to imply that the *purpose* of the parables is to prevent outsiders from understanding. *Matthew* 13:13-15 has a softer version of the same. "Therefore do I speak to them in parables: because seeing they do not see, and hearing they do not hear, neither do they understand. And the prophecy of Isaiah is fulfilled in them, who said: You shall really hear, but not understand, and really look but not see."

All three Gospels report Jesus quoting the same passage of *Isaiah*. There, God has just appointed Isaiah as a prophet, and He tells him, in the form of a command, "Go and thou shalt say to this people: Really hear, but do not understand, and really see, but do not perceive. Make thick the heart of this people, and make their ears heavy and shut their eyes, lest they see with their eyes and hear with their ears and understand with their heart and turn and be healed." (*Is.* 6:9-10).

Did not Jesus want people in general to hear His message? Obviously He did; otherwise, why would He go to such labors? Why then did He make these statements? Obviously, we need to investigate to find out.

There is a well-known Semitic speech pattern which Westerners cannot understand without help. Often, in fact most of the time, the Hebrews would speak as though God *positively did and intended things which He really only permitted.* For example in the book of Exodus, Pharaoh's heart was hardened several times, even after he had seen the displays of mighty power by Moses and Aaron, yet *Exodus* 10:1 says, "And the Lord said to Moses: Go in to Pharaoh; for I have hardened his heart, and the heart of his servants: that I may work these my signs in him."

Obviously, God does not want men to be hard, men harden themselves. Even more dramatically, in *1 Sam.* 4:3, after the Philistines had inflicted a great defeat on the Israelites, they said, "Why has the Lord struck us today before the face of Philistines?" Of course the Israelites knew it was the Philistines who had struck them, yet they said God did it.

Hence, in the way the Gospels depict Jesus quoting Isaiah, and in the original text of *1 Samuel* as well, when we find an expression that says God intended to close their eyes and ears so they would not repent, we should recognize the Hebrew pattern we have just explained and understand that the real meaning is that God has permitted, not caused, the hardening.

Therefore, Jesus did not *want* to blind His hearers. Rather, in *Matthew* 23:37 Jesus weeps over that hardness: "Jerusalem, Jerusalem . . . how often would I have gathered together your children, as the hen gathers her chickens under her wings, and you would not?"

Again, after the parable of the wedding dinner, when most of those invited not only refused to attend, but even killed the servants who called them, He sadly added, "For many are called, but few are chosen."[62] (*Matt.* 22:14).

St. Matthew observes (*Matt.* 21:45) that the Pharisees understood that the parable just before, the one about the wicked tenants, meant them. So they would understand that the wedding feast parable meant the same. Now the meaning of "many are called" is clear: He called all—Pharisees and all others of His people—to the wedding feast, to the Messianic Kingdom. But most of them were not chosen, because they refused to come.[63]

Thus, Jesus did want His people to understand, but when He found many of them so ill-disposed, He turned to parables. Later on, the Apostles, especially St. Paul, would find people better disposed and would be able to speak more openly.

There has been much discussion about the purpose of the parables: Were they meant to show mercy, or as blinding in justice? The real answer is that they were both at the same time. They were a device such that those with good dispositions would understand at least something at the start, and would grow in understanding; while the ill-disposed would understand less and less.

Thus, there really is a spiral pattern set up, in two opposite directions by the parable (and in many other things in Scripture as well). To begin to see the spirals, we will think of a man who has never been drunk before, but goes out and really gets drunk. The next morning he has a grand hangover, but also guilt feelings. Since this is a case in which the man has never been drunk before, after that first spree there will be a clash of two voices inside him. The voice of his beliefs says it is very wrong to get drunk; the voice of his actions (which speak more loudly than words) says it is all right.

Our nature dislikes such clashes and works hard to eliminate them. So, in due time, something has to give: either the man makes his actions fit his faith, or his faith will fit his actions. That is, if he continues in his pattern of drunkenness, he will reach a point at which he no longer believes it very wrong to get drunk. His faith has been forced into line with his actions. And he can go further down the spiral, for other beliefs are interlocked with the belief of the evil of drunkenness, so that in time he can be very dull indeed in perceiving *any* religious truths; he has gone far on a downward spiral, which feeds only on itself, making his mind darker and darker toward the truth.

But there is a spiral in the other direction as well. Faith tells us that this world, compared to the next, is worth very little. St. Paul (*Phil.* 3:8) even dares to speak of all the things of the world as "dung" in comparison to the things of eternity. So if a man lives vigorously in accord with such faith, he will continue going farther and farther into the spiral in the good direction. His ability to perceive religious truths will become greater and greater.

There is both mercy and justice in both spirals. The evil man deserves his blindness; it is due in justice; yet there is mercy for him in this because the more deeply one knows the truths of faith, the greater his responsibility. The man of faith, on the other hand, deserves the added light, and so receives it in justice; yet the fact that he gets it is most basically mercy: all gifts of God to us are, at bottom, mercy. We cannot by our own power generate any claim on Him.

We return to the parables and Scripture. They are designed to point out a distinction among people: those well-disposed, who will get more and more of the light; those ill-disposed, who will lose even what they seemed to have. Recall the line at the end of the parable of the talents: "For to everyone who has, more will be given, and he will abound; but from him who has not, even that which he has will be taken away." (*Matt.* 25:14-29). And, as we saw, there is both mercy and justice in both cases.

So we can easily see that teaching in parables was splendidly designed to address best the hardness in His audience, to set up the division based on good or bad dispositions. At the same time, He explained all to His inner circle, for use later on with those who would be better disposed.

We can see, too, why Jesus did not overwhelm people with miracles. Why did He not arrange to rise from the tomb before several hundred people, including unbelievers, so that people could not help believing? The answer is that faith should not be forced. If forced, it is not really faith at all.

When we accept things as true we use compulsive and noncompulsive evidence. Compulsive evidence leaves us no freedom of choice. For instance, two plus two equals four. Noncompulsive evidence covers a larger spectrum. At the upper end are facts so strongly based that no one can doubt their validity. For example, we know that Washington crossed the Delaware. Again, there is virtually no freedom to decide. But on the other end of the noncompulsive range of evidence, we meet *things for which there is ample proof, but yet, not such proof as to leave us no freedom of choice. Our minds are not forced into believing.* Precisely in that range there is freedom, and therefore room for faith. And it will be with faith in general, as it was with the parables: those well-disposed will see more and more, as they grow in holiness; those ill-disposed will see less and less, and they grow in iniquity.

We have seen that Jesus did have an inner circle to whom He explained things more clearly, not so much for immediate use, since the crowds were mostly hardened, but for later use. The Gentiles, as St. Paul witnessed repeatedly, would accept Christ in great numbers. Jesus wanted people to understand, but He did not want to coerce their belief. It is important that people freely choose the truth. Once they believe, grace is abundantly given so they can grow in holiness.

Chapter 14

BEHOLD, I AM WITH YOU ALL DAYS

We now reach the climax of our search: The proof that the messenger from God told His Apostles to teach, and promised that God would protect their teaching and that of their successors until the very End of Time. In this chapter, we will see the positive proof; in the next chapter, we will answer the chief objections raised to the validity of the foundation of the Church.

"And he went up to a mountain, and called those he wanted, and they came to him. And he caused the twelve to be with him, to send them to preach." Thus *Mark* 3:13-14 (cf. *Matt.* 10:5; *Luke* 9:2) describes the call of the Apostles and their appointment by Jesus to continue His mission of preaching and teaching.

This was at the beginning of the public ministry of Jesus Himself; at the end, after His Resurrection, *Matthew* (28:18-20) tells about the confirmation and extension of this mission: "And Jesus coming, spoke to them, saying: All power is given to me in heaven and earth. Going therefore, teach all nations; baptizing them in the name of the Father, and of the Son, and of the Holy Spirit. Teaching them to observe all things whatsoever I have commanded you: and behold I am with you all days, even to the consummation of the world."

After Pentecost had calmed their first fears and strengthened them, the Apostles went forth fearlessly, teaching the message of Jesus in spite of all threats of beatings, imprisonment, and death, as we see in the *Acts of the Apostles.*

Everyone then understood that only the Apostles were the official teachers appointed by Jesus, for *Acts* 5:13 states, "But of the rest no man dared join himself to them; but the people magnified them."

Paul too, commissioned by Jesus on the road to Damascus, went out, tirelessly preaching, in spite of every kind of obstacle and persecution. He, like the other Apostles, made provision for the continuance of the teaching of Jesus. Hence, he left Timothy at Ephesus,[64] and wrote to him, "These things command and teach . . . Till I come, attend to reading, to exhortation, and to doctrine . . . Take heed to yourself and to doctrine: be earnest in them. For in doing this you will save yourself and those who hear you." (*1 Tim.* 4:11, 13, 16).

And still more explicitly in *2 Timothy* 1:13-14, 2:2: "Hold the form of sound words, which you have heard from me in faith, and in the love which is in Christ Jesus. Keep the good deposit committed to your trust by the Holy Ghost . . . And the things which you have heard of me by many witnesses, the same commend to faithful men, who shall be fit to teach others also."

In the same vein, at the end of the first century, Pope St. Clement I, who was of the same generation as the Apostles Peter and Paul,[65] wrote to Corinth, where rebels had dared to oust and supplant the properly appointed successors of the Apostles, "Our Apostles knew through our Lord Jesus Christ that there would be strife over the name of Bishop. As a result, having received full foreknowledge, they appointed those we have mentioned, and meanwhile added a provision that if these would fall asleep [die], other approved men should receive their ministry."[66]

Jesus Himself had indicated that the mission He gave to the Apostles was not for the one generation only. He made this clear in the words recorded in *Matt.* 28:20, when He said, "Behold I am with you all days, even to the consummation of the world." He made it clear in other ways too, especially in the parables of the weeds (*Matt.* 13:24-43) and the net (*Matt.* 13:47-50). In the first, the kingdom of Heaven is compared to a field in which the master sowed good seed, but his enemy came at night and sowed weeds in the same field. The servants wanted to pull out the weeds but the master said, "No, lest in gathering the weeds, you root up the wheat along with them." He advised, "The harvest is the end of the world, and the reapers are angels. Just as the weeds are gathered and burned with fire, so will it be at the end of the world." So the Church, with both good and wicked men in it, is to last until the harvest, the end of the world. The same thought is clear in the parable of the net which gathered up fish of every kind. Afterwards, the fishers sorted out the good and the bad fish. "So it will be at the end of the world."

So, as one would naturally expect, Jesus wanted His teaching, by the Apostles and their successors, to go on until the very end.

As one would expect, too, He promised that God would protect that teaching. Really, any sensible leader, if he had the means to do so, would want to protect his organization and see that it would stay faithful to the teachings he imparted to it. Ordinary men cannot make such a provision, but a messenger sent from God could do it, if God so willed. We know that God did so will, for that messenger made the fact clear more than once.

As St. Luke records (*Luke* 10:16), Jesus told the Apostles, "He who hears you hears me; and he who rejects you rejects me, and he who rejects me, rejects him who sent me." That is, he rejects God Himself. So Jesus did, as a messenger from God, assure them that men in hearing them would hear Him—and so, in turn, would hear God's message. If not, they would be rejecting God, who sent Him as His messenger.

Similarly, in *Matthew* 18:17-18, He told the Apostles, "And if he will not hear them: tell the church. And if he will not hear the church, let him be to you as the heathen and publican." The words that follow make the case even more emphatic and clear: "Amen I say to you, whatsoever you shall bind upon earth, shall be bound also in heaven; and whatsoever you shall loose upon earth, shall be loosed also in heaven."

The words, "binding and loosing" were well known in the teaching of the rabbis of the time. Their regular meaning was to impose or remove an obligation by an authoritative decision or teaching. In the verse just quoted, they were spoken to all the Apostles. As we shall see in Chapter 16, they were also spoken individually and specially to Peter (*Matt.* 16:19). Commenting directly on the commission to Peter, and so indirectly on the same words to all the Apostles, W. F. Albright, a noted Protestant Scripture scholar often called in his last years "the dean of American Scripture scholars," wrote in his commentary on Matthew, "Peter's authority to 'bind' or 'release' will be a carrying out of decisions made in Heaven. His teaching and disciplinary activities will be similarly guided by the Spirit to carry out Heaven's will."[67]

We see then, the full import of the words Jesus used in His last farewell to the Apostles, which we quoted earlier (*Matt.* 28:18-20), "All power is given to me in heaven and earth. Going therefore, teach all nations; baptizing them in the name of the Father, and of the Son, and of the Holy Spirit. Teaching them to observe all things whatsoever I have commanded you: and behold I am with you all days, even to the consummation of the world."

Let us now determine at what point we have arrived in our study. We have seen that there lived a man named Jesus, who claimed to be a messenger sent by God, who proved it by miracles worked in special connections. We have seen that He, as we would expect, had an inner circle among the crowds that followed Him, and that He spoke more fully to them, and that, as we would also expect, He told them to continue His teaching. Finally, as we would also suppose from anyone having the means to do so, He arranged to protect their fidelity in continuing His teaching. He said that he who hears you, hears Me; and he who does not, rejects the One who sent Me. So He, by divine commission, sent them as He was sent, with authority, and promises to be with them as they taught men to observe all that He commanded. He will do this until the end of the world.

Now that we have established that there was a body commissioned by a messenger from God and promised protection in the name of God for its teaching, what is expected from us? *Intellectually, it is not only permissible to believe what that body teaches—if one is intelligent enough to follow our proofs, it is not just permissible, it is intellectually inescapable.* Thus, Catholics follow that teaching, not out of esteem for the humans who bear the commission—in fact, the first head of the body, Peter, even denied Jesus at His trial. No, Catholics accept that teaching because the Apostles and their successors are on the receiving end of the promises. "He who hears you hears me . . . I am with you always, to the end of the world."

Therefore, it is not only rational to have faith—it is intellectually *required*. It is *inescapable* intellectually, as we have said. As a result, now we can ask that same body to clarify many other things for us, to tell us if the Messenger might happen to be God Himself. We ask it to tell us if the Gospels are also inspired by the Holy Spirit, besides being ancient documents that pass the same tests other reliable records pass. Such assurance is needed, for in the first centuries there were in circulation many alleged Gospels and other alleged sacred books. We need to know which really are sacred and inspired. Now we can find out; for the body commissioned by the Divine Messenger can tell us, and has told us. Only in this way do we know what writings constitute the Bible. Anyone who does not accept that divinely-given teaching authority really has no logical right to appeal to the Gospels at all as sacred and inspired. How could he know if they are inspired or not?

Chapter 15

KÜNGLY OBJECTIONS

In spite of the clear Scriptural evidence that we have already presented, some objections have been raised by critics. The strongest come from Hans Küng.

Küng believes:

1) "Jesus did *not found a Church* during His lifetime."[69] His view was limited: "He regarded Himself ... as sent only to the children of Israel ... the missionary command (*Matt.* 28:19) is post-paschal."

2) "Jesus never required a membership of a Church as a condition of entry into God's kingdom."[70] The Dead Sea community insisted on many things. It had a sort of novitiate, with many rules, long prayers, ritual meals and baths, and regulations. Jesus made no such demands. With Him there was, instead, "criminal irregularity, casualness, spontaneity, freedom."[71] So "He offended the passive world-forsaking ascetics by His uninhibited worldliness."[72]

3) Hence, in contrast to the fasting of John the Baptist and his followers,[73] "for Jesus . . . the sign took the form of feasts held in an atmosphere of joy, in which people celebrated their membership in the future kingdom." According to Küng, He expected the end soon.[74] Even the Last Supper is just one more of these meals of celebration.[75] Jesus was just having a high time with friends, who continued the practice after He died.

Küng's views are extreme. But very many Catholic scholars do make approaches in varying degrees to certain of Küng's points.

First, the question: Did Jesus directly found the Church and institute the Sacraments? For example, Richard McBrien,[76] while not speaking too clearly, seems to say that Jesus did not *directly* found a Church, or institute Sacraments.[77] To say that Jesus did both of these things would be what McBrien calls "non-scholarly conservatism." Our position in this book would get that label from McBrien and many others. But we are in good company. The Council of Trent defined that Jesus instituted seven Sacraments.[78] In addition, the same Council explicitly defined that Jesus instituted the Sacrament of Penance when He said to the Apostles: "Receive the Holy Spirit, whose sins you shall forgive, they are forgiven them."[79] (*John* 20:22 ff.). It is likewise defined that Jesus at the Last Supper ordained the Apostles in saying: "Do this in commemoration of me." (*Luke* 22:19; *1 Cor.* 11:24).[80] It further defined specifically that Jesus instituted the Sacraments of the Anointing of the Sick and of Matrimony.[81]

In contrast, various scholars like to say that all Jesus did was to proclaim the kingdom, gather disciples, give them the holy Spirit—and that later the Church developed, and the priesthood developed too, along with it.

A chief root of such views is the widespread conviction that Jesus was ignorant, did not know enough about even His own work and character to lay out what many scholars like to call a "blueprint" for the future. They do not really mean to say that *He,* the Divine Person, had any ignorance—they mean that certain things did not, as it were, register on His human mind.

In my book, *The Consciousness of Christ,* I take up and answer every argument given by any scholar of note to prove ignorance in Jesus.[83] The same book also gives all the teachings of the Church, which definitely exclude ignorance in the human intellect of Jesus.[84]

Some think that Jesus spoke no words at all after

Easter: In such a case, He would have communicated with the Apostles and others by what mystical theologians call interior locutions.[85] Then, the objectors continue, the Apostles only later could have come to understand the command to teach all nations (*Matt.* 28:19)—or else this command was never given at all, but was simply a "community formulation"—something faked.

The objectors seem not to know the real nature of interior locutions. Actually, in them the recipient understands well, and at once.[86] It is only at a later time that the same soul may begin to wonder if it really came from God.[87] So this proposal will not explain why the Apostles did not seem at first to have heard the command to teach all nations.

Really, the objectors forget that over and over again the Gospels portray the Apostles as slow to understand. They did not grasp even the repeated predictions of Christ's death, and therefore seem to have given up faith when He died. Even when the women came and reported He had risen, they had difficulty comprehending or believing. Still later, the Apostles flunked their "final exam"; just before He ascended, they asked, "Lord will you at this time restore again the kingdom of Israel?" (*Acts* 1:6): It seems they still had not gotten over the notion of a conquering Messiah!

How could they fail to grasp? Much brighter, better-educated people than dull Galilean fishermen have been known to fail to grasp things. At the end of Chapter 8 we gave a short note on Form and Redaction Criticism. In it we saw how Norman Perrin, not an uneducated fisherman, but a highly-trained University of Chicago professor of Scripture, could fail to see what is so clear.

Take the example of the sad case of Dr. Semmelweis in the middle of the 19th century, whom other doctors put away for life in an insane asylum because they could not accept his discovery of the cause of puerperal fever. The proof of his claim was accurate and undeniable. His patients did not often get puerperal fever. The reason was so simple: he had used antiseptic precautions. The other doctors had been accustomed to ignoring them—not knowing about germs. They would even come from an autopsy room with blood on their aprons and go right into the delivery room. No wonder germs were passed from patient to patient! But the doctors could not see what was right in front of their noses.

Again, Teilhard de Chardin, a Jesuit priest, painted a glorious picture of the human race as he thought it would be just before the return of Christ. He predicted that all people would be bound together as closely as in a totalitarian state, but the bond would be love, and perhaps even telepathy.[88] Yet Chardin, as a Jesuit priest, must have read *Luke* 18:8, in which Jesus says, "But when the Son of man comes, do you think he will find faith on the earth?" And St. Paul in *2 Thess.* 2:3 joins in predicting a great apostasy just before the end. In *Matthew* 24:12 Jesus warns us that then, because wickedness will reach its peak, the love of most humans will grow cold.

2 Timothy 3:1-4 adds, "Know also this, that, in the last days, shall come dangerous times. Men shall be lovers of themselves, covetous, haughty, proud, blasphemers, disobedient to parents, ungrateful, wicked, without affection, without peace, slanderers, incontinent, unmerciful, without kindness, traitors, stubborn, puffed up, and lovers of pleasures more than of God." Yet a learned Jesuit could not see the obvious—nor so many of his devotees today, including many highly educated persons. So why be surprised at the *dullness* of poor Galilean fishermen?

In most of these cases, the reason for the lack of perception is clear. Some people establish a mental framework that will not allow any contrary idea to enter.

Thus, Perrin believed so firmly in Form Criticism that he could not see what was so evident. The Hungarian doctors knew nothing about germs, and so did not believe their own eyes which saw the results in patients helped by Dr. Semmelweis. Chardin could not see the Scripture passages that refuted his theory. And the Apostles shared the belief that the Messiah would be a glorious conqueror—and when Jesus tried to tell them the opposite, the idea just did not penetrate at all.

In defense of the Apostles, we must examine the command to teach all nations and the separation of Christianity from Judaism. We have spoken of the first of these two. As to the second, we must note that Christianity is really the fulfillment or completion of Judaism. Hence a modern Jewish convert, Father Arthur Klyber, C.SS.R., likes to speak of himself as a "completed Jew" (Cf. his outstanding book, *Once a Jew.* [89]) Jesus Himself insisted too (*Matt.* 5:17), "I am not come to destroy, [law and prophets] but to fulfill."

St. Matthew loves to point out over and over how Jesus fulfilled prophecies. St. Paul in *Romans* 11 speaks of a tame and a wild olive tree. The tame olive is the original people of God. Unfaithful Jews were branches of that people, but were broken off, by their infidelity or rejection of Christ. In their place the Gentiles were grafted as the new people of God, in continuity with the original people of God. St. Paul insists (*Rom.* 4:11; *Gal.* 3:6-9) that Christians are the true sons of Abraham, not by carnal descent, but by imitation of his faith.

Quite naturally then, the first Christians continued to frequent the Temple, while having their own Baptism and Eucharist separately.

Did Jesus, as Küng claims, "never require membership of a Church as a condition of entry into God's kingdom"? In *Matthew* 28:19 the final words of Jesus are, "Going therefore, teach all nations; baptizing them in the name of the Father, and of the Son, and of the Holy Spirit. Teaching them to observe all things whatsoever I have commanded you." Even the dull Apostles grasped the command to baptize. So on the first Pentecost, the crowds after hearing Peter, asked what to do. "And Peter said to them: Do penance and be baptized . . . for the remission of your sins." (*Acts* 2:37-38). Further, *Acts* 2:42 states, "And they were persevering in the doctrine of the Apostles, and in the communication of the breaking of bread, and in prayers." All recognized the preeminent position of the Apostles (*Acts* 5:13): "But of the rest no man dared join himself to them; but the people magnified them."

Was the Eucharist just part of "a long series of meals," just for fun, in "uninhibited worldliness" and "criminal irregularity" as Küng claims? First, the Last Supper was clearly a ritual meal, the observance of the Jewish Passover, as St. Luke makes clear (*Luke* 22:11). Within it Jesus took bread saying, "This is my body," and wine, saying, "This is my blood." One does not act or talk in such a serious manner at fun-meals with uninhibited worldliness. Jesus also at the Supper told them (*Matt.* 26:20; *Mark* 14:17), "Amen I say to you, that one of you is about to betray me"—hardly the way to have an uninhibited celebration. Nor would one knowing that He is about to die in a horrible manner take an interest in telling them to just continue these fun-meals with, "Do this in memory of me."

Küng also compares the Church to the Dead Sea Scroll community of Qumran, and finds in the Church no elaborate set-up of novitiate, initiation oath, long prayers, ritual meals etc. We reply that the important consideration is that Jesus did provide the essentials. He told them to teach all nations. He promised that God would protect their teaching. He instituted an entrance rite, Baptism, and He told them to continue the Eucharist. He told them to insist on teaching authority (*Matt.* 18:17), "And if he will not hear the Church, let him be to you as the heathen and publican." For He had given them authority (*Luke* 10:16): "He who hears you hears me; and he who rejects you rejects me, and he who rejects me, rejects him who sent me." And God Himself (*Matt.* 18:18) says, "Whatsoever you shall bind upon earth, shall be bound in heaven, and whatsoever you shall loose upon earth, shall be loosed also in heaven."

True, there were no chancery offices in the Apostolic Church! But there were authorities. St. Paul, in what is probably the first written book of the New Testament, told the Thessalonians: "Know those who labor among you, and are over you in the Lord, and admonish you, and . . . esteem them more abundantly in charity, for their work's sake." (*1 Thess.* 5:12).

This coincides with *Acts* 14:23, which reports that even before reaching Thessalonica, Paul, on his very first missionary expedition, appointed presbyters in every Church. The fact that we do not know the details of the function of the various officers in the early Church does not prove that those of whom Paul and Luke speak did not exist, or did not have authority. The words *presbyter* and *bishop* were at first generic words, even interchangeable—it takes time in any field of knowledge to develop precise technical terms.[90]

Finally, Küng claimed that Jesus "regarded himself . . . as sent only to the children of Israel." Here, Küng is being even duller than the slow Apostles. In *Matthew* 15:21-28 Jesus, in pagan territory, meets a Canaanite woman who asks Him to cure her daughter. Jesus at first did not answer at all. She insisted and He replied, "I was not sent but to the sheep that are lost of the house of Israel." Still she persisted, and He added, "It is not good to take the children's bread and to cast it to the dogs." She said, "Yes Lord for all the whelps also eat of the crumbs that fall from the table of their masters." Then Jesus praised her saying, "O woman, great is your faith: be it done to you as you wish."

Jesus, if we are not too dull to see it, was trying her, eliciting strong faith. He hardly meant to call her a dog. She, in faith and cleverness too, picked up that remark and said that even dogs get the crumbs. Jesus then stopped testing her, and praised her, and worked the cure.

Earlier, in *Matthew* 8:5, He cured the servant of the centurion, another pagan, and praised the pagan, saying, "I have not found so great faith in Israel."

What of the fact that in *Matthew* 10:5 Jesus told the Twelve, "Do not go into the way of the Gentiles, and into the city of the Samaritans enter not. But go rather to the lost sheep of the house of Israel." It is apparent that this was the instruction for a particular mission, a trial mission. It would not follow that He would always want them to stay away from pagans and Samaritans. As *John* 4:7-30 tells us, Jesus Himself did preach to the Samaritans. And on at least one occasion, He also preached in the Greek cities of the Decapolis (*Mark* 7:31) to the east of Jewish territory.

Consequently, there is more than enough proof to say there was a Church. There were authorities called Apostles, whom others did not dare to join and there were other authorities mentioned as early as 51 A.D. There was an entrance rite called Baptism. There was the sacred meal called the Eucharist and there was authority to teach, to bind, and to loose. All this was done, not by faked "community formulations," but by careful memory of Jesus. The Apostles were slow to realize some points but were still very concerned with facts, facts essential for eternity.

Chapter 16

YOU ARE PETER

We have carefully and solidly worked our way to the conclusion that it is not only intellectually possible, but even inescapable, to believe the body commissioned by the Divine Messenger, His Church, to whose teaching He promised divine protection, so that he who hears the Church hears Him, and hence, Him who sent Him.

We saw that His promises were spoken not to all followers, but to the Apostles and their successors, for Jesus intended His Church to last to the end of time. We saw that this fact was understood clearly from the beginning (*Acts* 5:13): "But of the rest no man dared join himself to them; but the people magnified them."

Next, we must explore the concept of the primacy of Peter and his successors. Since we have already established the fact that the teaching of the Church is divinely protected, obviously, the most secure and the easiest proof is simply to ask if the Church has taught that primacy. We can also, though it is not essential, examine the testimony of the Gospels regarding primacy.

1) THE TEACHING OF THE CHURCH

Even before a Council found occasion to teach the primacy of Rome, we find Christians in practice accepting that primacy. For example, there was acceptance when Pope St. Clement I, writing to Corinth around 95 A.D., intervened in a schism there, in which the lawful authorities had been ousted and supplanted by rebels. This Pope, who seems to have known Sts.

Peter and Paul personally—for he says that they "belonged to our own generation"[91]—began his letter saying, "Because of the sudden and repeated calamities and misfortunes, we think our attention has been slow in turning to the things debated among you."[92] Later in the same letter he adds, "If some are disobedient to the things He [Jesus] has spoken through us, they should know that they are enmeshing themselves in sin, and no small danger."[93] No ordinary person, without authority, would want or need to explain his slowness in taking up a case in a distant place, nor would he claim Jesus had spoken through him, so that it would be wrong not to comply.

In the second half of the next century, St. Irenaeus, who as we saw before, had listened to St. Polycarp tell things he had heard from the lips of St. John the Apostle himself, wrote a striking line. In the course of explaining that the way to be sure of getting sound doctrine is to be sure that the local church from which one receives it has unbroken continuity back to the Apostles, he adds, "Since it would be very long, in a volume of this sort, to go through the succession [of Bishops] in all the churches, by showing it in the most ancient one, known to all, founded by the two most glorious Apostles, Peter and Paul at Rome, which holds the tradition and faith announced by the Apostles, coming down by the successions of Bishops even to us—in this way we confound all those who in any way, out of self-pleasing, or vain glory, hold illicit assemblies. For it is necessary that every church, that is, the faithful who are everywhere, agree with this church because of its more important principality—this church in which the tradition coming from the Apostles has always been kept by those who are from every place."[94]

Some features of this text are not clear, and therefore are open to discussion. However, it is clear that the Church of Rome is the principal church and all other churches must agree with it because it has the doctrine of the Apostles Peter and Paul.

At the Council of Ephesus in 431 A.D., although the Nestorian heresy was an Eastern error, St. Cyril, patriarch of Alexandria in Egypt, went west to Pope Celestine for a decision before he went to the Council. The Pope then sent delegates to the Council who asserted without contradiction by anyone at the Council, "There is no doubt, it has been known to all centuries, that the holy and blessed Apostle Peter, the prince and head and pillar of the faith and foundation of the Catholic Church, received the keys of the kingdom from our Lord Jesus Christ . . . He [Peter] lives even to this time, and always in his successors gives judgment."[95]

Twenty years later the Council of Chalcedon, which again dealt with an Eastern heresy, accepted the decision of Pope Leo that, in Christ, there is one divine Person and two natures, divine and human. When the Pope's letter had been read, the bishops exclaimed, "This is the faith of the Fathers, this is the faith of the Apostles. We all believe thus . . . Anathema to him who does not so believe. Peter has spoken through Leo."[96]

In 680 A.D., the Third Council of Constantinople wrote to Pope Agatho, "And so we leave to you, the Bishop of the first See of the whole Church, what is to be done, you who stand on the firm rock of faith, and we gladly acquiesce in your letters of true doctrine . . . which we acknowledge as prescribed divinely from the supreme peak of the Apostles . . . Peter spoke through Agatho."[97]

The Council of Lyons, in 1274 A.D., taught in more general terms that, "The holy Roman Church holds the supreme and full primacy over the whole Catholic Church, together with fullness of power, which it truly and humbly recognizes it received from the Lord Himself in blessed Peter, prince and summit of the Apostles, whose successor is the Roman Pontiff."[98]

The Council of Florence, in 1439 A.D., taught, "We define that the holy Apostolic See and the Roman Pontiff holds the primacy in the whole world, and that the Roman Pontiff himself is the successor of blessed Peter, prince of the Apostles and true vicar of Christ, and that he is the head of the whole Church and the father and teacher of all Christians, and that to him, in blessed Peter, full power of ruling and governing the universal Church was given by our Lord Jesus Christ."[99]

Finally, Vatican Council I, in 1870, acting under the protection which Jesus Christ Himself promised to the teaching of the successors of the Apostles, taught, "We teach and define that it is a divinely revealed dogma that the Roman Pontiff, when he speaks *ex cathedra,* that is, when functioning as the pastor and teacher of all Christians, by his supreme Apostolic authority he defines a doctrine on faith or morals to be held by the whole Church, through the divine assistance promised him in blessed Peter, enjoys that infallibility with which the divine Redeemer willed His Church should be equipped in defining a doctrine of faith or morals, and so, that such definitions of the Roman Pontiff are irreformable, of themselves, and not from the consent of the Church. If anyone—which may God forbid—dares to contradict this our definition, let him be anathema."[100]

Vatican II reaffirmed this teaching, "His definitions of themselves, and not from the consent of the Church, are rightly called irreformable, for they are pronounced under the assistance of the Holy Spirit promised to him in blessed Peter, and so they need no approval of others, nor do they allow an appeal to any other judgment."[101]

Speaking of his lesser pronouncements, Vatican II said, ". . . religious submission of will and of mind must be shown in a special way to the authentic Magisterium of the Roman Pontiff even when he is not defining; that is, in such a way that his supreme Magisterium is acknowledged with reverence, the judgments made by him are sincerely adhered to, according to his manifest mind and will . . ."[102]

In regard to his authority of ruling, the same Council said, "The Roman Pontiff, by virtue of his function, that is, as Vicar of Christ and Pastor of the whole Church, has full, supreme, and universal power, which he can always exercise freely."[103] That is, even though most major decisions have been and are taken in a collegial fashion (by a council or group with the Pope), the Pope can act entirely alone whenever he so wishes, both in teaching, defining, and in ruling.

2) THE SCRIPTURAL DATA

The teachings of the Council rest on Scripture and on the Church's tradition, which is Her ongoing memory and teaching since the beginning. The Councils clarify, and, under the protection promised by the Divine Messenger, assure us of the correct meaning of the sources of revelation.

At this point, let us begin investigating the record of the Scriptures on Peter. In the Gospels, Peter is everywhere. He is always named first among the special three who were given the privilege of being with Jesus at special times: on the Mount of the Transfiguration, in the inner part of the Garden of Gethsemani, and on other occasions. When Jesus wanted to preach to the crowds pressing on Him, it was into Peter's boat that He went to sit and teach the crowds (*Luke* 5:3). A bit later, He said to the same Peter, "Launch out into the deep." (*Luke* 5:4). It was to Peter that Jesus said not long after, "Fear not, from henceforth you shall catch men." (*Luke* 5:10). It was Peter who was told to walk on the waters of the lake to meet Jesus (*Matt.* 28-30). It was Peter who alone was told to catch a fish and find in its mouth a coin to pay the tribute for Jesus and Peter

(*Matt.* 17:24-27). It was Peter who asked on behalf of all the Apostles, "Behold we have left all things, and have followed you: what therefore shall we have?" (*Matt.* 19:27).

The angel at the tomb of the risen Savior said, "But go, tell his disciples and Peter that he goes before you into Galilee." (*Mark* 16:7). Four times in the New Testament there appears a list of the Apostles, and, although the order of names is not the same in all, Peter is always listed first. (*Matt.* 10:2-5; *Mark* 3:16-20; *Luke* 6:14-16; *Acts* 1:13).

There are numerous other examples in which Peter is constantly first. In all, he is named 118 times in the Gospels, while John is named only 38 times. If we count the Gospels and Acts together, Peter is named 171 times, while John is mentioned by name only 46 times.

Most important are the words in *Matthew* 16:16-19. Jesus and the Apostles are in Caesarea Philippi. Jesus asks them who people say He is. They tell Him various things. Then Jesus asks the Apostles, "Whom do you say that I am?" Peter answers for all, "You are the Christ, the Son of the living God." And Jesus answers him, "Blessed are you Simon Bar-Jona: because flesh and blood has not revealed it to you, but my Father who is in heaven. And I say to you: That you are Peter; and upon this rock I will build my church, and the gates of hell shall not prevail against it. And I will give you the keys of the kingdom of heaven. And whatsoever you shall bind upon earth, it shall be bound also in heaven: And whatsoever you shall loose on earth, it shall be loosed also in heaven."

The passage is so clear that little explanation is needed. But, we will turn to two famous Protestant scholars for comment. W. F. Albright, often called in his last years the "Dean of U.S. Scripture scholars," and C. S. Mann, who wrote, "In view of the background of verse 19 . . . one must dismiss as confessional interpretation [biased by denominational views] any attempt to see *this rock* as meaning the faith, or the Messianic confession of Peter."[104] They strongly reject any attempts to deny the authenticity of the words, "On this rock I will build my Church." "Such attempts are biased," they say. Further, they observe, all Jews expected the Messiah to have a Messianic community. Then, to explain the gift of the *keys,* they add, "The *keys* are the symbol of authority."[105]

Finally, Albright and Mann say, "The general sense of the passage is indisputable . . . Peter is the rock on which the new community will be built, and in that community, Peter's authority to 'bind' or 'release' will be a carrying out of decisions made in heaven. His teaching and disciplinary activities will be similarly guided by the Spirit to carry out Heaven's will."[106]

As Albright and Mann said—and we agree—the sense of the passage is beyond doubt. Yet, as we might expect, some critics raise objections. They claim "retrojection" is the reason for Peter calling Jesus "The Christ, the son of the living God" and is also the reason for the praise Jesus gives Peter and the promise of the primacy.

What is retrojection? Some scholars believe that Jesus and Peter spoke those words *after* the Resurrection, but that the Evangelist decided to retroject when writing, that is, to record it as if the words were spoken *before* the Resurrection.

Is such retrojection possible? We ask first about the Synoptics, later about John. We established in Chapter 8 that the genre, the literary pattern of the Synoptics, is intent on giving *facts* needed for eternal salvation, plus the addition of *interpretations*. With regard to the Synoptics, a few distinctions must be made: 1) To retroject a *prophecy,* or even to make a vague prophecy clear, would be fakery. It would not be a prophecy at all if it were made later, after the event. As a result, the Synoptic genre cannot possibly include retrojection of prophecies. 2) To retroject a saying other than a prophecy, or to make it clearer with the help of post-resurrection words than it was when first uttered, would not really be a falsification, or contrary to facts, and so would be possible in the Synoptics. It has been established that Scripture writers did not always follow chronological order anyway. In this case, as long as Jesus really said it, the timing is not crucial.

Thus, it is possible within the Synoptic genre to suppose that the words in question were retrojected. Yet, even though the genre would not forbid it, the actual case makes it seem impossible. The scene created involves Peter's confession of Jesus as the Messiah (which is established in *Mark* 8:27-30 and *Luke* 9:18-21), Matthew's account of Jesus' praise of Peter, the words about the primacy, and especially the words, "the Son of the living God."

It would make no sense to suppose that this scene happened after the Resurrection. Jesus then appears glorified, not asking questions. For Peter, then, to call Him Messiah would be a tremendous anticlimax. So the basic scene must have happened before the death of Jesus.

What about the added words? If the basic scene happened before Jesus' death, it is still possible that Jesus promised the primacy to Peter only after the Resurrection; yet, there is no good reason to suppose it was done that way. And even if it was, it would still be true that Jesus said that to Peter, and that is all that matters.

It is most unlikely that the whole episode was retrojected. Jesus, in all three Synoptics, asks who people say He is. That question would make no sense after the Resurrection. And Matthew and Mark specify that it happened at Caesarea Philippi. Again, this would be very odd after the Resurrection because it was in pagan territory. There is no hint in any Gospel of appearances there after the Resurrection. Luke pictures Jesus praying before this event, as He did before many great events. There is no positive evidence of any retrojection unless one believes the false notion that Jesus was unaware of being the Messiah before the Resurrection. Nor is there a problem if Peter did not know the divinity of Jesus before the Resurrection. But it is not required by the words Matthew puts on his lips to suppose Peter did know that Christ was God. (See Appendix 1.7).

Further, if we suppose the whole scene was retrojected, what would we make of Mark, whose account lacks the words about the primacy and the words "the Son of the living God?" We would have to suppose Mark did not know when the scene took place—he would have no reason to retroject.

And even if we suppose the whole scene is retrojected, the fidelity of the Evangelists to truth—eternity depending on it—would not allow them to say what Jesus had not said at all. So Jesus still would have given the primacy to Peter.

What about the fact that Mark, who was a follower of Peter, does not record the words about the primacy? Quite simply, Mark was not present, but Matthew who was present did record them. Peter, quite plausibly, might not have been accustomed to preaching things laudatory to himself, and Mark would not have picked up these words.

In Chapter 8, we deliberately limited our discussion of genre to the Synoptics because many think the genre of John is somewhat different. Some believe he retrojects, since he represents Jesus as speaking clearly about His own divinity. We do not think that there is a lot of retrojection in John, but since it is so difficult to *prove,* we decided to bypass such debates. A very plausible explanation is that the clear statements about divinity are put by John at the very end of the preaching of Jesus. We know that Jesus deliberately chose to reveal things about Himself gradually. So it would be likely that at the end, when opposition to Him had so hardened, He would drop restraint and speak clearly.

Further, some authorities think the Gospel of John was revised several times by members of John's circle. This theory would be difficult to disprove; but if it happened, we know, by the teaching of the Church, that the final form is protected by the inspiration of the Holy Spirit.

So it is because of these difficulties that we decided to get our proofs without having to appeal to John's Gospel. This does not mean we do not value the history contained in this Gospel.

Since we have answered the questions concerning John, we can make use of a very important passage which no one can claim was retrojected, since it took place after the Resurrection. In Chapter 21 of John we read about the time Jesus appeared to the Apostles at the lake. They had been fishing and had caught nothing. He came to them and told them to try on the right side of the boat. They did and took in a huge catch. After that, Jesus ate some of the fish with them, to prove He was not just a ghost who had come. After eating, Jesus asked Peter, "Simon, son of John, do you love me more than these? He said to him: Yes, Lord, you know that I love you. He said to him: Feed my lambs." (*John* 21:15-17).

Jesus asked Peter the same question again and then, finally, a third time Scripture continues, "Peter was grieved, because he had said to him the third time: Do you love me? And he said to him: Lord, you know all things; you know that I love you. He said to him: Feed my sheep."

The imagery of this passage is easy to grasp if one knows the background. From Babylonian times (Hammurabi, 18th century B.C.) down through the Old Testament times, the shepherd stood for authority. In ancient Egypt, too, one of the symbols of the power of the Pharaohs was a shepherd's crook. Similarly, in Homer, kings are regularly given the epithet, "shepherds of the people." Therefore, this clearly was a grant of authority to Peter, the authority promised in *Matthew* 16:16-19. As R. Brown points out, "Two Protestant scholars of such different persuasions as Cullmann and Bultmann are quite firm in interpreting the command of 15-17 in terms of an authoritative commission for Peter, a view already espoused by Von Harnack, W. Bauer, Loisy and others."[107]

Thus, we have here more prime Scriptural support for Peter's authority, which even some very radical Protestant scholars have accepted.

Finally, many Scripture scholars have noted that Peter once denied Jesus three times; so it was quite fitting that Jesus would insist that Peter confess Him three times before actually receiving the promised primacy.

Chapter 17

PROTESTANT SCRIPTURE ALONE

Is there any great difference between Protestantism and Roman Catholicism? In our ecumenical striving for reunion today there is a strong tendency to gloss over differences. Vatican II had warned against straining doctrine to promote ecumenism: "It is altogether necessary that the complete doctrine [of the Church] be presented lucidly. Nothing is so foreign to ecumenism as that false peace-making, in which the purity of Catholic doctrine suffers loss, and its genuine and certain sense is made obscure."[108]

In other words, in discussions with Protestants, Catholics must still "tell it like it is," and not deceive people into joining us by false representations, though the Church admits the language could be improved to promote better understanding.[109]

Not only Vatican II, but good sense and common decency call for this honesty. In spite of the fact that there are some things on which Catholics and Protestants can agree, there is yet a great gulf between them. Unless this gulf is overcome, agreement on peripheral items is good and perhaps may help to prepare the way for real union, but *there can be no real union without agreement on the most basic principles of all, which we have examined thus far in this book.*

It could be expressed this way: There are two ways of seeking an answer to any Christian religious question, the Protestant way and the Catholic way. Both will agree we should study the sources of revelation—

Scripture alone for Protestants, or Scripture plus the ongoing teaching of the Church (Tradition) for Catholics. But that is only step one. The essential step reveals the complete gulf between the two. One can hardly claim that the meaning of Scripture, or even the Gospels, is clear on all points. Yes, we did see that we can clearly find six simple basic physical facts in the Gospels, on which faith depends. But there are so many other things: the divinity of Christ, His Presence in the Eucharist, the nature of the Mass, the means by which we try for salvation, and many more that are not so obvious. The number of churches listed in the yellow pages of the telephone book makes clear that things are not so obvious. Notice the multitude of denominations claiming to know what the Scriptures mean on the points we have mentioned, and many other things too.

So, since Scripture often needs interpretation, how do we get the correct interpretation? *For the Protestant, the only rule is: What do I think it means?* Yes, many Protestant bodies have creeds, which they often call "Confessions," such as the Augsburg Confession. But if a man were to tell his Lutheran pastor, "I cannot believe the Augsburg Confession," the pastor would not tell him, "You have an obligation, divinely imposed, by the authority of Christ, to accept it." He would merely say, "I guess you belong in some other denomination."

But for the Catholic, the principle always has been, and still is: *What does the Church teach?* For the Church is protected by the promises of Christ. Vatican II, contrary to sadly false reports about it, restated this principle vigorously: "The task of authoritatively interpreting the word of God, whether written or handed on [Scripture or Tradition] has been entrusted *exclusively* to the living teaching office [Magisterium] of the Church, whose authority is exercised in the name of Jesus Christ."[110] Thus, Vatican II appealed to the authority of Christ, that is, the promises of Christ to protect the teaching of the Church, which we studied in the past chapters.

We are not asked to think a particular Pope, with or without a Council, is holy, well-educated, brilliant, or anything of the sort. No, these qualities are good if present, but they are not essential. The important thing is that the Magisterium is on the receiving end of the promises of Christ. Nothing else matters. We may think a particular Pope or Bishop is a very disreputable person. Pope Alexander VI even had illegitimate children and made no secret of it. Yet, Christ could and did protect his teaching. In fact, someone said, "One of the better evidences of the divinity of the Church is that it can survive its churchmen." Those who have read Church history can smile and say, "Amen." So could Luther say, "Amen." Abuses in the Church were immense in his day. Yet the *teaching* of the Church then, as now, was still protected by Christ. It was not the *teaching* that was in error, it was rather a case of *mismanagement* of things and a lack of *prudence.* Imprudence is not the same as false doctrine.

So, the basic difference is that the Protestant founders all denied that Christ had protected the teaching of His Church, and asserted instead that Scripture was clear. As we said, the yellow pages prove that Scripture is not clear. What the Protestant founders claimed amounted to supposing that Christ had told the Apostles or others: "Write some books; get copies made; tell the people to figure them out for themselves." That would be unthinkable for multiple reasons. It was some time before the New Testament was complete (the earliest part was probably 51 A.D.); copies were very expensive before printing; and so many people were illiterate, or at least lacked the knowledge to interpret Scripture. The inspired Second Epistle of Peter says of the Epistles of St. Paul, "In them there are certain things hard to understand, which the unlearned and

unstable twist to their own destruction, as they also do
the other Scriptures." (*2 Peter* 3:16).

Actually, the Protestant founders and their followers
had no *logical* right even to appeal to the New Testament. In the first centuries, there were in circulation
many "gospels" bearing the names of Apostles: The
Gospel of Thomas, of James, of Peter, etc., not to mention many epistles. Many Protestants have searched
diligently for a way to know which books are inspired.
But it is not enough to say that a book which gives one
pious thoughts is inspired—many devotional books do
that. Nor is it enough to say that those books are inspired which proclaim salvation by faith alone—many
books outside Scripture do that. And how can one be
sure that is the test? Are there not other doctrines? And
what does "faith" mean, anyway? As we will see in the
next chapter, Luther was mistaken about the meaning
of the word "faith," as many fine Protestant scholars
today admit.

Should one say that: "Only Scripture itself can say in
a binding way what authority it claims and has . . .
Scripture considers itself as revelation." This proposal,
from the major Lutheran publishing house at Concordia, is really a fine case of begging the question.[111] It
really means: "inspired Scripture says it is inspired." If
so, we must first take for granted that Scripture is inspired and then let Scripture tell us that it is inspired.

The truth is, there is no other way to be certain what
books are part of the Bible except through the process
examined in Chapter 14. The conclusion was that a
body protected in its teaching by the Divine Messenger
can say which books are inspired. So without the teaching authority of the Church protected by Christ, one
cannot know that Scripture is inspired. Then what
becomes of the security of appealing to Scripture
alone? It is left resting on a cloud with no firm ground
beneath it for support.

So if some Protestants say, "We follow the Bible, not the Pope, who is just a man," we reply, "First, how can you know what is or is not part of the Bible? Only by the teaching authority of the Catholic Church can you be sure of that. Secondly, although the Pope is human, and is a man, he is not an ordinary man. He is the one who is on the receiving end of the promises of Christ. Nor are we, as people sometimes charge, 'putting the Church ahead of Scripture.' No, the role of the Church is, in part, that of making certain for us what Scripture really means—a function given it by Christ Himself."

It has been established that it is only part of the Church's role, for it has, in addition to Scripture, its own ongoing teaching coming down from the Apostles, in accord with His command to go and teach—not to go and write books. We recall that the Gospels are just part of the Church's ongoing teaching, written down under inspiration.

A similar response is in order when someone challenges, "Where in the Bible do you find that?" We reply again that he cannot even know what the Bible is without the Catholic Church, and that Church, like St. Paul, depends not just on the written word of Christ, but on its own ongoing teaching coming down from the Apostles and Christ. For St. Paul wrote, "And the things which you have heard from me before many witnesses, commend to faithful men, who shall be fit to teach others also." (*2 Tim.* 2:2).[112] St. Paul was making provision for the ongoing, living teaching of the Church, in response to the mandate of Christ to go and teach all nations.

Chapter 18

FAITH ALONE:
LUTHER'S DISCOVERY?

A basic Protestant claim is that Martin Luther's great discovery was the concept of salvation by faith alone, which he found stated in the Epistles to the Galatians and the Romans. What about this claim? As we saw in Chapter 17, it could not be true that Christ would let His Church teach the wrong method for salvation for most of the time throughout so many centuries. If He had so failed the Church, we would have to reject Christ Himself for making false promises.

Yet, we can gain insight by looking at Luther's claim. It often happens that when a person makes a major error, he has also seen something much more clearly than most men. The bright light of his insight can blind him, so that he misses the total picture and hence, falls into error. Luther had that type of experience. He did see an important truth more clearly than most Catholics of his time. The Church had never denied that truth; in fact, it had taught it, and even defined it, as we shall see. Yet in the practical abuses of the day, many did not have a good appreciation of this important fact.

So we can gain some added light by looking for what Luther saw.

1) SALVATION BY FAITH ALONE

Is it true that there is salvation by faith alone? Definitely, yes! St. Paul teaches it over and over and it is the chief theme of Galatians and Romans. But St.

James wrote in his Epistle (2:24), "See that a man is justified by works, and not by faith alone."

Because it was contrary to his personal philosophy, Luther rejected that Epistle. But if we look closely, we will see that the critical point lies in the meaning of the word *faith*. Not everyone uses every word in precisely the same sense. St. James and St. Paul, both working under inspiration, could not contradict each other. But they did use the word *faith* in different senses. St. James clearly uses *faith* to mean, narrowly, just intellectual acceptance of a revealed truth. So we can see why St. James feels the need to add works. Even St. Paul talks similarly at times; for instance, in *Romans* 2:6-13: "He will repay to every man according to his works . . . For not the hearers of the law are just before God, but the doers of the law shall be justified." As we will explore later, St. Paul does not mean that works *earn* salvatoon—but violations of the law can *earn* eternal ruin.

Thus, St. Paul does not disagree with St. James, but his use of the word *faith* is much broader. By *faith,* Paul means *total adherence of a person to God in mind and will.* This, in turn, implies several things: If God speaks a truth, we believe with our minds. This is the sense St. James had in mind (see *1 Thes.* 2:13; *2 Cor.* 5:7). If God makes a promise, we are confident He will keep it (see *Gal.* 5:5; *Rom.* 5:1; *1 Thes.* 5:8). If God gives a command, we obey (see *Rom.* 1:5). And all should be done in love (*Gal.* 5:6).

In contrast, the Lutheran Augsburg Confession taught (20:23), "Faith does not mean knowledge of an event . . . it means a faith which believes . . . also in the effect of an event, namely . . . the remission of sins, i.e., that we have, through Christ, grace, righteousness, and remission of sins." Modern Protestants often express this as meaning that *one takes Christ as his personal Savior,* or, has *confidence that the merits of Christ are credited to his account.* It is as if there were a ledger with a credit and a debit page for each man. If he "takes Christ as his personal Savior," he can write on the credit page the infinite merits of Christ. On the debit page go his sins: past, present and future. Of course the balance is always more than favorable.

Hence, they see no need for confession, no need even to make an act of contrition even out of love. Protestants believe that Jesus paid in advance for one's sins, and nothing more needs to be done. Hence, Luther wrote to his associate Melanchthon, "Sin greatly, but believe more greatly."[113] Luther has been unjustly maligned for saying this because it sounds as if he encouraged sin, which he surely did not mean to do. What he meant was that no matter how much you sin, you need do nothing to gain forgiveness except believe that Christ paid the bill in advance. You are *infallibly saved.*

The Council of Trent condemned this idea of *faith* as heretical.[114] Even many Protestant scholars today modify the old notion of faith substantially. A standard Protestant reference work on Scripture, the *Interpreter's Dictionary of the Bible,* Supplement Volume, tells us, "Paul uses *pistis/pisteuein* [Greek words for *faith* and *believe*] to mean, above all, belief in the Christ kerygma [proclamation or preaching], knowledge, obedience, trust in the Lord Jesus.[115] "Note the word *obedience.* The *Interpreter's Dictionary* admits St. Paul includes it in an important place in his idea of faith.

In fact, Paul sometimes identifies *faith* and *obedience* when he speaks of the "obedience of faith." Here, the *of* has the same sense as it does when we say the "city of Chicago." We mean: the City that *is* Chicago (see *Rom.* 1:5; 16:26, and in a similar sense, *Rom.* 10:16; 6:16; 15:18; *2 Thes.* 1:8). Similarly, Vatican II says, "the obedience of faith" is "an obedience in which man entrusts his entire self freely to God, offering 'the complete submission of intellect and will to God who reveals.'"[116]

Clearly, such a concept of *faith* as that given in the Councils of Trent and Vatican is radically different from Luther's concept. So, sadly, Luther's "discovery" is not really a discovery but a mistake, since he did not get the true Pauline meaning of *faith* in the words "salvation by faith."

We noted earlier that the Protestant view tells people they can be *infallibly saved once for all* by just one act, taking Christ as their personal Savior. St. Paul had no such notion. If anyone should have been saved that way, it ought to have been St. Paul. Yet Paul told the Corinthians, "But I chastise my body, and bring it into subjection: lest perhaps, when I have preached to others, I myself should become a castaway." (*1 Cor.* 9:27). So Paul knew he had to tame his flesh by mortification, much as athletes at the Isthmian games went into training. Hence, in *2 Cor.* 11:23-27, he added fasting to all the great hardships that came with his apostolic work. He did not want to fall and risk being rejected at the Judgment. If he were "infallibly saved," there would be no need of acts of mortification, because no matter how much he might fall, he would still be saved.

Again, in *1 Cor.* 10:1-12, he is trying to induce the Corinthians to be willing to give up meat at times to avoid scandal, and he tells them in effect, "Do not just say, we are the People of God—look at the first People of God. God did not approve of many of them, so He often had to strike them, even to strike them dead." So Paul concluded in *1 Cor.* 10:12, "Wherefore he who thinks that he stands, let him take heed lest he fall." If they were all infallibly saved there would be no need for such a warning.

Again in *Romans* 5:3-5, Paul wrote, "But we glory also in tribulations, knowing that tribulation produces patience; and patience trial; and trial hope; and hope does not disappoint us." These verses make "character" needed for salvation, character coming from endurance in suffering. This is hardly the same as an easy once-for-all declaration of "taking Christ as my personal Savior." Yes, the best Protestant teaching does urge good works, not to earn salvation, but as the fruit of faith. But according to that Protestant teaching, it is faith alone that gives hope—not endurance in suffering leading to character.

Still further, St. Paul told the Philippians (2:12), "Work out your own salvation with fear and trembling." The expression, "with fear and trembling" was a stereotyped one which meant only "reverently." Yet they had to *work out* their salvation—not get it in one quick stroke, infallibly, by "taking Christ as their personal Savior."

2) TOTAL DEPENDENCE ON GOD

Earlier in this chapter, it was suggested that Luther might have seen something true with special clarity. He did. He saw our total dependence on God for doing good and our inability to do good by ourselves, so that we cannot really *earn* salvation. Now this was not really a new concept. The second Council of Orange in 529 A.D. had defined the same concept, as we shall see. But the truth was obscured and almost forgotten by some; hence, it was good to have it re-emphasized.

The Second Council of Orange was not a general council, but because of a special confirmation by Pope Boniface II, its canons are recognized as having the force of solemn definitions. They teach most strikingly our total dependence on God. Canon 4 says, "If anyone contends that God waits for our will so we may be cleansed from sin—and does not admit that *the very fact that we even will to be cleansed* comes in us by the infusion and work of the Holy Spirit, he resists the same Holy Spirit . . . and the Apostle [Paul] preaching . . . 'It is God who works in you both the will and the doing.'"[117] Canon 7 adds, "If anyone asserts that we, by the good power of nature, are *able to think anything* that pertains to salvation ... or to *choose* or *consent* to the saving preaching ... he is deceived by a heretical spirit. He does not understand the word of God in the Gospel: 'Without me you can do nothing' and the words of the Apostle; not that we are sufficient to think anything by ourselves as from ourselves: our sufficiency is from God."

These definitions are utterly devastating to our pride and claims of self-sufficiency. The Council taught that we cannot even will to be cleansed from sin except by the work of the Holy Spirit in us, for He *causes* us to will good, and that we cannot even get a good thought leading towards salvation or make a good choice (decision of our will) towards salvation of our own power. For as Jesus Himself said, "Without me you can do nothing." (*John* 15:5). And St. Paul taught, "Not that we are sufficient to *think* anything by ourselves, as from ourselves, but our sufficiency is from God." (*1 Cor.* 3:5). St. Paul taught, too: "For it is God who works [produces] in you both the will and the doing, according to his good will." (*Phil* 2:13).

So we are totally dependent on God to get a good thought, to make a good decision and to carry out that decision. Neither Luther nor anyone else could have said it more bluntly. So Luther did not discover our dependence on God, though he did greatly emphasize it.

Are we then marionettes, unable even to make an act of will? Of course not. Scripture, over and over, urges men to repent, to return to God. St. Paul in *2 Cor.* 6:1 says, "And we exhort you not to receive the grace of God in vain." So it does depend on us in some way whether or not grace bears fruit in us. Just *how* to reconcile our inability and our freedom, St. Paul does not explain, nor has the Church completely explained thus far. Later, we will offer a suggested way.

But to return to Luther—he not only emphasized our

total dependence on God, which is fully true, he not only gave the basis for a belief in *infallible* salvation, which is false; he also provided—not intentionally—a basis for a belief or implication that God infallibly damns many persons, independent of anything or any condition in them.

Here is how it happens. Luther believed that human nature was totally corrupted by Original Sin, so much that he wrote a treatise called, *On the Bondage of the Will.* He was, of course, wrong about that total corruption.[118] But that idea, along with the teaching on total dependence, logically should lead to a belief in a blind, absolute predestination by God. The situation is well stated in the *Brief Statement of the Doctrinal Position* of the Missouri Synod of Lutherans: "As to the question why not all men are converted and saved, seeing that God's grace is universal and all men are equally and utterly corrupt, we confess that we cannot answer it."[119] Of course, they could not answer, for it is unanswerable *if there is nothing at all in man* to serve as a basis of whether he should be saved or lost. Then God alone, with no regard to any condition within man, must decide to damn some and to rescue others.

What the Lutherans feared—rightly—to teach, John Calvin did teach. He held the theory of an absolute predestination. Thanks be to God, very many of those descended from him now repudiate such an idea.[120] We do not even need the help of a teaching of the Church to know that concept is wrong. This belief makes God a terrifying monster, who really would not love anyone, but would just *use* people, some to show His "justice," some to show "mercy."

Is there a way out of this morass? Definitely, yes. We will see it in the next chapter. But for the time being, since we have dealt in difficult material to comprehend, let us briefly sum up what we have seen. Protestantism teaches salvation by faith alone. St. Paul did speak of salvation by faith, but St. Paul meant something quite different by *faith* from what Luther meant, as many Protestant scholars are seeing today. The error of teaching salvation by a mere confidence that the merits of Christ are credited to one's account leads logically to another error: infallible salvation once one has "made a decision for Christ." We saw that St. Paul did not at all believe that he was infallibly saved by his adherence to Christ.

Yet, we said that the Protestant error contained a good insight: our total dependence on God. But Luther's way of understanding that dependence led to still another great mistake. It led to thinking there is nothing at all in man on the basis of which God could decide who is to be saved or damned. The resulting belief—from which most Protestants rightly backed away—is a blind predestination or decision by God without considering anything in man to save some and damn others.

There is, as we said, a way out of this tangle. We will start to explore it in the next chapter.

Chapter 19

HELP FOR ECUMENISM:
ON PREDESTINATION

The Church, whose authority Luther rejected, assures us that we are saved by faith alone—provided we interpret *faith* in St. Paul's sense of a total adherence of a person to God, not in Luther's sense of just being confident Christ has paid all debt for sin in advance, with nothing else to be done. The Church tells us too that we are totally dependent on God, as Luther did, but the Church does not say we are totally corrupt. Luther's teaching on that point tended to imply a blind predestination to Heaven and a similarly blind reprobation to Hell. Luther did not explicitly say that; Calvin did.

The Catholic Church, in the second Council of Orange from which we quoted earlier, also said, "We not only do not believe that any persons have been predestined by divine power to evil, but also, if there are any who wish to believe so great an evil, with all detestation, we say anathema to them."[121] The detestation comes from the fact that such a view implies a denial of the goodness of God. A lesser Council, that of Quiersy in 853 A.D., added, "The fact that some are saved is the *gift* of Him who saves; the fact that some are lost, is the *merit* of those who are lost."[122] As we shall see, this is just a restatement of the teaching of St. Paul in *Romans* 6:23, "For the wages of sin is death. But the gift of God, life everlasting, in Christ Jesus our Lord."

But the Church has not given us a full and complete

114

explanation of the two important concepts just mentioned: predestination and human interaction with grace. Since the Church has not yet done so, we must make use of what information the Church provides to find the proper solution.

We hope our attempts may be of some help to ecumenism. The last chapter shows that these two questions are basic in ecumenism. We are going to propose some original, new solutions to these problems.[123] The solutions will be, on the one hand, well within the lines marked out by existing teachings of the Church; but yet they are closer to Protestant ideas than other proposals. We will treat predestination in this chapter, interaction with grace in the next chapter.

Students in high school have been known to put up a hand and say, "Since God knows where I am going in eternity, what is the use of trying to lead a good life and get to Heaven?" Their question is the result of inaccurate information about predestination. First, to *know* in advance is not the same as to *compel* or force anything. We remain free even if God does foresee. Second, we can say positively that God does not foresee anything. This may sound shocking, but it is not. Here is why: We know that God is completely unchangeable. But, time is a constant succession of restless changes. Ahead of me now is a moment I call future, but quickly it becomes present, and just as quickly, it turns into past. Unlike us, God is not immersed in such a sea of changes. He is in eternity, with no change. Therefore for Him there is no past and no future—everything is one great eternal present to Him! So He does not foresee anything—He sees all as present.

Here is another way to think of it: We say God *made* the world, in the *past*. But to Him it is *present*. We say Christ *will* return at the end. But to Him it is *present*. Our minds cannot grasp this concept. But it is good for us to begin to realize our minds are small compared to God.

Yet, as we implied, there is a real question about pre-destination. That word means *an arrangement of Divine Providence to see that something gets done.* What must get done? There are two things to remember here, though people commonly have in mind only the first when they use the word: a man may be predestined *to Heaven,* or *to full membership in the People of God,* the Church. Scripture rarely uses the word *predestine,* and when it does, it is always only in the second sense which we have mentioned. Failure to see that—for people forgot the Scriptural context—led to some long and bitter debates among Catholic theologians, and Protestants too. *Reprobation* means the unfavorable decision that a man is not to be saved.

Even though Scripture does not speak *explicitly* of predestination, it does so implicitly, as we shall see. And from just reasoning a bit, it is evident that there must be such a thing.

To see that, we first realize that people can be very different in good or evil. At one end of the scale, some spend most or practically all of their lives in the state of grace (that is, in God's favor with His transforming grace at work in their souls). They may be out of that state of grace for just a brief period. At the other end of the scale, there are those who are out of the state of grace for most of their lives and may be right for only one short stretch. And of course, there are all degrees in between these extremes.

Further, we realize that in this world of ours there are many natural causes at work set up by God. These can bring sudden death to anyone, at any age. For a teen-ager, such a thing happens more readily by an auto accident; for a person in his 50's, more easily from a sudden heart attack.

With these things in view, we must face the question: Will Divine Providence either order or permit death to strike a man who is out of grace most of his life—but who is good for just one short stretch? Providence makes that decision. If favorable, it is called predestination; if unfavorable, it is called reprobation. Similarly, picture a man who is in the state of grace most of his life, but out just briefly. Again will Divine Providence order or permit death to take him at just the wrong instant, causing him to be damned? Clearly, Providence decides these extreme cases, and all cases in between. So there is such a thing as predestination and reprobation.

Next, *on what basis* does God decide? Does He decide with or without looking at a person's merits or demerits or how he lives, his qualities in general?

Theologians have always assumed (wrongly, as we shall see) that if God decides predestination without looking at a person's life, He also decides reprobation the same way. Both predestination and reprobation are opposite sides of one coin: you are one or the other.

But this poses a great dilemma because both ways of deciding turn out to be impossible.

It is impossible to assume that God decides both predestination and reprobation *without* looking at a person's life, for He has revealed that He "wills all men to be saved." (*1 Tim.* 2:4). Imagine that Joe Doaks is a man who is reprobated, without God looking at his life at all. Can God reprobate Joe this way and also, at the same time say, "I want all men to be saved"? Of course, that is impossible.

On the other hand, if we suppose God decides by looking at peoples' good lives, we have another impossibility. For merit or good in our lives comes only as God's gift. St. Paul says, "What have you that you did not receive" from God? (*1 Cor.* 4:7). Nothing, of course. St. Augustine said, "When God crowns our merits, He crowns nothing other than His own gifts."[124] So merits, or a good life, are gifts of God. How then could He use as a *basis* of predestination something we will not have unless He gives it? Again impossible.

This dilemma can be solved by discovering that it is not necessary to say that He must decide *both* predestination and reprobation on the same footing, as theologians have been assuming. There are two possible explanations.

First, notice that Jesus constantly refers to God as "Father." Some foolish persons have said, "If God is a good Father, there can be no Hell." But Jesus taught us that there is a Hell. Without being emotional, examine Jesus' comparison of God as Father to a normal, human family situation. We could, logically, speak of three points or stages:

1) The Father (and Mother, too, of course) want all the children to turn out well. This is like *1 Tim.* 2:4 saying that God wants all to be saved.

2) Does a son say, "I know what I must do. I have to dry the dishes, cut the grass, help out in the house, and then I will get my father to love and care for me"? This is nonsense because the father loves and cares *not because the son is good, but because he, the father, is good.* This basic love and care is too great and fundamental to be earned. It does not have to be earned and cannot be earned.

3) But even though a son cannot earn and need not earn that great basic love from his father, he can earn punishment if he is bad. In fact, if he is bad enough, he can even earn being thrown out of the house permanently.

So it is with our Father in Heaven: 1) He wants all His children to be saved; 2) He looks ahead to see who will resist His grace so much that he cannot be saved. (This is just our way of speaking because there is no "future" for Him as we perceive it.) Remember, grace is a divine power to save us and if one throws it away too often, he cannot be saved. So then, sadly, God determines *to reprobate or reject those who have earned it fully.* (3) He then turns to all the rest, to those who are not forcing their own loss, and He decrees to predestine or save them. Why? Not because of their merits or good lives. He has not even looked at such things yet. He has been looking only at resistance to His grace. Further, it is not even because of their lack of such serious resistance. No, the bottom-line reason He will save them is simply this: He always wanted to do that—He wants to save all—and those He saves are not stopping Him by throwing away the means that could save them or His grace.

To sum it up, *predestination is determined without consideration of merits* or good living; *reprobation is decided with or because of consideration of demerits,* resistance to grace.

As we have shown, this is a very simple concept and many people, after hearing it explained, say, "What else would you expect?" Others, caught in a "theological puzzle," cannot grasp it. This brings to mind the strange case of the Inca Indians centuries ago in South America. They had a rather advanced civilization, yet nowhere in their civilization was a wheel found! No one had discovered a wheel. Now, a wheel is such a simple thing, but it is simple only *after* someone discovers it. *Before* that, it can be missed by a whole civilization for centuries.

Similarly, this answer we have found could be, and was, missed for centuries. It seemed not just difficult but impossible. Yet, once aware, we wonder how anyone could have missed it.

We said there was a second way to reach the same answer. It too is simple. St. Paul in *Romans* 6:23 wrote, "For the *wages* of sin is death. But the gift of God, life everlasting." So we can *earn punishment,* reprobation, but predestination, *eternal life,* is just a *free, unearned gift.*

How much resistance to grace will bring reprobation? We can hazard a guess. It is the amount which will bring spiritual blindness that makes us incapable of even perceiving that God is calling us by His grace, at a particular moment, to do His will. If we cannot even perceive His call, the rest of the process cannot happen either. Such blindness comes from repeated sinning, especially from sinning in *presumption,* in the attitude that says, "I will get my fill of evil, and then later tell God that I wish I had not done it." But would there be a real repentance, that is, a real wish not to have done it, when it was all planned that way? Further, it is conceivable that God might send death and the resultant Hell, after one mortal sin, to a man whom He foresees would sin even to blindness if allowed to live a full lifespan. That would be mercy to the man himself, for his eternal ruin would be less after one sin, and also to others, who would not be corrupted by him.

We now return to the *Doctrinal Position of the Missouri Synod of Lutherans,* "As to the question why not all men are converted and saved, seeing that God's grace is universal and all men are equally corrupt, we confess that we cannot answer it."[126] Part of this statement shows fine insight, yet it misses important points, with the result that it concludes without knowing the answer. The insight lies in seeing that predestination to Heaven cannot rest on merits, that we cannot *earn* salvation. Yet, the Lutheran Synod wound up with no answer, since they could not find anything on which to prove that there could be a difference in men. This happened partly because of their mistaken idea of the total corruption of man, and partly because they did not know how to solve the dilemma we have just broken. So they were led in the direction of supposing that God reprobates without looking at anything in people. They wisely pulled back from such an implication, for that, in turn, would imply a denial of the goodness of God.

Hence they concluded, "We cannot answer."

We hope they may be pleased with the alternative solution that God does indeed save us without our earning it (predestination without merits). But He never reprobates blindly; He does it only because of, and in consideration of our great resistance to His grace.

A NOTE ON A PAULINE PUZZLE

Our discovery, especially in view of *Romans* 6:23, provides the answer to another difficult puzzle in St. Paul. Examine the following two sets of statements:

First, Jesus Himself said, "Do not think that I am come to destroy the law, or the prophets. I am not come to destroy, but to fulfill." (*Matt.* 5:17). Similarly, in spite of his words about salvation by faith and not by law, St. Paul says many times that if one violates the law he will be eternally lost. For example, in *1 Cor.* 6:9-10, "Do you not know that the unjust shall not possess the kingdom of God? Do not err: neither fornicators, nor idolators, nor adulterers, nor the effeminate, nor those who lie with men, nor thieves, nor covetors, nor drunkards, nor slanderers, nor extortioners, shall inherit the kingdom of God." So if one breaks the law on a major point, he will not be saved. (St. Paul has similar statements in *Eph.* 5:5 and *Gal.* 5:19-21.)

Secondly, St. Paul insists equally, and over and over, that we are free from the law. For example, *Romans* 3:28 says, "For we judge that a man is justified by faith, without the works of the law." Or again in *1 Cor.* 6:12, "All things are lawful to me." Or in *Romans* 6:14, "For sin shall not have dominion over you; for you are not under the law, but under grace." (More similar statements: *Rom.* 3:21; *Gal.* 2:16, 5:18, 3:21.)

Yet, we can easily make sense of all these statements with the help of *Romans* 6:23, as we said, "For the wages of sin is death. But the gift of God, life everlasting." That is, eternal death can be earned by breaking the law; but eternal life is a free gift of God. Our keeping the law does not earn it; not even faith earns it. It is our "inheritance" as sons. Note the word "inherit" in *1 Cor.* 6:10—they who break the law will not "inherit the kingdom."

Consequently, a Christian must follow the Spirit of Christ, who teaches him to live as Christ did. Then he need not even look at the law. *1 Timothy* 1:9 says, "Knowing this, that the law is not made for the just man, but for the unjust and disobedient." If the just man breaks the law, he loses his inheritance.

A student in a discussion class once summed it all up neatly: "You can't earn it [salvation], but you can blow it."

Chapter 20

DO WE CONTRIBUTE
TO OUR SALVATION?

The second Epistle of St. Peter comments on the complexity of the Epistles of St. Paul: "In them [his Epistles], are certain things hard to be understood, which the unlearned and unstable twist, as they do also the other scriptures, to their own destruction." (3:16). From our own experience with St. Paul we can say a hearty, "Amen. Yes, St. Paul's writing can be puzzling."

Earlier, in speaking of Luther's idea of our total dependence on God, we quoted some texts from St. Paul and found them difficult to understand. We promised to return to them. Now is the time, since they are vital in ecumenism. Protestants insist strongly that we contribute nothing at all to our own salvation. The problem gets more complex because, as we began to see in Chapter 18, these texts of St. Paul seem to leave us no free will at all.

As a result, we are again faced with two sets of seemingly contradictory statements. First, St. Paul insists with devastating force our incapability of doing any good. *Philippians* 2:13 says, "For it is God who works in you, both the will and the doing, according to his good will." So we cannot even make a good act of will by ourselves, or carry it out. But, could we at least get the good thought that starts the process? No, for *2 Cor.* 3:5 says, "Not that we are sufficient to think any thing of ourselves, as of ourselves: but our sufficiency is from God."

Could *Philippians* 2:13 be softened by saying Paul is using a familiar Semitic pattern in which Scripture says that God positively does what He really just permits? Thus, in *Exodus* 10:1 God says of Pharaoh, "I have hardened his heart." Of course, God does not create evil. (See *1 Sam.* 4:3). Obviously, that language pattern is not used here, for then Paul would mean just that God *permits* us to do good. In that case, the good would be from us, not from Him. Whereas Paul says in *1 Cor.* 4:7, "What have you that you have not received?" In other words, "Every bit of good that you are or have or do is God's gift, you did not *originate* it."

Some weak translations of *Phil.* 2:13 imply that God only gives us the *desire*. If that means that *He* causes the desire, but *we* make the act of will, the same problem exists, for we would credit ourselves with the real good.

Consequently, we are forced to take the meaning of *Phil.* 2:13 and *2 Cor.* 3:5 fully. They deny us all ability to think good, to will good, to carry out good by ourselves. In fact, these verses say that even when God offers us grace to enable us to do good, we cannot even decide (make the act of will) to accept it! So where is our free will?

We know from experience, as well as from Scripture, that we do have free will. All the countless exhortations in Scripture to repent, to reform, to turn to God, imply that. So does St. Paul in *2 Cor.* 6:1: "And we exhort you, not to receive the grace of God in vain."

Semites did not mind believing two truths which seemed to clash. Faith made that easy for them, and their own mentality did not tend to make syntheses or harmonious patterns. For example, in *Matthew* 6:6 Jesus says, "But you when you pray, enter into your chamber, and having shut the door, pray to thy Father in secret."

Yet in *Matthew* 5:16, He said, "So let your light shine

before men, that they may see your good works, and glorify your Father who is in heaven." Both sayings are fully true, even though they seem to conflict. Semites might not even notice the seeming clash.

But people of our time do notice such incongruities, and naturally ask, "How can we be both dependent on God for decision of will and yet be free?"

As we said, since the Church has not given an answer to this problem, we must find one on our own. Our ecumenical spirit urges us to find a solution, since the question of the interaction of our freedom and God's grace is vital, and Protestants insist that we contribute nothing to our own salvation. So we are going to offer an original attempt at a solution. We did a similar thing in Chapter 19, when we proposed a solution to the problem of predestination. There we offered it confidently, for the answer, once found, was so completely simple and clear. But on this problem we cannot and do not claim the answer is so obvious. Even so, it is worth our time and effort.[127]

First, imagine God sending me grace to lead me to do a particular thing now. Without it I would be helpless, of course. His mere *favor*—smiling at me—would not be enough, for as Jesus insisted, "Without me you can do nothing." (*John* 15:5). So then grace has come to me. First, it must put the good idea into my mind because as *2 Cor.* 3:5 insists, I am not sufficient to do that. The very fact that I saw something as good makes me favorably disposed, for the will is naturally inclined to what is presented as good.

What are the possibilities now that this grace has come? We see that I could accept it or reject it. But we had better think twice before saying I could accept it, since that would be a *decision of my will,* a good decision. *Phil.* 2:13 warns, "It is God who works in you both the will and the doing." So then, it seems there would be only one option open to me: to reject. But if that is my only choice, I am not free. A person with just one choice is not free.

Thus, there has to be a third option to consider besides accepting and rejecting. Clearly, the only possibility would be *"non-rejecting."* This would have the same *effect* as accepting, but yet would not be the *same thing in itself.*

There are two ways to describe the concept of non-rejecting. The first will not hold up under study, but we will examine it anyway for completeness.

After I find that grace has put a good idea into my head, I sit back and say to myself, "I see that a grace has come to me. It wants me to do thus. What will I do?" After thinking it over I conclude, 'I hereby decide, I will not reject it.'" But St. Paul will not allow it to be so simple, since the example involves a *decision* to non-reject. Such a decision is ruled out again by *Phil.* 2:13, "For it is God who works in you, both the will and the doing."

There is a different way of looking at the same example. God has sent me a grace; it has put into my head the good idea of what He wants me to do. At this point I could reject it—I know that from sad experience. But—and this is the important point now—*at the very juncture at which I could reject it, I might just do nothing, make no decision at all.* Is that in my power? Of course, for it is merely doing nothing. Yes, that *lack of decision* at such a juncture, when I could have rejected it, can serve as the *condition* for the next step. If that condition is verified, God will then work in me both the will and the doing.

We should notice that though we have spelled out this process at length, it really would not have to take up any length of time. The complete process, from good thought to decision, can fit into just one instant of time. For clarity of explantion, we needed a *logical* division or spelling out of the stages.

Now we can see where we are at: *In doing a good act, our contribution at the critical instant which settles everything was zero or a lack of a decision, when we could have rejected it.* This fits well with the Protestant insistence that we refrain from saying we contribute anything to our own salvation. And yet, we would be controlling the outcome, even though we would do it by taking no action. So two elements are clear in our example: (1) we contribute nothing to salvation; (2) we control whether or not we receive the grace of God in vain—recalling *2 Corinthians* 6:1, which urges us not to receive grace in vain.

We may even add that our very ability to do nothing, to non-reject when we could reject, depends on the fact that grace causes us to see the thing proposed as good. If it did not do that, rejection would readily follow.

At this juncture, the Council of Trent demands one small addition to our picture. It teaches that under the action of grace, we are not totally passive.[128] So in this second stage, after omitting a decision to reject, two things are happening: I am both being moved by grace, and moving myself by power being received at the very instant from grace. Thus I am not fully passive.

St. Augustine said, as we saw earlier, "When God crowns our merits, He crowns nothing other than His own gifts."[129] We have accepted that idea completely. And we can agree most heartily too with St. Paul: "Or what have you that you have not received? And if you have received, why do you boast, as if you had not received it?" (*1 Cor.* 4:7).

Chapter 21

FALSE ANGELS

"I have met Jesus!" This statement is common today. Not all, but some will say that they have the Bible and Jesus: What more do they need? They say that the Church did not give them Jesus, they had to find Him for themselves, so they need not bother with the Church.

It is very difficult to deal with people of this belief; they claim that they have something that overrides and is superior to any reasoning or theology or proof: they feel they have met Jesus.

They are similar to Eve in Genesis. Eve was in the garden one day, and along came the tempter. He remarked, "My, what a nice garden. Do they let you eat from all the fine trees here?" "Yes," said Eve. "Oh, just a minute. There is one over there. God says we must not eat from it. If we do we will die." The tempter seemed surprised, "He said that! Why can't you see He is holding out on you. He knows if you eat that, you will be like gods. He wants to keep that just for Himself; He doesn't want anyone else to get in on it." Eve looked at the fruit. "Yes," she thought, "God may know things in general, but right now, why I can *just see for myself* that it is good." So she took a bite. "Yes, it is good. I can feel that for myself."

The inspired writer of Genesis was trying to make a point in this part of the narrative. Among other things, he was showing us the psychology of sin. In every sin, not just the first sin, the sinner in effect, says, "God may know in general, but right now, I can *feel* and *see* this thing is good."

So it is with some who have "met Jesus." They can *feel,* can almost touch Him. So they can know on their own. They do not have to take the word of stodgy churchmen, who probably have never met Jesus themselves.

As we said, it is difficult to get through to these people. They claim to have proof they can feel, so there is no need to take the word of anyone, including the Church.

If they really had met Jesus, they would know that He does not contradict Himself. The words He said long ago would still have meaning. For example, "And if he will not hear them: tell the Church. And if he will not hear the Church, let him be to you as the heathen and publican." (*Matt.* 18:17). For "He who hears you, hears me; and he that rejects me, rejects him who sent me." (*Luke* 10:16). As we saw in Chapter 14, "binding and loosing," as the words were used at the time of Jesus by the Jewish teachers, meant imposing or removing an obligation by an authoritative decision. So to be *certain* of divine truth, we cannot do without the Church.

Similarly, we need spiritual food. Jesus Himself said, "I am the living bread which came down from heaven. If any man eat of this bread, he shall live for ever ... He who eats my flesh, and drinks my blood, has everlasting life: and I will raise him up in the last day." (*John* 6:51 & 55). But we get that Flesh and Blood of Jesus only from the Church. Not to all, but to the Apostles, and thereby to their successors, He said, "Do this in remembrance of me." (*Luke* 22:10; and *1 Cor.* 11:24). So we *must* have the Church. If we do not, Jesus warns us, "Unless you eat the flesh of the Son of man, and drink his blood, you shall not have life in you." (*John* 6:54).

Simply, we have shown from the words of Jesus Himself that He established a Church, gave it the commis-

sion to teach and promised that its teaching would be
protected. One who wishes to ignore that, even if he
thinks he has "met Jesus," is not really a Catholic at
all. Instead, Jesus says we should look on him "as the
heathen and publican." (*Matt.* 18:17).

Also, if one looks for wonders which our senses can
take in, the Church has them in abundance. They include cures that are beyond the possible power of suggestion, cures completely proved by modern science, not
to mention the Host of Lanciano, the image of
Guadalupe, and many others. And it is only the Catholic
Church that has a Lourdes and other places where miracles have happened that have been scientifically
checked. No sect even tries to claim such miracles—except of course for the questionable cases we have mentioned, in which the power of suggestion can be a factor.

It is worthwhile, at this point, to review the sound
principles on "feelings" in religion. These principles
were established after centuries of experience on the
part of ordinary people and saints and are principles in
accord with the scientific studies of sound theology approved by the Church of Jesus.

Feelings in religion can stem from any one of three
sources: God or a good spirit, an evil spirit, or ourselves.
We will look at some of the characteristics of each.

God and His agents can and often do give us feelings.
St. John of the Cross, a saint who had an unusual
amount of supernatural experiences himself and who
was at the same time a great theologian, compares feelings to toys. When a person comes to what is often
called the "second conversion," that is, when he starts
to work in earnest on growing spiritually, God often
sends him feelings to wean him away from things of the
world. St. John tells us to think of "a child holding
something in one of its hands," such as a sharp knife.[130]
We dare not just try to take it away. So instead, "to
make it loosen its hold upon it, we give it something

else to hold in the other hand," some toy. Then the child will safely let go. But we should not need toys permanently, and so St. Francis de Sales, another saint of wide experience and theological learning, advises us, "We must from time to time make acts of renunciation of such feelings of sweetness, tenderness, and consolation."[131] Otherwise, the real motive that leads us to pray and try to serve God may not be He, but the pleasure we get out of it.

Satan, too, sometimes sends us religious feelings. He has a thousand wiles. He can lead us by feelings to make good resolutions that are too ambitious for our present state. Then we will soon fall and probably give up trying. Again, Satan helps people to feel pleasure in religion to make them proud. They may say, "We must be saints," or, "We do not need the Church." But Satan can exploit aridity or dryness, too (we mean lack of emotion). He can tempt us to say, "We are strong souls, we do not need such toys."

Finally, we ourselves can be the source of feelings, especially, but not solely, by way of suggestion. The great St. Teresa of Avila, who had such a profusion of divine favors—visions, revelations, feelings, etc.— wrote about people who want to see visions and such manifestations, "I will only warn you that, when you learn or hear that God is granting souls these graces, you must never beseech or desire Him to lead you along this road . . . there are certain reasons why such a course is not wise." She explains in detail: First, the desire shows a lack of humility; second, one thereby leaves himself open to "great peril, because the devil has only to see a door left slightly ajar to enter"; and third, the danger of suggestion: "When a person has a great desire for something, he persuades himself that he is seeing or hearing what he desires."[132]

A further word on that warning about lack of humility. There are two levels, or tiers, in the rules for the spiritual life. Among the first are the basic rules which everyone must follow, or take a loss. Among the second are the things in which great individual variations are possible, and even usual. For example, St. Francis de Sales was a highly refined gentleman; but St. Benedict Joseph Labre lived like a tramp, with body lice, and probably smelled bad. St. Francis of Assisi is said to have been reluctant to let his first followers have books at all; St. Thomas Aquinas lived his life surrounded by books. Each of these saints followed the same basic principles of the spiritual life—yet what differences in approaches![133]

Returning to the role of feelings in the Christian life, we could point out many more possibilities of deception from feelings—and many more good things about them too. But we trust we have shown that no feelings, no imagining that one has "met Jesus," can ever justify disregarding the words which we know came from Jesus in the Gospels. However good some things may *seem* to be, we must remember Eve—the fruit seemed obviously good to her.

Finally, St. Paul warned the Corinthians that at times Satan "transforms himself into an angel of light." (*2 Cor.* 11:14). It was true in St. Paul's day and is still true in our day.

Chapter 22

THE JEWISH MESSIAH

Is there any point in Jews becoming Christian since God Himself over and over in the Old Testament speaks of them as His people? The best and most direct answer is just to point out what we have proved in the body of this book thus far: Jesus, the Divine Messenger, did commission His Apostles and their successors to teach, and promised God's protection on that teaching. Hence, it is the will of God that all, including His ancient people, accept Jesus and His Church. In so doing, they are not rejecting Judaism and the ancient Patriarchs. Vatican II wrote, "The Church of Christ recognizes that the beginnings of faith and its being chosen are found already among the Patriarchs, Moses, and the Prophets... For the Church believes that Christ, our Peace, reconciled Jews and Gentiles by His cross, and made both into one in Himself."[134] Rabbi Israel Zolli, who had an international reputation as a master of Hebrew philosophy, Scripture and the Talmud, and who wrote many books on those subjects, became a Christian at age 65, though he was then Chief Rabbi of Rome, and knew it meant being reduced to poverty. After his conversion, he was asked if he still considered himself a Jew. He replied, "Once a Jew, always a Jew. Did Peter, James, John, Matthew, and hundreds of Hebrews like them cease to be Jews just because they followed Jesus the Messiah? Emphatically no. . . . I continue to hold unchanged love for the People of Israel."[135]

Jesus Himself said, "Do not think that I am come to destroy the law, or the prophets. I am not come to destroy, but to fulfill. For Amen I say to you, till heaven and earth pass, one jot, or one tittle shall not pass of the law, till all is fulfilled." (*Matt.* 5:17-18).

He told the Apostles, ". . . All things must be fulfilled, which are written in the law of Moses, and in the prophets, and in the psalms, concerning me." (*Luke* 24:44).

As we stated earlier, the only proof needed for the statement that Judaism is fulfilled, not destroyed in Christianity, is what is worked out in the body of this book and in the words of Jesus just quoted. But it is still worthwhile to review some of the chief prophecies of the Old Testament which He fulfilled. We are well aware that many scholars today dismiss these prophecies as so vague that they could be understood only by hindsight, even though Jesus Himself pointed to the prophecies about Himself, even though St. Paul, trained as a Rabbi, spoke of Jesus as dying and rising "according to the Scriptures." (*1 Cor.* 15:3-4). In fact, Vatican I taught that, "Moses and the Prophets, and especially Christ the Lord, put forth many and most manifest miracles and prophecies."[135] Let us see for ourselves how wrong these scholars are.

PROTOGOSPEL: *GENESIS* 3:15

Prophecy begins after the sin of Adam and Eve, when God speaks to them and to the serpent: "I will put enmity between you and the woman, between your seed and her seed. He will strike at your head and you will strike at his heel."[137] Vatican II comments thus: "These primeval documents, as they are read in the Church and are understood in the light of later and full revelation, gradually bring more clearly to light the figure of the woman, the Mother of the Redeemer. She, in this light, is already prophetically foreshadowed in the promise given to our first parents who had fallen into sin, of victory over the serpent (see *Gen.* 3:15)."[138]

Notice the carefully qualified language of the Council. Passages such as *Genesis* 3:15 became clearer in time, and now, with the help of full revelation, we can see even the Mother of the Redeemer, as well as the Redeemer Himself, "prophetically foreshadowed." Leave aside for the moment the question of the identification of the "woman" of *Gen.* 3:15 as the Mother of the Redeemer. But notice that in some way the prophecy refers to the Messiah. Could this be a passage understood *only* later on?

In answering this question we are fortunate in having a great help that has been often ignored called the Targums. By the time of Christ many Jews no longer spoke Hebrew; their language was Aramaic. So in reading Scripture in the synagogues, there was need of the Aramaic version called the Targum. We are not sure of the date of the Targums which we now have, but many are likely to come within a century before or after Christ. The important point is that they do not depend on hindsight because the Jews who wrote them would not accept Christ, regardless of the time frame.

The Targums are really a free translation plus commentary. So we can see how Jews, without Christ, understood the Old Testament. The Neofiti, Pseudo-Jonathan and the Fragmentary Targums interpret *Gen.* 3:15 as Messianic. Their interpretation is partly allegorical, saying that the sons of the woman will observe the commandments of the Torah and will fight the sons of the serpent, who are disobedient. Further, the Targums see a victory for the son or sons of the woman. Thus Neofiti reads, "There will be a remedy [for his wound] for the son of the woman, but for you, serpent, no remedy."[139] The other two Targums speak in the plural, i.e., of a remedy for *them,* rather than for the son, singular.

It is interesting to recall the interpretation of Vatican

II that the woman stands for the Mother of the Messiah. Really, this is obvious because if the text refers to the Messiah, then the woman whose "seed" the Messiah is must be His Mother. Yet modern commentators have been reluctant to acknowledge Mary in this verse. They point out that the only woman mentioned alive at all is Eve. To that we reply: (1) This is a prophecy, which can look ahead, beyond the time when it was given; (2) There was a tendency in ancient times to see prophecies as having more than one fulfillment. We see this in the New Testament. For example, in *2 Tim.* 3:1, where most scholars take "the last days" to refer both to all time from the Ascension of Jesus until His return, and more narrowly, to the time just before His return.[140] Again, St. Matthew's Gospel seems to take this attitude in *Matt.* 2:15 to understand *Hosea* 11:1 (which originally referred to the Exodus) and the return of the child Jesus from Egypt, and in interpreting *Isaiah* 7:14 to mean the virgin birth (*Matt.* 1:22-23). Some scholars think the entire mysterious Chapter 24 of Matthew follows this pattern too.

Similarly, Samson H. Levey, a Jewish scholar, in commenting on *Exodus* 12:42 says that the fact that the Targum links together Moses and the Messiah could indicate that the final phase of the history of Israel will be a type of repetition of the deliverance from Egypt at its beginning.[141]

In this light, we could easily say that the "woman" of *Gen.* 3:15 stands for both Eve and Mary. The Fathers of the Church over and over speak of Mary as the new Eve.[142]

THE PROPHECY OF THE DYING JACOB
GENESIS 49:10

When Jacob was dying in Egypt, he gave a prophecy about his sons, and especially Judah: "The scepter shall not depart from Juda, nor the ruler's staff from between his feet, until Shiloh comes, and his shall be the obedience of the peoples." There has been much discussion of the translation of this verse. Yet, the Targum Neofiti confidently renders it: "Kings shall not be lacking from the house of Judah ... until the time at which King Messiah will come."[144] Levey comments that this supposes the restoration of the dynasty of David and adds that other rabbinic sources, Midrashic and Talmudic, agree that the passage is Messianic.[145]

The question is raised: What of the fact that Judah fell under the rule of Babylonia, and that there were no kings of the line of David after the Babylonian exile? There are two replies: First, the tribe of Judah did maintain supremacy and power even after the exile, as David's tribe and as the place of the Temple, until Herod, the first foreign-born king, was installed in that land. Secondly, although God spoke in a seemingly absolute way to Solomon after the Temple was dedicated—"My eyes and my heart shall be there always" (*Kgs.* 9:3)—yet a few lines later, He warned, "But if you turn away from following me ... I will cut off Israel from the face of the land which I have given them ... and this house I will cast out of my sight." (*Kgs.* 6-8). This actually happened. Therefore we could say that the prophecy of Jacob was still realized, but not as fully as it would have been if the people had been faithful to God.

THE VIRGIN SHALL CONCEIVE: *ISAIAH* 7:14

There was a period of crisis for the southern kingdom, Judah, in the years 735-33 B.C. A coalition of the kings of Israel, the northern kingdom, and Damascus wanted to overthrow King Ahaz of Judah, and put in a ruler who would join them in an alliance against Assyria. Ahaz was more inclined to ask Assyria for help. He was a wicked king who had burned his own son in sacrifice (*2 Kgs.* 16:3) probably not long before the day of his meeting with Isaiah the prophet just outside Jerusalem. Isaiah told the king he must put his trust in God, not in the Assyrians, and added that God would give the king any sign he might ask, whether in the sky or in the depths. Ahaz pretended to be too pious to accept because it would be "tempting" God. In reply, the prophet rebuked him and said he was tiresome not only to men, but even to God, "Therefore the Lord himself shall give you a sign. Behold a virgin shall conceive, and bear a son, and shall call his name: Emmanuel." (*Isa.* 7:14).

Scholars have been divided on the meaning of *Isaiah* 7:14. Some have said the child promised is just Hezekiah, the son born naturally not virginally, to Ahaz. That birth could be taken as a "sign" in that it would be a continuation of the line of David. Others say the son is virginally born, and therefore is Christ. The solemnity of the whole scene suggests the birth of more than just an ordinary son—after offering a sign in the heavens or in the depths, to give just an ordinary child would not be striking, even though it would continue David's line. Further, God had promised (*2 Sam.* 7:11-16) that David's line would *last forever*. It was commonly thought that the Messiah would rule *forever*.[146] When the Septuagint was made, centuries after Isaiah and Hezekiah, the translators believed the prophecy was still to be fulfilled—which is another indication that it referred to Jesus.

St. Matthew (*Matt.* 22-23) quotes this prophecy and says it was fulfilled in Jesus. We noted above that Matthew, and other parts of Scripture, at times see multiple fulfillments of prophecies. This is just such a case since the child promised was both Hezekiah and Jesus.

Still further, *Isaiah* 7:1 through 12:6 is often called the book of *Emmanuel*. It seems that the child spoken of in Isaiah 9:6 is the same as the child of *Isaiah* 7:14. Plus, there is an indirect help in our interpretation from the Targums, for they see *Isaiah* 9:6 as Messianic. Levey says that all versions take the line as Messianic.[147] Hezekiah hardly matches the description of *Isaiah* 9:5.

A CHILD IS BORN: *ISAIAH* 9:6

It was earlier established that the Targums do consider *Isaiah* 9:6 as Messianic. However, there is a problem in that verse, which does not affect its messianic character. The problem is whether or not the child is called God.

The translation of this verse is much debated, and with reason, for the implications can be astounding. Levey twists the sentence structure to avoid a statement of divinity. In his translation, God calls the newborn child "Prince of Peace."[148] The Soncino version, another scholarly Jewish publication, reads it, "And his name is called 'Pele-joez-el-gibbor-abi-ad-sar-shalom.'" Thus the critical words are turned into an extremely long name, which means: "Wonderful in counsel is God the Mighty, the Everlasting Father, the Ruler of Peace."[149] The New American Bible for the same words has: "They name him Wonder-Counselor, God-Hero, Father-Forever, Prince of Peace." The Protestant Revised Standard version is: "And his name will be called 'Wonderful Counselor, Mighty God, Everlasting Father, Prince of Peace.'"

The Hebrew text will allow any of these translations—though the New American Bible strains the usual sense of *El-gibbor,* "God the Mighty." The Targums also present problems in translation. Levey translates in a manner parallel to his twisting of sentence structure in the Hebrew. He claims to follow the Targumic sentence structure beyond question. But J. F. Stenning of Oxford thinks it is not beyond question. He translates: "And his name has been called from of old, Wonderful counsellor Mighty God, He who lives forever, the Anointed one (or, Messiah) in whose days peace shall increase upon us."[151] Again, the Aramaic will allow either translation.

The Septuagint greatly reduces the wording, and omits the phrase "Mighty God." It reads, "And his name shall be called, messenger of the great council." One wonders if the Septuagint is, as Shakespeare puts it, "protesting too much" to avoid saying the child is to be God.[152] For the Hebrew *El gibbor* means God in every occurrence in the Old Testament. To put it mildly, it would be a great problem for an ancient Jew to find a prophecy saying the Messiah would be God. It would *seem* to violate the truth that was so strongly hammered in that there is only one God. Those who had had no hint of the Blessed Trinity would have immense difficulty.

However, as we said above, in spite of all this, the Targums do clearly consider *Isaiah* 9:6 as Messianic,[153] and so, since the child of *Isaiah* 7:14 seems to be the same as the child of *Isaiah* 9:6, we have another proof that the child of 7:14 is the Messiah, virginally born.

THE SUFFERING, ATONING SERVANT: *ISAIAH* 53

One of the most striking prophecies is that of Isaiah Chapter 53, which tells of the atoning, suffering and death of the Servant of God who will have "no form or comeliness," who will be "despised and rejected by men," who "has borne our griefs... [and] was wounded for our transgressions ... was oppressed and afflicted, yet did not open his mouth ... like a lamb being led to the slaughter."

But when we turn to the Targum, we have the clearest case of Shakespeare's example of protesting too much. For while the Targum clearly makes the servant of God to be the Messiah, as Levey says, it does extreme violence to the sense, giving the text the very opposite meaning. Instead of the meek sufferer, like the lamb led to the slaughter, the Targums show a proud, arrogant man who brings ruin to the enemies of Israel, and who overcomes mighty kings.

For example, in verse 3, the Hebrew says, "He was despised and rejected by men." But the Targum says, "Then the glory of all kingdoms will be despised and cease."[154] Verse 5 says, "He was wounded for our transgressions, he was bruised for our iniquities." But the Targum says, "He will [re]build the sanctuary, polluted because of our sins, [and] handed over because of our iniquities." Where the Hebrew in verse 7 has that He was "like a lamb being led to the slaughter," the Targum says instead, "He will hand over the mighty ones of the peoples, like a lamb to the slaughter."

Clearly, the Targumist had no notion of a suffering Messiah, even though he knew the servant was the Messiah.[155] However, the Targum does make the passage Messianic, and by its extreme reverse of meaning gives away the truth. Even some modern Jewish scholars are candid enough to admit that the Targumists at times deliberately distorted the sense of such prophecies to try to keep the Christians from using them.[156] A very prominent modern Jewish scholar, H. J. Schoeps, admits the same thing: ". . . it was felt to be undesirable to lend support to the Christian interpretation. Again with the same motive and in order to eliminate the reference of *Isaiah* 53 to Christ, atoning power was imputed to the death of Moses."[157]

BETHLEHEM: *MICAH* 5:1-3

When the Magi came to King Herod and asked where the King of the Jews was to be born, Herod, "assembling together all the chief priests and scribes of the people, inquired of them where the Christ should be born." (*Matt.* 2:4). Without hesitation "They said to him: In Bethlehem of Juda. For so it is written by the prophet: And you Bethlehem of the land of Judah are not the least among the rulers of Juda: for out of you shall come forth the captain who shall govern my people Israel." (*Matt.* 2:5).

They were, of course, quoting *Micah* 5:2: "And you Bethlehem Ephrathah, you are little to be among the thousands of Judah, from you shall come for me one who is to be ruler in Israel, whose origin is from of old, from the days of eternity." The Targum Jonathan is quite clear: "From you will come forth before me the Messiah . . . whose name was spoken from days of old, from the days of eternity." In fact, the last part of verse 2 in the Hebrew could suggest even a pre-existence for the Messiah: "Whose origin is from of old, from the days of eternity." The Targums concur: "whose name was spoken from days of old, from the days of eternity."

CONCLUSION

There are many other prophecies that the Targums recognize as Messianic. We have cited enough to show that even in ancient times, Jews did understand that the Messiah was foretold to our first parents, and that He was to come when the dominion had finally passed from Judah (to Herod), and that He would be born in Bethlehem. We gathered with their help that He would be born of a virgin, and if we accept the normal Hebrew sense of *"El gibbor"* in *Isaiah* 9:6 ("God the Mighty") and Stenning's translation of the Targum Jonathan, that He would be divine. His divinity was hinted at in *Micah* 5:2 where the Hebrew says His "origin is from old, from the days of eternity" which, as we saw, can mean pre-existence.[160]

We gathered too, because of the very distortion of the Targum on *Isaiah* 53, making the meek lamb into an arrogant conqueror, that the Messiah would suffer from our sins.

All these things, of course, Jesus fulfilled most clearly and abundantly. Again, we emphasize that He came not to destroy, but to fulfill the law, the prophets and the hopes of His people Israel.

Chapter 23

OTHER SHEEP I HAVE

There are many non-Christian religions and philosophies that have numerous followers in the world. Yet, there is not one of them that would even attempt to give a carefully worked out, rational basis for its faith such as we have given in the main part of this book. Yes, Muhammad, founder of Islam, claimed to be a prophet. But he did not even try to prove it by miracles worked in the connected framework we saw for the miracles that prove Jesus was a messenger sent by God. Nor is there any such thing as an Islamic Lourdes, a center where miracles still happen, which are meticulously checked by the best resources of modern science. Only the Catholic Church can and does claim such proven wonders.

But another question can and must be raised about these sects. St. Paul in *Romans* 3:29 asked: "Is he the God of the Jews only? Is he not also of the Gentiles?" St. Paul meant that if we say that one could only be saved by keeping the law of Moses, then what of the countless people who have never heard of Moses? Did God desert them, as if He were not their God at all? St. Paul says that He is their God too, for He has provided for salvation by faith (we recall the meaning of that expression in Chapter 18).

Clearly, we have to ask the same question about the millions who have never heard of Christianity. Is God not their God too? With St. Paul we say, "Of course He is."

But here we must carefully distinguish two things: the *fact* that it is true, and *how* this is accomplished. The fact

143

that God makes salvation possible for them is beyond doubt—just how it is done is a different question.

As to the fact that it is true: Pope Pius IX taught, "God, who clearly sees, examines, and knows the minds, souls, thoughts and attitudes of all, in His supreme goodness definitely does not allow anyone to be punished with eternal punishments who does not have the guilt of voluntary fault."[161] When Father Leonard Feeney said that all who did not have their names on a parish register were lost, Pope Pius XII directed the Holy Office to condemn his error. In its declaration, the Holy Office quoted from the Mystical Body Encyclical of Pius XII, saying people can be saved, "who are ordered to the Church by a sort of unrecognized [by them] desire and wish."[162] Vatican II taught the same concept: "They who without their own fault do not know the Gospel of Christ and His Church, but yet seek God with a sincere heart, and try, with the help of grace, to carry out His will which they know by conscience can attain eternal salvation . . ."[163] This does not mean a person who knows that the Church has been founded by Jesus as the means to salvation can choose merely to obey the moral law and ignore the Church: "Those persons cannot be saved who while knowing that the Catholic Church was founded by God through Jesus Christ as necessary, still refuse to enter it or to continue in it."[164]

Thus, it is certain that these millions who are not officially part of the Church are not excluded from eternal salvation. But, as we said, just how this works out in practice is another question. Pius XII made clear that in some way people can by an implicit desire (which they themselves do not recognize as such) pertain to the Church, or be "ordered to the Church" and so, if they fulfill the moral law as they know it, can be saved. (Modern anthropology shows that primitives do know the moral law surprisingly well).

In exploring farther, we recognize that the Church has not given us more information than what we have just quoted. That of course does not forbid us, without denying the Church's words, to add to them to clarify the issue.

HOW CAN PAGANS BE SAVED?

The question of how pagans are saved presents a puzzle. On the one hand, we have the modern, authoritative statements which we have just quoted; on the other hand, some older texts which sound contrastingly severe. For example, the Fourth Lateran Council in 1215 A.D. taught, "There is one universal Church of the faithful, outside of which no one at all is saved."[165]

Now before going ahead, it must be recognized that in matters of divine revelation, we may easily come upon two truths, and know both are true—yet we may not be able to see how to reconcile them. We saw examples of this conflict from St. Paul in Chapters 19 and 20, and there are more. The *way* to reconcile seemingly opposite things may be to accept that we can never resolve them, at least in this life. For example, the mystery of the Blessed Trinity is unsolvable in this life. But in other cases, after some time, the answer may be discovered, as we saw previously. *It is of major importance to work using the right method. We must take care not to deny, or even to strain the interpretation of either of the two truths. So here we must hold that membership in the Church is required—yet that some can be saved who seem not to have that membership.*

Pope St. Clement I, who was of the same generation at Rome as Sts. Peter and Paul, wrote in about 95 A.D. to the Church of Corinth, "Let us go through all generations, and learn that in generation and generation the Master has given a place of repentance for those willing to turn to Him. Those who repented for their sins, appeased God in praying and received salvation, *even though they were aliens to God.*"[166]

Even more striking are the words of St. Justin, Martyr, written in his First Apology, in Rome, around 150 A.D.: "Those who lived according to *Logos* are Christians, even if they were considered atheists, as among the Greeks, Socrates and Heraclitus."[167] We left the word *Logos* in Greek because it has several meanings including *word, Word of God,* and *reason.* St. Justin seems to mean the *Word of God,* the Second Person of the Blessed Trinity, who in the fullness of time took flesh for our salvation.

How could Justin say some followed Christ the Logos centuries before His birth? In his Second Apology, St. Justin explains: "Christ . . . was and is *the Logos who is in everyone,* who foretold through the prophets the things that were to come, and, when He became like us in experience, taught these things Himself."[168] St. Justin is saying that even before the incarnation, the Divine Word could speak to men—to the Jews through the prophets and to outsiders in a purely interior way. Those who followed the Word were Christians, even centuries before Christ.

St. Justin is elaborating on an idea of St. Paul's found in *Romans* 2:14-16 which states, "For when the Gentiles, who have not the law, do by nature those things that are of the law; these having not the law are a law to themselves: They show the work of the law written in their hearts, their conscience bears witness to them, and their thoughts in turn will be either accusing or even defending them, in the day when God shall judge the secrets of men by Jesus Christ, according to my gospel."

St. Paul echoes *Jeremiah* 31:33, where God says, "I will put my law within them, and I will write it in their heart." If the Gentiles obey the law written on their hearts, then their consciences will defend them at the Judgment and they will be saved. If we compare these words with what St. Paul adds later in *Romans* 8:9: "Now if any man does not have the spirit of Christ, he does not belong to him," we can see that it must be that the Spirit of Christ—the Divine Logos, the Word— writes the law in hearts. If one does not have and follow that Spirit, he does not belong to Christ—but if he does have and follow it, he does belong to Christ. The implications are tremendous and we will explore them in greater detail later.

About the same time as St. Justin, a remarkable lay- man called Hermas, the brother of Pope St. Pius I, wrote a work on the Church and the Sacrament of Pen- ance called *The Shepherd.* In it, he reports a vision which perhaps is just a device of the genre in which he was working. In that vision an old woman appears. An angel asks Hermas, "The old woman ... who do you think it is?" Hermas thinks it is a pagan prophetess, a Sibyl. But the angel tells him, "You are wrong ... it is not." "Who then is it," asks Hermas. The angel ex- plains, "It is the Church." But then Hermas asks, "Why the appearance as an old woman?" The angel explains, "Because She was created first of all, and for this reason, She is an old woman."[169] According to this vi- sion, the Church has always existed, since the begin- ning; She is the first creation.

The same idea exists in a very early sermon from about the time of Hermas which was once thought to come from Pope St. Clement I: "The books of the prophets and the Apostles [say] that the Church is not [only] now, but from the beginning. She was spiritual ... She was manifested in the last days to save us."[170]

St. Justin had said that some people centuries before Christ were really Christians, since they followed the Logos, the Divine Word. St. Irenaeus, the martyr Bishop of Lyons (died c. 200 A.D.), had listened when he was young to St. Polycarp telling what he in turn had heard from St. John the Apostle himself. St. Irenaeus wrote,

"There is one and the same God the Father, and His Logos, always assisting the human race, with varied arrangements, doing many things, and saving from the beginning those who are saved—they are those who love God and . . . follow the Logos of God."[171]

The idea that the Church is ancient, from the beginning of time, is put forth by Clement of Alexandria, head of the great catechetical school of Alexandria: "It is clear that there is one true Church, which is really ancient, into which those who are just . . . are enrolled."[172]

The next head of the school at Alexandria was Clement's pupil Origen. The pagan Celsus had attacked the Church, saying: "Did God then only, after so long a time, think of making the life of man just, while before He did not care?" Origen replied, "But He always cared, and gave occasions of virtue to make reasonable beings right. For generation by generation, the wisdom of God came to souls it found holy, and made them friends of God and prophets."[173]

The objection of Celsus appears again, and is answered, in the work of Arnobius around 305 A.D. Arnobius had long been an opponent of Christianity. When he finally asked for Baptism, the bishop was suspicious. To prove his sincerity, Arnobius wrote *Against the Nations*. In it he said: "Put aside these cares, and leave the questions you do not know. Royal mercy was imparted to them, and the divine benefits ran equally through all. They were conserved, they were liberated."[174]

Not long after Arnobius, a dialogue presented as between Manes, founder of Manichaeism, and Archelaus, Bishop of Charchar, speaks similarly. Manes had raised the same objection as Celsus. Archelaus replied, "From the creation of the world, He has always been with just men . . . Were they not just from the fact that they kept the law? 'each of them showing the work of the law on their hearts, their conscience testifying to them.' "[175] Archelaus, we easily see, is appealing to *Romans* 2:14-16, which taught the salvation of pagans who followed the law that the Spirit of Christ, the Logos, made known to them in their hearts.

One of the greatest of the Latin Fathers, St. Augustine, wrote in his *Epistle 102,* "From the beginning of the human race, whoever believed in Him and understood Him somewhat, and lived according to His precepts . . . whoever and wherever they may have been, doubtless were saved through Him."[176] And again later in the same Epistle: "The salvation of this religion, through which alone true salvation is truly promised, was never lacking to anyone who was worthy, and he to whom it was lacking, was not worthy."

Near the end of his life, when he made a long review of all his works, called *Retractations,* we find: "This very thing, which is now called the Christian religion, existed among the ancients, nor was it lacking from the beginning of the human race until Christ Himself came in the flesh, whence the true religion, that already existed, began to be called Christian."[177]

We could quote many more statements from the Fathers, but let us be content with brief mention of a few more. St. Gregory of Naziansus, at the funeral of his father, who had been pagan but died a bishop, said, "He was ours even before he was of our fold."[178] St. John Chrysostom interpreted *Romans* 2:14-16 just as we did.[179] Pope St. Leo the Great spoke of Christ establishing one and the same cause of salvation since the foundation of the world.[180] Pope St. Gregory the Great spoke much as did St. Augustine, and in a *Homily on Ezechiel* added, "They were, then, outside, but yet not divided from the Holy Church, because in mind, in work, in preaching, they already held the Sacraments of faith, and saw that loftiness of Holy Church." Although they were outside the Church in that they were not official members, they were "not divided" from the true Church.[181]

FINALLY AN ANSWER

It has been proven that many Fathers held that the Church existed from the beginning of the human race. Others, like St. Justin, said that some before Christ were really Christians because they followed the Logos, the Divine Word. So now we ask: In what sense was and is the Logos in each man, so that, by listening and obeying, men could be Christians even before Christ?

As we hinted above, the answer lies in the great *Epistle to the Romans.* In *Romans* 2:14-16, the Spirit of Christ was sent into the hearts of pagans who had not heard the revealed law of Moses. The Spirit wrote the law on their hearts—anthropology today says that primitives did and do know the moral law. Those pagans, of course, did not know it was the Spirit of Christ. Yet, objectively, many of them did follow that Spirit, and so, objectively, if they complied, they were following the Spirit of Christ. We saw further, from Chapter 8 of *Romans,* that those who do not have and follow that Spirit do not belong to Christ, but those who do have and follow the Spirit of Christ do belong to Christ. Now, in St. Paul's language, to "belong to Christ" means to be a member of the Body of Christ—but that Body of Christ is the Church. Hence, this remarkable conclusion is evident: *The good pagans really did belong to Christ, or belonged to His Body, the Church.* They were unaware of that, of course, and so did not turn in their names to a parish register, as it were. In that respect, they were members in a lesser way or lesser degree, but yet, in a basic and true sense, they were members of the Church.

Were this not true, St. Paul could not have written, "Is he the God of the Jews only? Is he not also of the Gentiles?" (*Rom.* 3:29).

It is apparent that many of the Fathers could say the Church existed from the beginning. It was in this way that it did exist.

It is also obvious how the Fourth Lateran Council could say flatly that only those who belong to the Church are saved. This statement is quite right since these pagans we have described, who followed the Logos, the Spirit of Christ, really were Christians and were members of the Church.

Consequently, there is an answer to what seemed a great puzzle: How can we reconcile the opposing views that one must be a member to be saved; yet many who never get their names on the parish register are saved. Now we can have it both ways.

Whether or not they realized it, the Fathers of Vatican II expressed the same idea: "All who belong to Christ, having His Spirit, coalesce into one Church."[182]

But a further objection can be raised. Some say that before Christ, there was provision for those who did not know the revelation given to the Jews; after Christ, anyone who does not get his name on a parish register, as it were, is damned, even if he had really no chance to get to know the Church. This is a horrendous error, really, the most hideous of heresies, for it makes God, who is Love, to be a monster, damning untold millions through no fault of their own. On the contrary, St. Paul, in five different ways, repeats in *Romans* 5:15-21, that the redemption is more abundant than the fall. These people would make it far less abundant!

Further, the words of the Magisterium, cited above, clearly rule out the heresy of the objectors. Pius IX said that God . . . "*does not* allow anyone to be punished with eternal punishments who *does not* have the guilt of voluntary fault." He was referring to the present, not to the time before Christ, for he used the *present tense.* Similarly Vatican II says: "They who without their own fault do not know the Gospels of Christ and His

Church" can be saved if they do what they know. If the Council meant only people who formally get into the Church, there would be no point in writing these words. Pius XII too said those who are merely "ordered to the Church by a sort of unrecognized [by them] desire and wish" can be saved.

All this does not mean that we should not work and pray for the conversion of those whose names are not on the parish register. We should, definitely. It is the will of God that they should enter fully, for there they find more abundant, more secure means of salvation, and "God desires all men to be saved, and to come to the knowledge of the truth." (*1 Tim.* 2:4).

Chapter 24

WE HAVE HERE NO LASTING CITY

In Chapter 5, the question was posed: "If there is a good God, how can there be such evils in the world?" We were able to give only a partial answer then, since we could not use Scripture until we had shown that Scripture can be trusted, and is even inspired. But now we can return to more completely address the question.

It was established that evil is not a positive thing, a substance; it is a negative, a lack of what should be there. So evil does not need or have a Creator.

The worst evils are moral evils. These are permitted by God in an indirect way; that is, the very gift of free will makes such things possible. He could have created a race similar to ours, but lacking free will. But it would not be human, and we really would not want to be without freedom.

With regard to moral evil, nature itself strikes those who do wrong with automatic penalties. For example, if someone gets drunk, nature imposes a hangover. If someone grows up being completely self-indulgent, never having discipline, never denying self—such a person will be immature.

Marriage is not for children. If one immature person is part of a marriage, that marriage is very apt to fail. Again, the biochemistry of sex can cause feelings of tenderness—but these are not real love. Real love is a deep concern or desire (in the spiritual will) for the well-being and happiness of the other. Chemistry fools people into thinking they have such a concern—but

153

they really do not. They may think they can cheat, by violating moral laws, which only spell out what our nature needs—and later wake up to find themselves locked into a marriage without love. Again, nature strikes, without mercy. God is merciful but nature is not. A failed marriage is one of the greatest tragedies in life.

Something else about the immature and the self-indulgent must be added. They not only are likely to fail at marriage, but they cannot really enjoy life in other respects. And, if they go very far into their self-indulgence, they may pay a dear penalty at the hands of nature. The great pagan Roman historian, Tacitus, quotes for us part of a letter from the Emperor Tiberius to the Senate. It was written near the end, when Tiberius had corrupted himself in all sorts of terrible excesses. Tiberius wrote, "If I know what to write to you at this time, senators, or how to write it, or what not to write—may the gods sink me into even a worse ruin than I feel overtaking me daily!"[183]

Imagine, an all-powerful despot, able to gratify his every whim, feeling this way! Tacitus continues and explains, "Not in vain was the wisest of men wont to affirm that the souls of despots if uncovered would show manglings and wounds, tearings left on the spirit, like lash-marks on a body, by cruelty, lust, and malevolence. Neither Tiberius' power nor isolation could save him from confessing the inner torments of heart which were his penalty." That "wisest of men" to whom Tacitus refers was Socrates, who, in Plato's *Theatetus* says, "They [people who try to get away with wrongdoing] do not know the penalty of wickedness [is] . . . not beatings and death . . . which evil-doers often escape, but a penalty that cannot be escaped . . . that they lead a life that matches the pattern to which they are growing like."[184]

We have been talking thus far about moral evils. But

there are also physical evils, such as sickness, hardships, death. What of these? Many today have lost sight of, or have never known, a tremendous perspective which alone can explain physical evils. St. Paul knew it well. In *1 Corinthians* 7:17-24, he was explaining to his converts that the fact they had become Christians did not require a change in the externals of their lives (except, of course, things that were sinful). In that context he makes a statement that is very surprising: "Were you called [to the faith] as a slave? Let it not concern you. But even if you are able to become free, rather use [it]."[184] The words "use it" are ambiguous.

They could either advise using the chance to become free, or to use the chance for humility as a slave. The fact that Paul is developing the idea that the fact one becomes Christian does not have to mean a change in the externals of his life, strongly suggests Paul means that one should stay a slave. When we see his attitudes on this subject elsewhere, this view is somewhat strengthened. In *Colossians* 3:22-24 (and *Eph.* 6:5-8) he tells slaves to obey not only when their masters are watching, but even when they are not looking, and they will be rewarded by Christ.

Paul could talk this way because he saw a great vista which most people do not see. It becomes clearer in *Phillippians* 3:7-8: "But the things that were gain to me, these I have considered as loss on account of Christ. Furthermore I count all things to be but loss for the outstandingness of the knowledge of Christ Jesus My Lord; for whom I have suffered the loss of all things, and count them but as dung, that I may gain Christ." He means that in comparison to having Christ, everything else is worthless, is mere dung. For St. Paul knew that *we are saved and made holy if, and to the extent that we are not only members of Christ, but like Him.* Now in the life of Christ there were two phases. First there was a hard life, suffering, and death; second, eternal glory. St. Paul knew the more we are like Him in the first phase, the more we will be like Him in the second, in glory.

In such a perspective, St. Paul, without meaning to approve slavery, could still think it of little moment.

But now we must ask why Christ chose such a life—for He, in His divine nature, could and did choose every detail of His earthly life. The answer is twofold: Such things are good for us, and are needed for reparation of sin.

Why needed for us? Human nature includes both body and soul, and within each there are many drives and needs. They are legitimate in themselves, but the problem is that each drive operates without considering the other's needs; each one is automatic, blind. So, to keep ourselves in good condition—needed even for happiness in the present life—we must tame these drives. If we have a piece of springy steel, we cannot just push it once to straight position; it must be bent many times over to make it finally stay straight. So it is with our nature. It needs a lot of straightening. Acceptance of difficult things, whether permitted by God, or taken on voluntarily, is the way to real freedom, to wholeness, to the ability to enjoy even this life.

So Jesus took on a heavy measure of these things to induce us to do what is good for us, and as a reparation for sin.

But there is more: St. Paul knew we need these things for the present life, but we need them still more for the life to come because greater likeness to Christ here means greater likeness to His glory.

How satisfactory is this present life? At best it is short, and includes many things that are unpleasant. Suppose we think back to second grade: How long did a school year seem then, compared to a year now? So it is for all normal persons; as we age, time picks up speed. A span of fifty years seems long before we start it, but when it is over, it seems like little. Further, we contrast this short, and not too satisfactory life with an unending span, including satisfaction and happiness beyond our ability to imagine it! No wonder St. Paul took the attitude: Why worry about your situation here—the important thing is to get the best possible in the future life. For St. Paul knew that thanks to the goodness of God, these present evils, which human frailty and a material world make inevitable, can be turned into pure gold for that unending glorious life.

The very "Fatherliness" of God leads Him to give us this training and preparation (earthly parents who are always indulgent to children do them ill service because they stay immature and are unable to enjoy life as they should. They are in danger of failed marriages, and of eternal misery.) In the *Book of Proverbs* in the Old Testament we read (3:11-12), "My son, reject not the correction of the Lord: and do not faint when you are chastised by him: For whom the Lord loves, he chastises: and as a father in the son he takes pleasure." So difficulties are really a sign of special love: God is preparing us the more fully, the more surely, for that life that really counts. The *Epistle to the Hebrews* says the same thing (12:6), "For whom the Lord loves, he chastises; and he scourges every son whom he accepts."

Further, on the more positive side, St. Paul tells us that even small, difficult things now bring a reward all out of proportion later: "For that which is at present momentary and light of our troubles is working beyond all measure an eternal weight of glory for us." (*2 Cor.* 4:17). And again in *Romans* 8:18," For I judge that the sufferings of this time are not worthy to be compared with the glory to come, that shall be revealed to us."

St. Augustine, in his *Confessions,* spoke to God saying, "You have made us for yourself, and restless is our heart until it rests in you."[186] Augustine knew this because he tried illegitimate pleasures to excess, yet found none of them really satisfying. How many times have we looked forward to an event, only to be let down or disappointed after its arrival? Somehow, the reality is less than our anticipation of it and does not fully satisfy. No earthly pleasure provides the "happily ever after" we seek. Even sex, the most intense of pleasures, becomes routine and people try to recapture lost intensity through sex manuals or unnatural perversions.

The only thing that can really fill us, make us utterly happy, and will never grow old or monotonous is the sharing in the life of God Himself. For each animal, God has provided satisfaction proper to its species. But for men, He was not content to provide a merely human kind of happiness. He made us to enjoy being part divine. This phrase, "part divine" is not rhetoric, poetry, or exaggeration. It is most strictly true. *The Second Epistle of St. Peter* (1:4) says we are, "partakers of the divine nature." *The First Epistle of St. John* speaks similarly (*1 Jn.* 3:2), "We are now the sons of God; and it has not yet appeared what we shall be. We know, that, when he shall appear, we shall be like to him: because we shall see him as he is."

We are His children by adoption. In human adoption, a good couple takes in a child and treats it as if it were a natural member of the family. Yet they cannot give the child any of their genes or blood. It is only by a legal document that he is called their child. But what human couples cannot do, God can and does. He not only calls us His sons, He gives us a share in His own life, very literally.

St. Cyril of Jerusalem, a great Father of the Church, compared this transformation of our souls by grace to a piece of iron in a blacksmith's forge.[187] At first the iron is cold and dark, but then it warms up in the fire, and finally glows so that it seems to have turned into fire. Another good example is of a diamond that could float in the air in the brilliant noontime summer sun, so that it would seem to have been changed into the sun.

But these are only comparisons and do not get to the literal heart of the matter. St. Paul told the Corinthians (*1 Cor.* 13:12), "We see now through a mirror, dimly, but then face to face." Mirrors then did not have the brilliance of ours. Similarly, in this life we know God only in a dark manner, through the mirror of creation. Whatever good there is must be in Him in the supreme degree, for He made it. But in the world to come we will see Him "face to face." That is, of course, a figure of speech. What does it mean literally? When I see you, I do not take you into my head, I take in an image of you. Now an image is finite or limited; but so are you. Hence, an image can let me see you well. But no image—since images have to be finite—could let me see God. Hence, Pope Benedict XII defined that when we see God, there is no image at all in between Him and us.[188] How can that be? St. Thomas Aquinas made the obvious addition: If there is no image, then God must join Himself directly to our intellect to do the work of an image.[189] That really is seeing "face to face."

Now, this sort of vision is possible only for a creature that is part divine. Within the Blessed Trinity there are two infinite streams of knowledge and love. Chapter 1 of St. John's Gospel tells us that the Father speaks a Word. That Word is not the quickly passing vibration of the air that our words are. No, it is substantial and it fully expresses Him. It is a Divine Person, the Word, the Second Person of the Blessed Trinity. That is the infinite stream of knowledge, that IS a Divine Person. Between these Divine Persons there arises equally infinite love. Again, that love is no mere vibration, it is substantial, it is, again, a Person, the Holy Spirit, who IS the love of the Father for the Son, and the Son for the Father.

Can it ever become dull, as events in daily life, in these infinite streams? Of course not—we are finite, they are infinite, and hence inexhaustible. A modern writer, J. P. Arendzen, gives us a comparison that is helpful: "God, then, remains unfathomable even to the greatest of His saints. They see Him, but none can see to the very depths of His divine being. God is a world, a wide universe, which none of the Blessed has ever totally explored. Even after millions of cycles of ages, neither Mary, the Queen of Heaven, nor Michael, the Prince of the heavenly host, shall exhaust the greatness of the divine Majesty. It is an ocean on which the little craft of created intelligences can forever press forward in all directions, for it is a sea without a shore."[190]

It is necessary to note too that we are finite vessels, trying to take in the Infinite. But these vessels, our souls, can be enlarged to be capable of taking in God more and more fully, even though no one can exhaust the vision. Each soul will be completely full and satisfied, having all it can "contain." Yet some can contain more than others. To make us capable of containing more is the work of suffering in this life.

Thus, if our Father gives us more difficult tasks, it means He wants us to have ever greater joy forever. And, to return to St. Paul, His generosity is such that whatever is "light and momentary in our troubles is working beyond all measure an eternal weight of glory for us," (*2 Cor.* 4:17), so that "the sufferings of this time are not worthy to be compared with the glory to come, that shall be revealed to us." (*Romans* 8:18).

The marvelous story of a modern woman illustrates this: Marthe Robin was a simple peasant woman in Southern France, who died on February 6, 1981. For more than fifty years she had been blind and paralyzed, unable to move in her bed. In 1930, she had received the sacred stigmata, and she went through the Passion every Friday. She never ate anything, or even drank a drop of water for more than fifty years. Although difficult for us to believe, she lived solely on the Holy

Eucharist. In spite of her afflictions, she was always patient, gentle, peaceful, humble, joyful, charitable, self-giving, and interested in others. She really could say with St. Paul, "Now I rejoice in my sufferings for you, and fill up those things that are wanting of the sufferings of Christ, in my flesh, for his body, which is the Church." (*Col.* 1:24). If what is light and momentary in affliction works an eternal weight of glory—what of such a soul? Her sufferings were a privilege for her and for the Church.[191]

The sane man sees things as they are and reacts appropriately; the insane man sees things as they are not. He may think someone is chasing him, or that he is Napoleon, etc. Within this framework, who is the sanest of men? He, who sees this world as it is, as no lasting city, but as the waiting room where we await our flight to our real home. This person is not too concerned with affairs in the waiting room, or with accumulating all sorts of baggage. No, his concern is to get home, to enjoy home most fully. Hence it is that the saints were the sanest people, the only totally sane people, because they saw this world as it is and reacted appropriately. St. Paul said that in comparison to what is to come, this world is mere "dung" (*Phil.* 3:3), on which we should set no store, knowing that "the sufferings of this time are not worthy to be compared with the glory to come, that shall be revealed to us." (*Rom.* 8:18).

Appendix 1

ERRORS IN CHURCH TEACHING?

1) THE LAY OF THE LAND

There are many claims today that the Church really has reversed past teaching. If that were true, one or both of the teachings would be in error. But we know from what we saw in the body of this book that this cannot happen. We know that Christ, the Divine Messenger, promised divine protection for the teaching of His Church. So we are assured that these claims simply must be untrue.

Further, we need to notice an important point: A thousand difficulties, even if not yet solved, do not add up to one doubt. Yes, if we were depending *only on human reasoning*, we might doubt a previously reached conclusion because of new objections. For we know that mere human reason, when it gets into complex issues, can err. But here things are different because we are not relying only on the power of any human mind, however sharp. No, we are relying on a divine promise, which cannot fail. Hence we must keep clearly in mind the principle that in this study a thousand difficulties do not make one doubt.

Of course, it is not wrong to want to know the answer to an objection; that is only human. So we will find those answers in this appendix: we will take up all the strongest objections we can find, and answer each, one at a time.

Strangely, some scholars today have developed a faith in reverse; instead of believing that the promises of Christ do protect the teaching of the Church, they are inclined to believe—without even taking a good look—that there are many errors in Scripture and in the teachings of the Church. What is utterly astounding is that they are claiming that problems in Scripture cannot be solved at *precisely the time when there are new techniques and means of solving problems that past ages did not have.*

Early in this century, Scripture scholars, both Catholic and Protestant, lacked these new means. They saw quite a few problems in Scripture that appeared to be errors or contradictions. Some of these problems were solvable. But many others seemed impossible. Yet they were men of great faith, whose attitude was that there must be an answer, even if they could not find it, because Scripture is the Word of God. Their attitude was precisely right. Yet, as we said, now is the time scholars pick to claim that the problems cannot be solved. They have a *faith in reverse: a blind faith that Scripture must be wrong!* They even claim that problems cannot be solved whose answers have been known for many years!

As we saw in Chapter 15, many today accuse even Jesus Himself of ignorance and error.

These claims demand study in two areas. In this first appendix, we will examine all the most impressive charges that say the Church has erred or reversed teaching. In a second appendix, we will solve the most impressive claims that Scripture is in error, that even Jesus was in error.

2) SORTING OUT CLAIMS OF CHURCH ERROR

Most of the charges that the Church has erred can be handled very simply if one makes distinctions, and knows a few basic, simple principles.

First of all, we must carefully distinguish and keep separate three areas: (1) The *teachings* of the Church (doctrine); (2) the *rules or commands* of the Church (legislation); (3) the question of *how prudently* the Church has acted in a given case.

As to the first, namely teaching, we saw that Christ, the Divine Messenger, promised to protect that teaching; so we believe. As to the second, that is legislation or commands, Christ gave authority to rule to the Church; so we obey. But the third is different: There are no promises by Christ that the Church would always act *prudently,* and would do things in the best way. It is one thing to teach truth or give binding laws and another to act in the best, most prudent way. On this third point, prudence, there are no promises of Christ nor any commission from Christ. So the Church does not now claim, and never has claimed, assurance of prudence.

This distinction is of capital importance because many good people today find themselves unable to think that some new ways of doing things, for example, the ceremonies of the Mass, are very good ways compared to older ways. Often such people, not knowing the distinction we have just made, mistakenly think that they are obliged to think the new rites are better, or are more conducive to devotion. Yet, they cannot force themselves really to think that way, so they fear they have broken with the Church. Worse, since they do not know about the three areas we mentioned, they think that since they have broken once, they might as well break some more; and they wind up breaking with the Church even in matters guaranteed by Christ, in matters of doctrine or legislation.

There is immense confusion, too, about the first area, doctrine. Many, even priests who should know better, take this attitude: If a matter is not covered by a solemn definition, we can take it or leave it. But such is not and has never been the case. What of the centuries before 325 A.D., the first General Council, at Nicea?

Was everything optional matter up to then? And, since after that, only one point was defined, the divinity of Christ, could people doubt all else?

Vatican II, in the *Constitution on the Church,* clearly restated the traditional teaching of the Church on this matter. It said that there are three levels of teaching. The first two of them are infallible; the third, not. We will look at each.

At the first level, the solemn definition is sufficiently familiar, yet there are some misunderstandings. Vatican II taught that the relation between Pope and Bishops is parallel to that between Peter and the Apostles, so that the Pope and Bishops form a college of which the Pope is the head. This is called collegiality. This teaching is not really new. Most major decisions in all past centuries have actually been made following this pattern.

However, the Pope does retain the right to act alone, even in defining. Vatican II taught: "His [the Pope's] definitions, of themselves, and not from the consent of the Church, are justly called irreformable, for they are pronounced with the assistance of the Holy Spirit, which was promised to him in blessed Peter. Therefore they need no approval of others, nor is there room for an appeal to any other judgment."[193] If the Pope can even define alone, clearly he also can make lesser statements alone.

The second level seems to be overlooked by many Catholics, even theologians. On it, Vatican II said, "Although the individual Bishops do not have the prerogative of infallibility, yet they can proclaim Christ's doctrine infallibly. This is so even when they are scattered around the world, provided that, while keeping the bond of unity among themselves and with Peter's successor, and while teaching authoritatively on a matter of faith or morals, they agree that a particular teaching is to be held definitively."[194] That is: The day-to-day teaching of the whole Church, in which the

Church tells us certain things, are part of Catholic belief—such teaching is infallible.

Therefore, many doctrines are guaranteed in this way which are not defined, yet many people act as though they can be ignored. It is the decision of the Church which teachings meet these conditions. Yet, it would not seem rash to suppose that the existence of angels, for example, is such a doctrine.

Thirdly, we meet with lesser, undefined teachings. Pius XII commented on such things in *Humani generis* in 1950: "Nor must it be thought that what is contained in Encyclical letters does not in itself require assent, on the pretext that in them the Popes are not using the supreme power of their teaching authority [are not defining]. Rather, these teachings pertain to the ordinary teaching authority, about which it is also true to say: 'He who hears you, hears me.' . . . If the Popes in their official acts deliberately pass judgment on a matter that has been debated up to then, it is clear to all that the matter . . . cannot be considered any longer a question open for discussion among theologians."[195] Vatican II makes a similar statement: "Religious submission of will and of mind must be shown in a special way to the authentic Magisterium of the Roman Pontiff even when he is not defining. That is, it must be shown in such a way that his supreme Magisterium is acknowledged with reverence, the judgments made by him are sincerely adhered to, according to his manifest mind and will."[196]

There follows a loud objection from those who say, "How can we be told to believe something which is admittedly not infallible?" At first, the objection seems valid. Yet when we stop to think, the answer is easy. There are many things in life for which there is no infallible guarantee, and yet we believe them, and even stake our very lives on them. For example, suppose at dinner someone points to a dish of food and says, "Did that come from a can?" The answer is yes. "But was it sent to a lab to be checked for botulism?" (Botulism is a deadly food poisoning that would not be detected in routine opening of cans). We answer, "No." The person then exclaims, "Do you expect me to stake my life on the noninfallible assurance that this food is safe?" We look at him and think him very odd. Of course, there is a chance of botulism, but that chance is very, very remote. The normal person not only may, but probably should ignore it.

Another example is a criminal court in which the judge instructs the jury on a capital case. He tells the jurors that they must find the defendant *proved* guilty "beyond reasonable doubt" if they are to condemn him. But notice that the judge does not ask, nor does the jury guarantee, that all possible doubt will be eliminated, only *reasonable* doubt.

Thus, in many areas of life we believe things when there is no infallible guarantee. In believing, we might or might not stop to realize that there is a remote possibility of a mistake. But whether we think of it or not, we ignore the possibility.

So it is with the noninfallible teachings of the Church, except that with them the possibility of error is much more remote than is the chance with the canned food or the criminal court. Further, if there were any mistake, the Divine Judge would never charge it against us if we had believed His Church. But He would penalize us if we did not believe.

Still further, there is not one case in nearly two thousand years in which the Pope himself has erred in this noninfallible type of teaching. Only one case even came close, that of Galileo. There are, however, many charges that such errors have been committed in the past. In the following sections, we will look at all of the most important of them.

3) GALILEO

On February 19, 1616, two statements by Galileo were submitted to the Holy Office: (1) The sun is the center of the galaxy; (2) the earth is not the center.[197] On February 24, the Qualifiers (theological experts) of the Holy Office reported that this contradicted Scripture. Pope Paul V told Cardinal Bellarmine to warn Galileo to stop teaching his views as *fact*. He could consider them as a *hypothesis*.

Galileo submitted; but in 1632, he was reported as going back on his agreement. So, on June 16, 1633, Pope Urban VIII ordered an interrogation in the Holy Office. The Holy Office decided that Galileo had made himself "vehemently *suspected* of heresy." We note he was only called suspected, not flatly heretical.

So, did a Pope, on the noninfallible level, teach error here? Definitely not. Already in 1624, Pope Urban VIII stated about the theory that the earth went around the sun, that "the Holy Church had never, and would never, condemn it as heretical, but only as rash, though there was no danger that anyone would ever demonstrate it to be necessarily true."[198] Accordingly, Pope Paul V did not personally teach what the experts of the Holy Office said.

Further, Galileo's idea was not really original nor new. The ancient Greek astronomer, Aristarchus of Samos, in about 280 B.C. had taught the theory but received scant support from other astronomers of his day or later, either. Copernicus (1473-1543) also taught it. Cardinal Bellarmine, who conducted the first investigation, did not consider Galileo's idea heretical. In a letter written in 1615 he said, "I say that if a real proof be found that the sun is fixed, and does not revolve round the earth . . . then it will be necessary to proceed to the explanation of the passages of Scripture which appear to be contrary . . ."[199]

A considerable part of the trouble with Galileo was his unscientific presumption. His "proofs" did not impress even the astronomers of that day—nor would they impress astronomers today. Even though today we know that the earth goes around the sun, we do not know it because of Galileo's reasons. First, he said he would prove the earth moved by the *tides.* But, we know tides are caused by the moon, not by the earth's movement. Second, he thought that the planets travel in circles. They really travel in ellipses. Another astronomer, Kepler, had shown that Galileo's circles were implausible, but Galileo refused to consider Kepler's evidence. Third, not even with his telescope did he find the stellar parallax, which his arguments presupposed.

We conclude that the incident was regrettable and a case of *imprudence,* but yet, no Pope taught error in it. We note that even the Holy Office just said Galileo was "vehemently *suspected*" of heresy—not that he was strictly heretical.

In more recent times, in the middle of the 19th century, some scientists suffered more severely at the hands of other scientists. Pasteur and Lister met much opposition from their own ranks for their discoveries about germs. Still worse, Semmelweis, a Hungarian doctor who discovered the cause of puerperal fever and proved it by results with his patients, was railroaded by other doctors into an insane asylum, where he remained for the rest of his life.

4) NO SALVATION OUTSIDE THE CHURCH

Some charge that we understand the teaching of "no salvation outside the Church" differently from the way it was understood in early centuries; hence, the Church has erred at least once.

The basic answer to this difficulty is found in the reply from the Holy Office in the Father Feeney case, which we quoted in Chapter 23. It pointed out that Pius XII explained that persons who have not put their names on a parish register can "pertain to" or "be ordered to" the Church in a way sufficient to fulfill the requirements for salvation. In Chapter 23 we went still further—without contradicting Pius XII. We presented a summary of a long survey of how the axiom, "no salvation outside the Church," really was understood in the first centuries, and found no contradiction with present teaching.

A special objection in this matter is raised from the Bull, *Unam Sanctam,* of Pope Boniface VIII, on November 18, 1302. In it the Pope made two points: "We are forced to believe that there is one holy Catholic Church ... outside which there is neither salvation nor the remission of sins ... in this his power [the Pope's] there are two swords, that is, the spiritual and the temporal ... Further, we declare, say, and define that it is altogether necessary for salvation to be subject to the Roman Pontiff."[200]

The best explanation of the point about the two swords comes from Boniface VIII himself. In a consistory of June 24, 1302, before legates from France, he complained that he had been falsely accused, as if "we had ordered the king to acknowledge his royal power was from us. For forty years we have been a legal specialist, and we know that there are two powers ordained by God. Can or should anyone believe, then, that there is such folly in our head? We say that in no way have we desired to usurp the jurisdiction of the king, and thus our brother Portuensis said [he seems to be the one who composed the text of the Bull]. The king cannot deny, nor can any other one of the faithful, that he is subject to us in regard to sin."[201] In other words, "We can give moral teachings, telling what morality requires. No one, not even the king, can ignore them."

This proves that the Pope did not claim that he gave kings their power. Hence Pius XII, in his Address to the International Congress of Historical Sciences, September 7, 1955, explained, "Even for them [men of that age] it was normally only a question of the transmission of authority as such, and not a question of the designation of its holder."[202] For Popes did then crown kings, and could, by the power of the keys, release subjects from their oath of allegiance to kings. So much then, for the teaching of the two swords.

The other statements quoted (before and after the words about the two swords) regarding the need to be subject to the Pope for salvation, refer to the obligation to believe the teaching of the Pope on morals—which Boniface VIII himself pointed out. The statements also express that there is "no salvation outside the Church." Actually, the very wording of the last sentence that says men must be subject to the Pope comes word for word from St. Thomas Aquinas.[203] Considering the context of St. Thomas' statement it is just a statement of no salvation outside the Church.

5) USURY

Did the Church once prohibit usury, although it now permits it? The key to this conflict is in the meaning of the word *usury*. At one time, the Latin word *usura* was a word of broad meaning covering excessive interest or, in some cases, any interest at all.

Looking at general moral principles, it is obvious that how much interest can be justified will vary with the type of economy. In some economies, money is virtually sterile; in others, it is highly productive. Further, if there is risk in a loan, more interest is justified.

The Church has always understood this. Even back in the period envisioned by the objection, we find this distinction. Thus the Fifth Lateran Council in 1515 taught, "This is the proper interpretation of usury [namely] when gain and increase is sought from the use of a thing that is nonproductive, and with no labor, no expense, and no risk."[204]

6) REVERSAL ON SCRIPTURE STUDIES BY PIUS XII

It is common today for scholars to say that the Church did an about face in Scripture studies with the *Divino afflante Spiritu* of Pius XII in 1943. For example, Wilfrid Harrington writes, "the effect of that document had changed Roman Catholic biblical studies beyond recognition."[205]

More specifically, the usual claims are these: One need not hold the belief any longer that Moses was the substantial author of the Pentateuch [first five books of The Old Testament] or that the early chapters of Genesis were historical, or that there was only one author for Isaiah, or that Matthew was the first Gospel, and was written by an eyewitness, or that Luke and Acts were written in the 60s, or that Paul wrote Hebrews. There is a further assertion that this dramatic change of positions was acknowledged in 1955 by a secretary or secretaries of the Pontifical Biblical Commission who said that now Catholic scholars had "complete freedom" in regard to the old decrees of 1905-15, except where they touched on faith and morals—and few of the decrees did that.

Those who make this remark about a secretary of the Biblical Commission authorizing an about-face are not well informed. Msgr. John Steinmueller, a member of the Commission at that time, tells us in his book, *The Sword of the Spirit,* that there were really two articles of that sort, by A. Miller and A. Kleinhans; but that the articles were "unauthorized" and "condemned by the voting Cardinal members of the Commission."[206] The authors were to have been charged before the Holy Office, but were saved by the personal intervention of

Cardinal Tisserant with the Pope.

But, let us examine these claims individually. There are chiefly three: (a) Pius XII, in *Divino afflante Spiritu,* called for translations from the original languages; (b) he also encouraged the approach of literary genres which had been "hitherto forbidden"; (c) the Biblical Commission's decrees are obsolete.

(a) ORIGINAL LANGUAGES

Pius XII did encourage translations from the original languages. But it had never been forbidden, though it was not done in general. The reason it was not done was a misunderstanding of a decree of the Council of Trent which said that the Vulgate (St. Jerome's Latin version) was "authentic." Pius XII explained that the decree meant only that the Vulgate was approved as a basis for religious argumentation.[207] It did not mean that scholars should not use the original languages.

(b) LITERARY GENRES

This second point, on literary genres, is more important. First, let us recall what we saw about genres in Chapter 8. Just as today we use many genres or patterns in writing, each with its own special rules for how to understand them, so too did the writers of Scripture. Today we use, among others, the genre of the historical novel, which is a mixture of history and fictional fill-ins. No one expects the fill-ins to be historical, nor does anyone charge the author with error or deception for making these fill-ins. The key is this: What did the author mean to *assert?* Did he really mean to assert that he heard, for example, word-for-word conversations between Lincoln and Grant? Not at all. So we must not make the mistake of thinking he asserted what he did not assert.

We saw how this applied to the first chapters of Genesis. They are historical in that they report things that really happened. Chiefly, that God made the world by a word; that He in some special way made man, and gave him grace and privileges, and that He gave a command to the first pair which they disobeyed, and which caused their fall from favor. But what the scene was like, whether a garden, or something else, and other similar details, are not *asserted*. Nor did the sacred author *assert* that God made everything in six spans of 24 hours each. Such was the nature of Genesis. It is historical in that it reported things that actually happened; but not in precisely our genre of history writing.

Similarly, it is not clear that the author of Jonah *asserted* that the events really happened. He might have been writing *a sort of expanded parable.*[208] Again, the author of Daniel, in the narrative parts, might not have meant to assert that all the things that were narrated really happened. He might have meant to write something more like a religious novel.

This approach, through genres, makes it possible to solve numerous problems in Scripture which we could not otherwise explain.

Now that we have established what is meant by interpretation via genres, we ask: Is it true that this approach was once "forbidden" as some claim? On June 23, 1905, the Biblical Commission gave a reply: "Can it be accepted as a principle of sound interpretation that holds that some books of Scripture that are considered as historical—partly or totally—do not, at times, give history strictly and objectively so called, but instead, have just the appearance of history, so as to convey something other than a strict literal or historical sense of the words?"[209]

The answer was, "No, except in the case in which the sense of the Church does not oppose it, and subject to the judgment of the Church, it is proved by solid arguments and the sacred writer did not *intend* to hand down true history. But, under the appearance and form of history the author gave a parable, an allegory, or a sense differing from the properly literal or historical sense of the words."

Does this *forbid* the use of literary genres? Not at all. We must notice the wording carefully, for it is heavily and carefully qualified. First, the question deals only with writings that *present the appearance of history,* the chief area of concern. There was no mention of other types of writing. Can works that seem to be history ever be considered as not strictly history, but of some other genre? The reply is a qualified no. Namely, we can take such writings as of a category other than history—as a parable, an allegory, or of some other method—if we have solid arguments to show that the sacred writer *intended* something other than strict history. Again, the critical point is what the author *intended to assert.* And it adds what is obvious, that we must not act contrary to the "sense of the Church" and must be subject, finally, to the judgment of the Church.

Thus, we may suppose there is a different genre being employed than what the first appearance would indicate, provided that we have solid reasons. Nothing is forbidden except an interpretation that is sadly so common today, in which the presumption is against historical character. Pius XII too, the supposed author of a "reversal," insisted on care and solid arguments in *Divino afflante Spiritu:* "What these [genres] were, the scholars cannot decide in advance, but only after a careful investigation of the literature of the ancient Near East."[210] Pius XII wrote this in 1943. Just a few years later, in 1950, seeing that many scholars were getting too loose in their interpretations, he issued a warning in his *Humani generis:* "We must specially deplore a certain excessively free way of interpreting the historical books of the Old Testament . . . the first eleven chapters of Genesis, even though they do not fully match the pattern of historical composition used by the great Greek and Latin writers of history, or by modern historians, yet in a certain true sense—which needs further investigation by scholars—do pertain to the genre of history."[211]

A concrete way to do this was presented earlier by explaining that Genesis taught things "that *really happened*: that God made the world by a word, that He in some special way made man, that He gave a command to the first men, that they disobeyed and fell . . ." even though the setting was not meant to be strictly historical.[212]

The Biblical Commission in 1905 warned that we must heed the "sense of the Church," and be ready to accept the judgment of the Church. Pius XII said the same: "Let Scripture scholars, mindful of the fact that there is here question of a divinely inspired word, whose care and interpretation is entrusted by God Himself to the Church—let them not less carefully take into account the explanations and declarations of the Magisterium of the Church, and likewise of the explanations given by the Holy Fathers, and also of the 'analogy of faith,' as Leo XIII . . . wisely noted."[213]

The "analogy of faith" means the entire structure of the teachings of the Church. It must be definite, in other words, that an interpretation does not clash with anything in that structure even by implication. Vatican II taught, "Since Sacred Scripture must be read and interpreted according to the same Spirit by whom it was written, no less attention must be devoted to the content and unity of the whole of Scripture, taking into account the Tradition of the entire Church and the analogy of faith."[214]

This is far from the "about-face" some claim it implies. Instead, there is only a shift in *emphasis,* not in doctrine or principle. The 1905 statement approved the use of genres with care and with heed to the analogy of faith. Pius XII was more encouraging, yet insisted on care, and when he saw scholars getting too loose in their interpretations, he warned them.

An interesting question comes to mind here about the use of genres. This approach became fully known only in our own century. So the Church for about 19 centuries interpreted Scripture without knowing about it. Does not this leave room for errors by the Church?

We must say no. Now that we do have this approach, and have checked past statements of the Church with this resource as a help, we cannot find any place where the Church has erred in doctrine.

The reasons are obvious: (1) The Church enjoys the promised protection of the Holy Spirit, the Chief Author of Scripture. Even if Churchmen did not know about genres, the Chief Author did not need them to understand His own work. (2) The Church has always had something more basic than Scripture, namely, its own ongoing teaching. As we said, Jesus did not tell the Apostles or others, "Write some books, get copies made, pass them out and tell people to figure them out for themselves." That would have been foolish. Instead, He told the Church to teach, and promised protection for that teaching.

Form Criticism, which we will examine in Section Seven, underscores this last remark because it definitely insists that the Church has something more basic than Scripture.

(c) OLD DECREES OBSOLETE?

We saw that some like to quote an article by men from the Biblical commission saying scholars had "complete freedom" with regard to those decrees of 1905-1915 except where they touched on faith or morals (and very few of them did).[215]

We saw earlier that they are ill-informed. The men cited were rebuked, and narrowly escaped being called before the Holy Office.

But it is true that most of the decrees of 1905-15 did not bear on faith or morals. They dealt largely with *authorship* of Scriptural books. That question is not a problem of faith. It is proven that ancient Near Eastern writers not only used the equivalent of pen names, but might even have chosen as pen names those of famous men. We know too that rights of authorship were not thought so strict then. A later man might revise, without admitting it, the work of an earlier man. This could have happened in parts of Scripture, but if so, divine inspiration protects at least the final product.

But it is good to examine some of the matters of authorship. These include Moses as substantial author of the Pentateuch, historicity of the first chapters of Genesis, unity of author for the book of Isaiah, Matthew as writer of the first Gospel, the date of composition of Luke and Acts, and Pauline authorship of Hebrews. Some think scholars now abandon all these positions.

We spoke earlier about the historicity of the first chapters of Genesis. Do all scholars really think Moses was not the author of the first five books of the Old Testament, the Pentateuch? Not at all. Eugene Maly, writing in *Jerome Biblical Commentary* said, "Moses is at the heart of the Pentateuch, and can, in accord with the common acceptance of the ancient period, correctly be called its author."[216] The Biblical Commission on June 27, 1906, said the same.[217] The Commission stated that we can admit that there were modifications in the original work of Moses, that he used sources written or oral, that Moses may even have given his ideas to secretaries, and let them do the actual composition.

Was there more than one author for the Book of Isaiah? Even though this is not a point of faith, it must be noted that the arguments used to prove two or three authors are not conclusive. The chief argument is that

Chapters 1-39 of Isaiah are addressed to inhabitants of Jerusalem, in a tone of condemnation, with a threat of divine punishment. But Chapters 40-66 seem to speak to a community that has suffered a great disaster. It seems not to think of Assyria now, but of Babylon, and even of Cyrus of Persia. So the second part is to a people in exile, and offers hope of restoration. Although these arguments are not worthless, yet neither are they at all conclusive. Isaiah, being a prophet, could have been given a vision of the later times. Of course, many today reject the notion of such prophetic sight, even though in Chapter 22 we saw that the ancient Jews did see the Messiah in many prophecies.

Did Matthew or Mark write first? For a long time most scholars said that Mark was the first to write. The tide is now turning, and many think Matthew was first (at least Hebrew Matthew). In agreement are W. R. Farmer, *The Synoptic Problem* (Dillsboro, N.C., 1976); Bernard Orchard, *Matthew, Luke and Mark* (Manchester, 1977); E. P. Sanders, *The Tendencies of the Synoptic Tradition* (Cambridge, 1969); John M. Rist, *On the Independence of Matthew and Mark* (Cambridge, 1978); and Hans-Herbert Stoldt, *History and Criticism of the Marcan Hypothesis* (Edinburgh, 1980). As we saw in Chapter 10, the ancient witnesses do put Matthew first.

Regarding the date of the composition of Luke-Acts: the chief arguments for a late date, after the fall of Jerusalem in 70 A.D., are that the prophecy Luke gives is quite clear, and the belief that Luke depended on Mark (whom many think wrote only a bit before 70 A.D.). The claim that the prophecy is too clear rests on a faith in reverse which holds that there are few true prophecies. Yet John A. T. Robinson, a respected, but far from conservative Anglican scholar, in his *Redating the New Testament*[218] tried to prove all books of the New Testament were written by 70 A.D. And a Protestant scholar, Johannes Munck, in the *Anchor Bible* edition of *Acts,* argues at length to show Acts was written in the 60s A.D.[219]

Only in the case of Pauline authorship of Hebrews can we concede that most scholars disagree with the old decree. And even there, the argument rests largely on style and thought framework—which are never conclusive.

7) BIBLICAL COMMISSION INSTRUCTION OF 1964 ON FORM CRITICISM

Many scholars today cite this instruction as an example of a reversal by the Church. Of course, it would not be a *doctrinal* reversal, just a change in the use of a *technique* in Scripture study, namely Form Criticism. Yet, form critics often do fall into doctrinal errors, and many seem to claim that the Church has approved. So let us see.

Form Criticism assumes that the Gospels arose in three stages. This is clearly true. First were the words and deeds of Jesus; we take it for granted that He, like any good speaker, adapted His presentation to the audience at hand. Second, the Apostles and others of the first generation preached what He did and said. Again, they would adapt their presentation. Third, some individuals in the Church, moved by the Holy Spirit, decided to write down some part of this basic preaching, thus producing the Gospels. So the Gospels are just part of the basic teaching of the Church, written down under inspiration. *Hence the teaching of the Church is more basic than even the Gospels.*

Further, each of the Evangelists had his own special purpose, and would present things to help prove a particular concept. For instance, Matthew was intent on revealing the fulfillment of prophecies in Jesus. The early form critics thought the Evangelists should not be called authors at all. They thought they did nothing but stitch together the individual sayings or acts of Jesus. But today the pendulum has swung the other way and critics claim to see the most intricate design and artistry in the Gospels.

Thus far we find no basic fault with Form Criticism. But the next step the critics take brings problems. They would like to find out at which of the three stages any of the "forms" or units took its present wording and pattern, to see what light this information could shed on interpretation. The trouble is how to determine where one part begins and another ends.

They propose to do this chiefly by noting the several different forms or patterns of writing that are used within a passage. We might even call these mini-genres. Thus, for example, Rudolf Bultmann, the greatest pioneer in New Testament Form Criticism, first distinguishes *sayings* from *narratives*. He subdivides sayings into apothegms and dominical sayings. Apothegms are sayings of greater importance. They are further subdivided into controversy dialogues, scholastic dialogues (talking with sincere inquirers) and biographical apothegms. Dominical sayings include proverbs, prophetic and apocalyptic sayings, laws and community regulations. The second major group, narratives, includes miracle stories, historical stories, and legends.

Further help is supposed to come from noting the *Sitz-im-Leben,* the community-life situation which called for the choice of a particular form.

Of course, other Form Critics have modified this outline and there is far from unanimity of opinion about it. But this will provide a good frame from which to build our study.

After identifying the units out of which a passage is composed, the critics say the history of the tradition can be determined, noting what happened at which of the three stages. This is very good. But our essential question is "What does this show us of the reliability of various things in the Gospels?"

At this point we meet with quite a difference of opinion among critics. Some are almost totally skeptical, saying we cannot be sure of much of anything; others are more open-minded.

Among the more severe positions is the use of the so-called principle of dual irreducibility. This means briefly that a saying of Jesus can be considered authentic only if it meets two tests: (1) it does not fit with the Jewish thinking of the time; (2) it does not fit with the viewpoints of the later Church. This view is founded on extreme skepticism about the honesty of the Evangelists and others in the early Church. So they call the community "creative."

A special example of this creativity is supposed to appear in the Controversy Dialogues. Bultmann wrote about this in his *History of the Synoptic Tradition* (p. 40, n. 2): "The Controversy Dialogues as we have them . . . are creations of the Church." In other words, imagine two groups within the Church disputing. Group A has no saying of Jesus to support what they believe, so they just invent one; Group B has none either, so they too invent a saying. No respect for the truth whatsoever! This, of course, is ridiculous. Can we really imagine people, who know that their eternity depended on getting the facts about Jesus, just making up things? We know that they could use different major genres of the sort we saw in Chapter 8. But we can, with the principles we saw in that chapter, determine what they meant to *assert* was factual. Bultmann himself admits his ideas on Controversy Dialogues are subjective. So he adds, "Naturally enough, our judgment will not be made in terms of objective criteria, but will depend on taste and discrimination." (p. 47).

Subjectivity shows again in the fact that Bultmann thinks the Controversy Dialogues arose "in the apologetic and polemic of the Palestinian Church ... It is quite inappropriate to call those passages paradigms, i.e., examples of preaching as Dibelius does." (pp. 40-41). For Dibelius said the community life situation (*Sitz-im-Leben*) had been preaching for missionary purposes. Two great pioneers cannot agree on so simple and basic a point.

As we said, the critics like to claim that the early community was "creative" and that it ran with no check at all by the Apostles, or by the Truth. The 1964 Instruction warned against this error. "Finally, there are others who make light of the authority of the Apostles as witnesses of Christ and their function and influence on the primitive community, but magnify the creativity of the community. All these things are not only opposed to Catholic doctrine, but lack a scientific foundation and are foreign to the true principles of the historical method."[221]

Acts 5:12-13 tells us about the real position and control exercised by the Apostles: "And by the hands of the apostles were many signs and wonders done among the people. And they were all with one accord in Solomon's porch. But of the rest no one of the rest dared to join himself to them; but the people magnified them." *Acts* 2:42 says, "And they were persevering in the doctrine of the apostles, and in the communication of the breaking of bread, and in prayers."

The critics see much creativity in miracle stories. They commonly try to compare them to pagan or rabbinic miracles saying they have the same pattern, and then give little value to the accounts. A large part of the reason is that, in varying degrees, critics reject in advance the possibility of anything supernatural. But we showed in Chapter 3 of this book that miracles, checked thoroughly by modern science, still occur today. As for the alleged similarities to pagan or rabbinic miracles, even if they did exist, they would not disprove anything. Actually, there is scant similarity, as detailed studies have shown (summary of these studies and references to the original studies can be found in W. Most, *The Consciousness of Christ,* pp. 218-19). Besides, as we have said often, the fact that their eternity depended on getting at least the basic facts right about Jesus would assure that the community, *led by the Apostles* who had seen for themselves, would get the basic facts right.

(a) DID THE EVANGELISTS CHANGE THE SENSE?

At first, the critics thought the Evangelists should not be called authors at all. They were compared to stringers of beads because they supposedly just put together, in hardly any set order, what bits about Jesus they had gathered. Now the pendulum, predictably, has swung in the other direction and the Evangelists are called high artists, showing magnificent skill.

We do not deny some skill and artistry in the Evangelists; we admit that each had his own purpose or theological framework to stress. But this would not lead them to falsify anything at all. Nor could one Evangelist contradict another, for all were instruments of the Holy Spirit, the Chief Author of Scripture.

However now we must deal with the claim that by putting things in different orders or settings, the Evangelists could change the sense of things.[222] To get at the truth, we need to distinguish two kinds of material, namely, simple, straightforward things, in contrast to things that are by nature enigmatic or of flexible meaning (such as proverbs and similar sayings).

About the simple things: the six basic points we have concluded surely cannot be affected by what setting they are put in: There was a man Jesus, who claimed to be a messenger from God, and proved it by miracles worked in special connections. He had an inner circle within His followers, told them to continue His teaching, and promised that God would protect it. Clearly, a change of setting for these items will not affect their meaning, and hence what we need to prove the teaching authority of the Church is intact. Really, most sayings of Jesus would mean precisely the same no matter what setting they were put in.

But there are some Biblical sayings that could shift in setting. Form criticism does a good service in pointing out that *Mark* 13:30 probably was first written with a setting referring to the fall of Jerusalem (most of *Mark* 13 seems that way): "This generation shall not pass until all these things be done." But in its present setting, after *Mark* 13:27, which seems to refer to the return of Jesus at the end, *Mark* 13:30 could be puzzling. Though we could still take *generation* to refer to the Christian era, which is to last to the end and would make all of *Mark* 13 a multiple fulfillment pattern.

Examine how the meaning of these two verses changes when we know the setting. *Matthew* 10:27 says, "That which I tell you in the dark, speak in the light: and that which you hear in the ear, preach upon the housetops." *Luke* 12:2-3 says, "For there is nothing covered, that shall not be revealed: nor hidden, that shall not be known. For whatsoever things you have spoken in darkness, shall be published in the light: and that which you have spoken in the ear in the chambers, shall be preached on the housetops."

Now, if we check the contexts, Matthew refers to public preaching by the Apostles later, of what Jesus told them in private. But in Luke the saying seems to refer to the hypocrisy of the Pharisees eventually being brought to light. So it does seem that this change of setting changed the sense of the passage.

What shall we say about this? First of all, Jesus was a travelling speaker. Anyone familiar with public speaking knows that speakers will often repeat things in different places, using slightly different language, or even with some shifts of idea. Jesus easily could have said the same thing in two different settings. Further, we happen to know from the Targum on *Qoheleth* 12:13 that this saying really was a *proverb*. The meaning of proverbs is flexible.[223] Even beyond that, it would not be unfaithful for an Evangelist to make different applications of some *nonessential* sayings—particularly proverbs and enigmatic things, which are flexible by nature. We know too that St. Paul could change the setting of quotations he made from the Old Testament. Yet he always did it in such a way that the thought was really faithful to the teaching of Christ.

We conclude that there can be such variations in applications, and on proverbs, and perhaps a few other sayings too; but they are not an instance of infidelity to the teachings of Jesus. And for certain they simply cannot touch the basic truths that we enumerated above, which are part of the foundation of faith. We say this for two reasons: first, the intense concern for facts stemming from concern for their own eternity on the part of the writers; second, the basic truths are, as we said, such that their meaning is simply *by nature incapable of shifting* when placed in a different setting.

(b) RETROJECTION

In Chapter 16, we spoke briefly about retrojection—taking a scene that really happened *after* the Resurrection, and placing it *before* that. We saw in Chapter 16 that some types of retrojection would involve falsification, such as retrojecting a prophecy. A prophecy has no meaning if it does not refer to the future. But other kinds of retrojection would not be falsification, as long as the things really happened and the words were really said, in substance at least. However, we also said that it does not seem likely that the Synoptic Gospels would do this because it does not seem to fit with their unfanciful and factual genre or pattern.[224]

Form critics are quite inclined to claim retrojection, i.e., to say that certain things presented by the Gospels as though happening before Easter really took place after Easter. Various reasons are given for such claims, especially: the belief that the Gospels are not factual reports, the belief that Matthew and Mark clash in their picture of how much the disciples understood, and the belief that Jesus was ignorant.

Let us examine each of these points separately.

Fitzmyer forcefully expresses the first of these notions (italics all his): *"The Biblical Commission calmly and frankly admitted that what is contained in the Gospels . . . is not the record of the words and deeds of Jesus in the first stage of the tradition."*[225] We recall from above that there were three stages: first, the words and actions of Jesus (who adapted His presentation to the audience), second, the way the Apostles and others preached these, adapting also the presentation to the audiences, and third, the recording of part of this ongoing preaching by the Evangelists under inspiration.

Of course, the Biblical Commission did admit that there are these three stages, and did admit what is obvious, that the Apostles, like any good teachers or speakers, would adapt their presentation. However, we need to stress a statement of the 1964 Instruction of the Biblical Commission that the critics are apt to leave out: "The fact that the Evangelists report the words and deeds of the Lord in different sequences, and that they express His statements in varied ways, not word for word, but yet keeping the sense—these things do not at all affect the truth of the narrative."[226]

So we can admit a difference in presentation, and even in wording of the sayings of Jesus. However, the 1964 Instruction insists that the revised wording and presentation still faithfully report what was really said and done. The concern of the Evangelists and Apostles and of the Christians in general for their eternity would ensure that they wanted facts.

The 1964 Instruction added something to which the critics like to point: "After Jesus rose from the dead and His divinity was *clearly* seen, the faith of the disciples not only did not wipe out the memory of the things that happened, but rather strengthened that [memory]. . . . There is no reason to deny, however, that the Apostles handed down to their hearers *what the Lord had really said and done* in the light of the fuller understanding which they gained by being instructed by the glorious events of Christ, and being taught by the light of the Spirit of truth."[227]

We notice first that the Instruction insists on the fact that the disciples by then saw His divinity *clearly* and not only did not want to distort their memory of "what the Lord had really said and done." So again, there is an insistence on the truth of the Gospels. Yet, to say that they wrote in the light of better understanding, *could* leave room for some retrojection. We must explore precisely in what areas that claim could consist.

A special case is clearly the second reason for supposing the retrojection which we mentioned above. Namely, the fact that Mark consistently pictures the disciples as slow to understand, while Matthew, chiefly in *Matt.* 14:33 and 16:16 has Peter and even the others calling Jesus "Son of [the living] God." How can we explain this seeming difference? One way is surely to say Matthew is retrojecting. Yet it is far from certain that he did so. First, that phrase, "Son of God" could be applied to any devout Jew. However, in context it surely means something more in *Matt.* 14:33 and 16:16. How much more? Commentators are much divided. So, even though we grant that the Evangelists did write in the light of fuller understanding, we would not have to say 14:33 and 16:16 involve *clear* and *full* knowledge of the divinity of Jesus.

Some[228] commentators do say that Peter fully under-
stood His divinity; others [229] say Peter did not. They say
Peter had only a slight grasp of the fact that Jesus was
Son *in some special, perhaps even unique sense.* J. D.
Kingsbury puts it this way: "The title Son of God in
Matthew's Gospel refers to the deepest mystery of the
person of Jesus, viz. that in Him God draws near with
His eschatological rule to dwell with humankind."[230]
This of course is not the same as saying clearly that
Jesus was the natural Son of God.

If one says Peter did not know the divinity of Jesus,
he must still explain the fact that Jesus praises Peter in
16:16 ff. as having a revelation from the Father, and
with the fact that Peter later on can still deny Jesus. In
(c) below we will take up these problems.

Critics also like to claim ignorance in Jesus.[231]
Almost all scholars today insist on this, in spite of the
clear teachings of the Church.[232] My book, *The Consciousness of Christ,* quotes all of these documents, and
answers every argument for ignorance advanced by any
scholar of note. Of course, if they claim the ignorance
of Jesus, they then can say that Jesus did not understand enough to directly found the Church—and so
they have an added reason for saying the promise of
primacy was really given after Easter.

(c) RETROJECTION OF PETER'S CONFESSION

Quite understandably, Protestants like to try to do
away with a grant of real primacy to Peter. Thus J. D.
Kingsbury, in the article cited above, argues at some
length to try to show that Peter was merely presented as
the typical disciple and spokesman for the others, but
yet is not given any more power than the others. In
Chapter 16 we saw that regardless of all debates about
Matt. 16:16, we know from the teaching of the
Church—protected by the promises of the Messenger
sent from God, Jesus, that there is a *real papal primacy.*

These critics will, of course, favor retrojection. Many Catholic scholars also contend retrojection of *Matt.* 16:16 ff. e.g., Joseph Fitzmyer.[233]

So let us evaluate separately the two possibilities about Peter's understanding.

a) The first possibility is that *Peter did not know the divinity of Jesus before Easter.* If so, we might have retrojection of two points, the confession of divinity (if Peter's words mean that) and the promise of primacy. Even then, these two points would remain true in themselves. And we have seen, in Chapter 16, that *John* 21 does report the actual grant after Easter. One reason against retrojection would be the strongly factual character of the Synoptics, plus the fact that Mark and Luke paint the Apostles as dull—how Matthew represents them is unclear, since, as we said, the sense of the words, "Son of [the living] God" is difficult to fix. Still further, would a special revelation to Peter have been needed after Easter? It is not so likely.

b) The second possibility is that *Peter did know.* This seems the more likely option. But there is a problem: if Peter did know, how could he have been so slow later in accepting the Resurrection, and even, before that, deny Jesus? Mystical theology provides the answer. When one gets an interior revelation, a locution, it will seem fully certain at the time it is given, but later, saints have often become uncertain about the revelation. God permits this, to try them. St. Teresa of Avila, a Doctor of the Church, who knew about these things from personal experience, reports in her *Interior Castle* 6.3.7, "When time has passed since it was heard, and the workings and the certainty it [the soul] had that it was God have passed; doubts can come, thinking if it was the devil, if it was imagination. None of these things was there when it was present; it [the soul] would have died for the truth [of the locution]."

So Peter could have had a revelation, and have

believed it firmly and so have confessed the divinity of
Jesus. Yet, as St. Teresa says, the certainty could fade.
This is especially likely in Peter, who had a strong
belief that the Messiah would be a great conqueror.
When Peter saw Jesus failing and being condemned to
death, we see how Peter could have given up his previous belief and even denied Jesus.

As we said in Chapter 16, the lack of these added
words in Mark and Luke could be explained by noting
that neither Mark nor Luke were present. Especially,
Mark depended, as we saw in Chapter 10, on Peter;
Peter's modesty could have led him not to preach the
additions.

(d) AN IGNORANT JESUS?

Many attempts at interpretation by form critics have
resulted in ideas that are gravely erroneous. A major
example is the way Reginald H. Fuller, one of the most
prominent form critics, treats *Mark* 8:29-33. Jesus and
the Apostles are in Caesarea Philippi, pagan territory.
Jesus asks what people are saying about Him and they
tell Him various things. Then, according to Fuller,
there are four units:

1) Jesus asks the Apostles who they say He is? Peter
answers, "You are the Messiah."

2) Jesus tells them not to tell that He is Messiah.

3) Jesus then predicts His Passion. Peter objects.

4) Jesus turns on Peter, saying, "Get behind Me
Satan!"

The critics see no problem with units 1 and 4; but
they think that the Church faked units 2 and 3.

They say that the second unit resulted from the fact
that Jesus did not know He was Messiah. Later, the
Church was embarrassed that He never said He was
Messiah. So, to cover up, the Church faked conversa-
tions in which He would admit it, but command silence.
The critics call this the "messianic secret."

First, the fidelity of the Evangelists and Apostles, and their concern for their own eternity, would not permit such faking.

Further, the support the critics offer for their claims of fakery is no good. They appeal to cases where Jesus works miracles and commands silence. Their strongest case is *Mark* 5:43, in which Jesus raises the daughter of Jairus.[237] W. Wrede, a major critic, comments that there is no sense in a command to silence in this instance because anyone could see that the girl was alive. But the critics have missed an important element: *How long* did the fact need to be hidden? In this case, just long enough for Jesus to slip out (for the miracle was done in the house, with only a few present) and get on His way. He did not want the crowds to know because they might have seized Him and proclaimed Him King Messiah, in their false notion of a messiah as a mighty conqueror.

So if those in the house would have been quiet for a short while, Jesus could be on His way.

Would not the crowds remember? People are surprisingly fickle; proof is Palm Sunday with its Hosannas followed less than a week later with "Crucify Him!" Or remember Paul and Barnabas in Lystra (*Acts* 14:8-19). They had cured a cripple, and the crowds went wild wanting to offer sacrifice to them as gods. Yet, a few minutes later, some Jews arrived from the last place Paul had preached and inflamed the crowds so that they stoned Paul and left him for dead.

Still further, the critics think Mark was an excellent artist. A fine artist knows that if he produces fiction, and that is what the critics think this is, that fiction must be *plausible*. If he cannot make it plausible, he will just omit an episode. So, if Mark had thought of *faking* an implausible incident in the story of the daughter of Jairus, he would have had the sense to drop the idea if it had not *really happened*. The case is similar to many other incidents which the critics cite as proof for the "messianic secret."

We turn to the third unit, in which Jesus predicts His Passion, and Peter objects. Here the critics say that the Passion prophecies were also faked by the Church. They say, if He had really foretold His death and resurrection, the Apostles would not have been so surprised when it happened.

Here again, the fact that the Evangelists and the Church were so concerned with their own eternity would exclude the possibility of fakery. But in addition, there is no need to be surprised at the behavior of the Apostles. Far more educated men, even today, show a quite similar lack of perception, as we explained at length in Chapter 15.

So we return to Fuller's form-critical analysis of *Mark* 8:29-33. He had said that two of the four units had been faked by the Church. We have examined his reasons, and found them without merit. But he, and countless others with him have not understood and have concluded that units 2 and 3 are fakes and the truth is found in units 1 and 4. They believe that Jesus did not know He was Messiah and resented the very idea. Thus, when Peter says, "You are Messiah," Jesus angrily turns on him and retorts, "Get behind Me Satan!"

Very interestingly, the same R. H. Fuller now has second thoughts about Form Criticism and the whole "historical-critical method" in general. Fuller now thinks that the historical-critical method is bankrupt. He says that bankruptcy should be overcome by feedback received from the believing community.[238] So should we just ask what people feel or think, instead of finding what Scripture says?

Many other scholars too are giving up on the historical-critical method today.[239] That is regrettable, for the method itself is not basically bad and has good potential if used properly. It is another case of the pendulum reaction in which scholars went too far and abused Form Criticism, not realizing that *seldom does it really prove anything,* since the evidence it works with is almost totally *internal* or *subjective.* So, they reached conclusions on unsolid premises, ignoring more solid proofs and thinking the conclusions solid, presumed to build still more on top of them with equally unsolid footing. No wonder they now give up. If only they would see it as it really is, and make proper use of the method!

(e) WARNINGS IN THE 1964 INSTRUCTION

Many today quote the Instruction telling us we may use Form Criticism. But oddly they quote only parts of it, and do not add the stern warnings the Instruction contains: "He [the scholar] should act circumspectly because philosophical and theological principles that cannot at all be approved are often found mixed with this method, [principles] which not rarely vitiate both the method and the conclusions on literary matters. For certain practitioners of this method, led astray by prejudiced opinions of rationalism often refuse to admit the existence of the supernatural order, and the intervention of a personal God in the world by revelation properly so called, and the possibility and actual existence of miracles and prophecies." Even some Catholics have failed in these respects, saying the Old Testament prophecies of Christ were hindsight and denying many miracles. They have forgotten that Vatican I insisted, "Moses and the prophets and especially Christ the Lord put forth many most manifest miracles and prophecies."[241] They have also forgotten the Targums, which we studied earlier.

Had the critics heeded the sound advice of that Instruction, they would not now be in despair over the historical-critical method. Nor would they have reason to say this method proves the Church is wrong on things. (Recall the sad error of Norman Perrin on form criticism of *Mark* 9:1, which we saw earlier).

(f) DID VATICAN II UNDERMINE TEACHING AUTHORITY?

Fr. Avery Dulles, S.J., in his presidential address to the Catholic Theological Society of America in 1976 said, "Indirectly . . . the Council worked powerfully to undermine the authoritarian theory and to legitimate dissent in the Church . . . Vatican II quietly reversed earlier positions . . . on a number of important issues."[242] He gives several examples.

First, he says that in biblical studies, the Council approved of a critical approach to the New Testament, in line with the *Divino afflante Spiritu* of Pius XII, and thereby delivered the Church "from the incubus of the earlier decrees of the Biblical Commission." Secondly, he says the *Decree on Ecumenism* reversed earlier attitudes to the ecumenical movement. Next, the *Declaration on Religious Freedom* "accepted the religiously neutral State" and so reversed earlier teaching. Further, he claims that the *Constitution on the Church in the Modern World* "adopted an evolutionary view of history" and that this ended "more than a century of vehement denunciations of modern civilization." Therefore, he said, the Council admitted that "the ordinary magisterium of the Roman pontiff had fallen into error." So, he asserts the Popes had unjustly treated and damaged the careers of loyal theologians.

Fr. Dulles did refer to the statement of Vatican II (*On the Church* §25) on the teaching authority of even noninfallible statements, but dismissed it lightly. (We examined that text in studying the three levels of teaching, in Section 2 of this Appendix).

First, in a way, Dulles charges a reversal by Pius XII on Scripture study techniques. My book, *Free From All*

Error (Prow, 1985), answers this claim in detail, and shows that the early decrees of the Biblical Commission are not really an "incubus"—a mythological male devil who attempts to force intercourse on human women!

The Council favored the ecumenical movement but gave cautions about it. It warned against a tendency, often seen in ecumenists, to strain interpretations of doctrine. It said, "It is altogether necessary that the full doctrine be lucidly explained. Nothing is so foreign to ecumenism as that false peace-making in which the purity of Catholic doctrine suffers detriment, and its genuine and certain sense is obscured."[243]

Did the *Declaration on Religious Freedom* "accept the neutral state" and so reverse the previous view "that the State should formally profess the truth of Catholicism"? Dulles has missed something. In the very first section of that *Declaration,* the Council said, "It leaves untouched [*integram*] the traditional Catholic doctrine about the moral duty of men *and societies* toward the true religion and the one-only Church of Christ."[244] The Council did add, in Section 2, that people have a right not to be threatened with prison, death, etc., if they are wrong. But it did not say they have a right to be wrong. The reason is clear: A right is a claim to have or to do something. Basic rights come from God. As the U.S. Declaration of Independence says, "All men are endowed by their Creator with certain inalienable rights." Does God really give someone a claim or right to *be* wrong? Hardly. It is enough to give the claim or right not to be *penalized* by the state for being wrong. The Church has never denied that, though some today, especially followers of Archbishop Lefebvre, claim it did deny it. We will see about that claim in detail in Appendix I.10.

If men have a right not to be coerced, does the Church lose the right to teach with authority? Not at all. It is one thing to teach, with the authority of Christ, what is true and another thing to threaten force if one does not believe. As we saw earlier in 2 of this Appendix, the same Council also strongly asserted the rights of the Church to teach, and our obligation in conscience to believe.

Did the *Constitution on the Church in the Modern World* adopt an evolutionary view of history, and modified optimism regarding secular systems of thought? Fr. Dulles gives no reference to any part of that constitution that would say such things. He just refers us to an article in *Theological Studies* by L. J. O'Donovan for support.[245] O'Donovan makes clear that what Dulles has in mind is a supposed influence of the ideas of De Chardin on the Council. The strongest *opinion* favoring Chardin at the Council came from Bishop Spulbeck of Meissen, Germany, who thought Chapter 3 of that Constitution showed much of his influence. Does it? First, there is no mention even of evolution of the human body in that chapter, or of evolution of doctrine. It does speak of progress in material civilization, but it also warns: "Sacred Scripture teaches . . . that the great advantages of human progress bring with them grave temptation: the hierarchy of values is disturbed, good and evil intermingle . . . Dour combat with the powers of darkness pervades all human history . . . Hence the Church . . . trusting in the design of the Creator, and admitting that progress can contribute to the true happiness of man, cannot help making heard the saying of the Apostle: 'Be not conformed to this world.' [*Rom.* 12] . . . man can and should love the things God has created . . . in giving thanks to the Benefactor for them, and using and enjoying them in poverty and freedom of spirit, he is brought into the true possession of the world, as if nothing, and possessing all things."

We find neither a trace of De Chardin in this, nor any contradiction of past teaching. Nor do we know of "vehement denunciations of modern civilization" coming from the Church—just warnings against abusing creatures, which is the same thing we find in the quote we just read from Vatican II. (On De Chardin, see Chapter 15 above).

So Fr. Dulles failed to prove that the Council had said that the Pope had "fallen into error" and had "unjustly harmed the careers of loyal and able theologians." Yes, there have been restrictive actions by Rome, but with good reason. We will see a fine case of that later in treating of evolution.

(g) DID VATICAN II REVOLUTIONIZE ALL THEOLOGY?

If such a claim were true, we would suspect that the Church had been wrong before, or is wrong now. How do we check such a claim?

First, we must be careful to notice that this question concerns only *doctrine* and does not concern *legislation,* such as changes in the Mass or questions of *prudence,* which we discussed in Appendix I.1.

Next, it is obvious that the right way to find out about such a claim is to read carefully every one of the 16 documents of Vatican II, comparing each statement with previous teaching on the same point. Clearly, we need to know well what the previous teaching was. Whenever we find a difference, we should make a note of it; at the end, we should add them all up. This is a lot of work, but it is the only way to really know for sure.

I did precisely that, as soon as each document was available. Of course anyone could overlook something; but it is not likely he would overlook something large and striking, especially, a reverse in previous teaching. Further, in giving public lectures in many places in the U.S., I have challenged audiences, "If you think you have found a change I missed, please say so." Also, I have published the list of changes given below several times, making the same request of readers.[247]

Only the changes listed below are legitimate; other alleged changes do not stand up under examination. In these appendices we examine every other alleged change.

Not one of the changes I found was a reverse of doctrine. All changes were of a different nature in that they consisted of giving answers to previously debated points. There are at most only ten such changes, which we will now list. Some of these are not entirely new, but we will mention them because of important renewed emphasis.

1) The Council probably, though not clearly, taught that baptized Protestants are members of the Church in some lesser way. (*On the Church* §§ 9,14,15,49; *On Ecumenism* 3,22. Also Chapter 23 above.).

2) The Pope and the Bishops form a body or college with the Pope as head. This is parallel to the relation of Peter and the Apostles. This is not really new, since most major decisions have always been made in this collegial way, though the Pope can even define alone. (*On the Church,* Chapter 3, esp. §25.)

3) Not all Jews bear the special guilt for the death of Christ, just those who shouted for His blood before Pilate. (*On Non-Christians* §4.)

4) All men are to be immune from *coercion* in religious matters. This does not mean they have a right to be wrong, nor does it take back what we quoted earlier about the obligations of men and societies to the one true Church (*On Religious Freedom* §§1,2). The Council did recognize, in the area of noncoercion, some aspects not taught before. But it did not contradict previous teaching in that. We will examine this in detail in Appendix I.10.

5) By Baptism and Confirmation all are called to the lay apostolate—not necessarily to join an organization,

but at least to make Christ's principles present and operative in their own places in the world. (*On the Church* §33.)

6) Every priestly ministry shares in the universality of the mission Christ entrusted to His Apostles. (*On Priests* §10.)

7) The Mystical Body, the Church, will still exist as such in Heaven. (*On the Church* §48.)

8) Public authority should see to it, out of justice, that public funds for education are given in such a way that parents are really free to follow their consciences in picking schools. (*On Christian Education* §6.)

9) The legitimate use of marriage is noble and worthy. (*Church in Modern World* §49.) The Church never denied this, though some theologians had spoken too dimly of marriage. Section §50 reaffirms that procreation is the primary purpose of marriage, mutual love being subordinate: "Marriage and conjugal love are ordered by their nature to procreate and educate offspring." (There have been claims that the Council reversed teaching on the ends of marriage.)

10) If the whole Church, people and authorities, have ever believed a doctrine as revealed, this belief cannot be wrong, is infallible. (*On the Church* §12.)

It is obvious then that Vatican II did not create a revolution in theology. There are no reversals of teaching at all, and some of the above are only a little different or stronger than previous teachings, but all are in the same direction.

(h) VATICAN II VS. PIUS IX, GREGORY XVI, AND LEO XIII ON RELIGIOUS FREEDOM.

The charge is made that Vatican II, in saying that all have a right to freedom from coercion in their beliefs and worship, and even that no one is to be "forced to act contrary to his conscience, or impeded from acting according to his conscience, in private and in public, either alone, or associated with others, within due limits," contradicted earlier teachings.[248]

We will compare the strongest texts of the earlier Popes with Vatican II. But first, we must make an important observation. God has made two commitments, which at times can seem to contradict each other. He has given us human free will; and He has promised to protect the teaching of the Church. Clearly, when these run in opposite directions, He will need to draw a very tight line, to keep both commitments; i.e., He will not allow the Church to teach error, yet He will not do more than what is strictly needed for that purpose. Therefore we must interpret all texts with precision, just as they were all drawn up with precision. Further, even if we know that as a matter of fact certain ideas were popular at the time a text was drafted, only what is explicitly set down on paper will be protected—not also things that we may know were simply *within the minds* of the drafters, but *not expressed.*

Still further, just as we must avoid private interpretation of Scripture, so too we must avoid private interpretation of the documents of the Church.[249] Otherwise, someone could take two documents, interpret each as he pleases—and lo! they clash. Of course, he made them clash by his own private interpretations. An instance of this is Feeney's error in interpreting the teaching "no salvation outside the Church."

Gregory XVI said that it is "an evil opinion that souls can attain eternal salvation by just any profession of faith, if their morals follow the right norm," and he called it absurd "that anyone should defend and vindicate for just anyone freedom of conscience."[250] Pius IX wrote, in his *Quanta cura,* that it is wrong to say "that the best condition of society is one in which there is no recognition of the duty of the government to repress violators of the Catholic religion . . ." Finally, Leo

XIII, in his *Immortale Dei,* said, "So too that liberty of thinking and of publishing anything whatsoever (*quidlibet*), with no restraint at all (*omni moderatione posthabita*) is not a good by its own nature over which human society should rightly *rejoice,* but is [on the contrary] the font and origin of many evils . . . for this reason, a state errs from the rule and prescription of nature if it allows a license of opinion and actions to such an extent that without penalty it is permitted to lead minds away from the truth and souls from virtue."

We added the Latin to the text of Leo XIII, since the version found in *The Church Speaks to the Modern World: The Social Teachings of Leo XIII* (Doubleday, 1954) is not fully accurate. If one had to depend on that version alone he might readily think that Vatican II clashed with Leo XIII.

The key word in the first statement we quoted from Gregory XVI is *by.* It is wrong to say one can be saved *by* just any religious beliefs. Of course he cannot, but he might be saved *in spite of them.* Pius IX, who speaks as strongly as Gregory XVI against the errors in question, also wrote, in his *Quanto conficiamur moerore,* "God . . . because of His supreme goodness and clemency, by no means allows anyone to be punished with eternal punishment who does not have the guilt of *voluntary fault.*"[251] In effect, Pius IX taught that if one follows the moral law as he knows it, somehow the needed faith will be supplied.

In the second part, Gregory XVI objected to "freedom of conscience." There are two possible interpretations: a man has (a) a *right to be wrong,* or (b) a right not to be jailed etc. for his false beliefs. Clearly, Gregory XVI condemned the first. No one has a right to be wrong, as we saw earlier in this Appendix, in Section 8. But the Pope said nothing that had to mean a man could not have a right to be free from jail for being wrong. Centuries ago, about 212 A.D., Tertullian wrote to Scapula, Roman Governor of Africa, "It is not proper for religion to compel religion."[252] Really, the very thought would be foolish. What a man believes in his mind cannot be changed by any threat. His outward behavior might change, but not his inner belief.

We turn next to Leo XIII, since his words will shed some light on how to understand Pius IX. The key to the text we cited above from him is to note the *extreme* position he is condemning. Every theologian knows that the Church often teaches via condemned propositions, and will mark a text as in error if even one thing is wrong with it. So Leo XIII condemned a libertinism that would permit publishing *anything whatsoever*— which could include teaching the grossest immorality, a proposal to overthrow a good government by force, even headhunting—all *without any restraint at all* (*omni moderatione posthabita*). He said such a state of affairs is not one over which society should *rejoice*. Obviously not. Later in the same document, the same Pope adds careful qualification: "Really, if the Church judges that it is not permitted that various kinds of divine worship have equal rights with the true religion, yet it does not for this reason condemn the rulers of states who, to attain some great good or prevent evil, patiently allow each [kind of cult] to have a place in the state."

Again, Leo XII carefully qualifies his words in his *Libertas Praestantissimum*. Speaking of the "freedom of speaking and publishing *whatsoever* one pleases" (*quodcumque libeat*), he comments, "It is scarcely necessary to say that there can be no *right* for a freedom that is *not moderately tempered,* but which *goes beyond measure and bounds* . . . For if a boundless license (*infinita licentia*) of speaking and writing be conceded to *just anyone* (*cuilibet*), *nothing* is going to remain holy and inviolate, not even those greatest, most true judgments of nature, which are to be considered as the common and most noble patrimony of the human race, will be spared."

A bit earlier in the same document, the Pope had said, "For these reasons, while not conceding *any right* to things that are not true and honorable, it [the Church] does not refuse to let public authority endure these, that is, to avoid some greater evil, or to attain or keep some greater good. The most provident God, though He is infinite in power, and can do all things, yet permits evils in the world, in part, so as not to impede greater good, in part, lest greater evils follow. In ruling states, it is right to imitate the Ruler of the World."

We turn to Pius IX. Besides the text quoted above from him, he also condemned the notion that, "The best condition of civil society . . . requires that human society be structured and governed with no considera- tion of religion, as if it did not exist."[253] Of course, that is not the "best." Just as each individual needs God's help, so too does the state. Hence the state as a state really should worship God. Vatican II taught the same, in §1 of its *Declaration on Religious Freedom.* "It leaves untouched the traditional Catholic doctrine about the moral duty of men *and societies* toward *the true religion* and the one-only Church of Christ." That doctrine to which Vatican II referred is precisely what Pius IX taught. Some have wondered if, though the state should worship God, needing His help, yet, does history show the state so incapable of finding the truth that it is excused by inability?

In the same document, Pius IX gave his strongest statement. He tells us it is wrong to say "that the best condition of society is one in which there is no recogni- tion of the duty of the government to repress *violatores* of the Catholic religion, except to the extent that public order demands." We left the word *violatores* in Latin, since the nearest English, "violators," is much too weak. A parking meter will show a sign, "violation" if one stays a few minutes too long. But Latin would not express it that way. The authoritative *Harper's Latin Dictionary* says the corresponding Latin verb, *violare* means "to treat with violence, injure, invade, profane, outrage." *Violatores,* then, are those who commit *violare.*

So here are the boundaries of the critical zone, as it were, in which we need to check for contradictions:

1) Pius IX says it is not the *best* state of things if there is no recognition of the duty of the state to repress *violatores.*

2) Pius IX adds that the state must do more than just repress what public order would insist on anyway.

3) Vatican II insists we must not force anyone to act against his conscience, or to fail to do what conscience commands "within due limits."

We need to note carefully that Vatican II focuses on the other's *conscience.* We must not force a person to do what it forbids, or to omit what it *commands,* so as not to force a man into sin. But if conscience *merely permits,* there is no such problem. So let us check all the chief possibilities against this list.

First, to bomb a church, or to publish false charges (slander) against the Catholic Church would surely be *violare.* But any normal state, for the sake of public order, stops people from bombing and slandering because they are clearly outside the "due limits" of Vatican II.

Second, what if a Protestant, orally or in print, defends his own doctrine? Again, no problem because this is not strong enough to be *violare,* so Pius IX would not wish for repression. Vatican II would insist that one must not be forced to go against, or be ordered not to do what conscience commands.

Third, what if a Protestant, orally or in print, not merely defends his own doctrine, but positively attacks the doctrine of the Catholic Church? Here we must notice there are many degrees and varieties. At one end of the scale there are attacks so virulent that Pius IX would call them *violare,* and want, *at least ideally,* to have the state stop them. What would Vatican II say? That Council only wanted us not to force one to act against what conscience commands, or to omit what conscience commands.

Would a Protestant's conscience really *command* him to make a rather vicious attack on Catholic doctrine? Not likely. It might *permit* him to, but Vatican II insists only that we must not force him to omit what it *commands.* In other words, we must not force him to sin. Even if he would think conscience commands, we could and would say that such an alleged command as this is "beyond due limits," for he would still have all the rights mentioned above, to believe, to worship, to defend his own doctrine. He need not be given the right to make vicious attacks on another church.

If his attacks were mild, the case would be less clear. We would have a hard time to be sure they should be called *violare* and also a hard time determining if they were "within due limits." Now a teaching that is unclear is not binding to the extent that it is unclear. Hence, no one can say that there is a contradiction of two teachings on points on which they are not clear.

We must add that Pius IX merely said we must not call it the *best* or *ideal* condition in which the state does not act at all. This fits well with what Pius XII said in his *Ci riesce* of Dec. 6, 1953. In it the Pope asked, "Can it be that in determined circumstances, He [God] does not give to man any mandate, or impose a duty, finally that *He gives no right to impede and to repress* that which is erroneous or false?"[254] He answers his own question by an appeal to the Gospel. Christ in the parable of the cockle gives the following admonition: "Let the cockle grow along with the good seed, for the sake of the harvest." So "in determined circumstances" God does not even give the state *a right* to suppress error by force. As the parable says, there would be too much danger of damaging the good crop at the same time.

Some objectors still persist and say that Pius IX had written that the state must suppress even some things which public order would not require suppressed. Vatican II said that the state must not suppress as long as a person is "within due limits." The objectors then say that the two expressions, "public order" and "within due limits" are identical in extent of meaning. If that were true, there would be a clash of two texts.

However, we must notice that the words of Vatican II "within due limits" are vague by nature. And so no one can *prove* that there is a clash. In a civil court, a person is considered innocent until *proved* guilty. No one can *prove* Vatican II had to mean the very same spread or extension as Pius IX. Even if some at the Council had such a sense in mind, as we said in the introduction to this section, only what is explicitly set down on paper counts, only that is providentially protected.

Still further in working out step by step the various possibilities, we showed concretely how it is easily possible to take Vatican II in such a way that it does not clash with Pius IX.

Therefore, if we believe the promises of Christ to protect His Church, we will not say Vatican II is guilty even when not proved such. As we saw above (Section 2 of this Appendix), Pius XII told us in *Humani Generis* that even the non-solemn theological decisions of a Pope in encyclicals are protected by the promise of Christ, "He who hears you, hears Me." Of course the same applies to the teaching of a Pope with a General Council. To say without proof or support, "I think the two expressions mean the same" reveals not a faith that the promise of Christ is valid, but a baseless "faith" that His promises have failed.

(i) REVERSAL BY THE CHURCH
ON EVOLUTION?

A cute story—whether true or not—will help us here. Little Johnnie came running to his mother, saying, "Mommie, I found out there ain't no Santy Claus, and I'm going to look into this little Jesus story too!"

The psychology is interesting. Both beliefs were on the same level in the child's mind, even though both are very different in reality. But when one was shaken, it was natural that the other should be shaken too.

Similarly, when Darwin first proposed his theory of evolution, many Catholics and Protestants thought it contradicted Scripture. It really did not, or did not have to, at least. It would contradict only if one thought there could be a development of humans from primates without any intervention of God to create a human soul. This concept is called atheistic evolution. But the important thing is that many people *thought* this was a challenge to Scripture, and it seemed so scientific, even though the evidence Darwin had was very poor.[255] Many thought this way because they held fundamentalistic notions about the first chapters of Genesis. They were wrong. The Church, as we shall see, never had taught such fundamentalism. But people would say that since the teaching on Genesis is wrong, perhaps the whole faith is wrong.

It was for this reason that the Church used *disciplinary,* not *doctrinal* restrictions on publications on evolution for some time. The Church never taught that it was false or contrary to the Faith. But it was dangerous, for the psychological reason we explained. So the Church attempted to hold back on such writings. Today we know there is no contradiction, unless as we said one believes an atheistic brand of evolution, and so the Church no longer objects to writings favoring evolution.

So we need to ask if the Church ever really taught fundamentalism on Genesis. First, let us be sure we know what fundamentalism means. A fundamentalist is one who acts as if Genesis were written by a 20th century American, in 20th century forms of expression. He says, "The Bible tells us everything was created in six days. That means 6 times 24 hours. And it says God took clay, made a figure, and breathed on it, and it came to life." The real trouble is that such a person ignores the use of literary genres (which we explained in Chapter 8). Fundamentalists think they are being strictly faithful to Scripture. Sadly, we must say they are being unfaithful. The supreme rule is that *we must find out what the inspired writer meant to convey or assert.* To really find that we must consider what devices of writing, genres and other features too, he used. Only then do we know what he meant or what he *asserted.* What he asserted is the true sense of Scripture. So the fundamentalists are not faithful to Scripture. They are *imposing* their own meaning on Scripture, instead of trying to find what the inspired writer meant to say.

To put it another way, the phrase "literal sense" is used in two ways today: (1) the fundamentalist way, which acts as if the writer were a modern American, and (2) the true literal way, when we do as we just described and find out what the writer intended to assert.

So we return to our question of whether the Church ever taught fundamentalism. The answer is *no.* We start with the Patristic age in which most of the Fathers were looking for what they called the "spiritual sense," which is really an allegorical sense. It is not the sense basically intended by the writers, but neither is it fundamentalistic. Hence, since we need to find the Fathers virtually unanimous to prove something is revealed, we see at once we cannot prove they taught fundamentalism, for they were not even trying to find the literal sense, no matter in which of the two ways mentioned we take the phrase.

St. Augustine, who himself dealt mostly in the allegorical sense, nevertheless wrote a work, *De Genesi Ad Litteram,* an attempt at a literal commentary on Genesis. In it he commented, "That God made man with bodily hands from the clay is an excessively childish thought, so that if Scripture had said this, we should rather believe that the writer used a metaphorical term, than to suppose God is bounded by such lines of limbs as we see in our bodies."

Similarly, St. John Chrysostom, in speaking of the account of the creation of Eve from a rib of Adam in *Gen.* 2:21-22 said, "See the condescendence [adaptation to human weakness] of divine Scripture, what words it uses because of our weakness. 'And He took,' it says, 'one of his ribs.' Do not take what is said in a human way, but understand that the crassness of the words fits human weakness."[257]

In much the same way, when in that age and later, speakers in the Church recounted the story of creation in the same words as Genesis, or in very similar, equivalent words, that did not constitute an interpretation, a statement that we must take Genesis fundamentalistically.

Yet, even though the Church never taught fundamentalism, many people had such notions. Hence evolution shook them, and hence, the Church wanted to protect them until the time when people had adjusted as they should.

Today we have an explicit statement by Pius XII in *Humani generis* (1950). "The teaching office of the Church does not forbid that the theory of evolution . . . be investigated and discussed by experts in both science and theology . . . [but] the Catholic faith orders us to retain that souls are immediately created by God.

. . . they are rash and go too far who act as if the origin of the human body from preexisting and living matter . . . were certain and fully proved."[258]

Unfortunately, the media today commonly offer only two options: (1) atheistic evolution, and (2) fundamentalism on Genesis. Both are wrong. Matter cannot lift itself from methane soup to life, from fish to bird, and on to ever higher and higher life. There must be a cause, a source for the higher being at each level (we recall some things in Chapter 4). So atheistic evolution is foolish, even when viewed by reason alone without the help of revelation. Fundamentalism is regrettable too.

But there are two other options people do not see: (1) Creation by God without the use of any evolutionary process. This would be similar *in effect* to what fundamentalism holds, but it would not rest on a fundamentalistic view that ignores genre, and so would not have to suppose 6 days of 24 hours, nor would it have to suppose just the sequence of things created listed in Genesis; (2) Creation by God with the use of an evolutionary process, in which He would make use of laws He Himself had established, and in which He would create the added new being or higher being at each point where a higher form of life would appear.

We might add that Fundamentalist creationists, in spite of their unfortunate ignoring of literary genre, yet have amassed much impressive evidence to show that the purely scientific evidence in favor of human evolution is very scanty. In fact, most evolutionists today have radically changed the theory of Darwin, and they admit that the fossil record simply does not provide the many intermediate forms of life that his theory would suppose.[259]

(j) FALSE TEACHINGS BY POPES LIBERIUS, VIGILIUS, AND HONORIUS

1) POPE LIBERIUS

Did this Pope sign an Arian creed? At the Synod of Arles in 353 A.D. which condemned St. Athanasius, the great defender of the sound doctrine of the Council of Nicea, even the Pope's legates gave in and voted for the condemnation. Of course, such a vote, taken under duress, had no doctrinal force. Further, the Pope repudiated his own legates, and called for another local council. This one met at Milan in 355. Again there were threats, but the Pope refused to condemn St. Athanasius. So Emperor Constantius had the Pope arrested at night, and taken to Milan. When the Pope still held out, he was sent into exile to Thrace.

Subsequent events are not fully clear. We know the Pope went into exile in 357, and returned the next year. It seems he did submit somewhat. But any statement made under duress, while a personal failing, would not be a false teaching given to the whole Church.

But more importantly, there were several creeds worked out by bishops at Sirmium in Pannonia, where the Emperor's court was in residence. Only one of these creeds was strictly heretical; the others were only ambiguous. It seems that the Pope signed one of the ambiguous creeds under duress. So for a double reason, he did not teach doctrinal error to the Church. He acted under duress, which made his actions invalid, and what he actually signed was not heretical anyway, just ambiguous.

2) POPE VIGILIUS

Emperor Justinian (527-65) was convinced he could bring the heretical Monophysites back to the Church if he could get a papal condemnation of certain writings of Theodore of Mopsuestia, Theodoret of Cyrus, and Ibas of Edessa. The latter two had taught the heresy of Nestorianism (two persons in Jesus). The first, Theodore, at least paved the way for it. Theodoret and Ibas had retracted their errors, and so were cleared by the Council of Chalcedon.

So the issue was largely tactical or political. *The Three Chapters,* as they were called, could be condemned for they had taught error; but since Theodoret and Ibas retracted their errors, the two could be declared valid.

Vigilius was at first an antipope, backed by the Empress Theodora, to whom he had promised he would approve three heretical Monophysites, Anthimus, Severus, and Theodosius. Vigilius, while antipope, did indeed keep that promise. However, when he finally became the legitimate Pope, he quickly retracted what he had done as antipope.

Severe pressure came a few years later from Justinian. The Pope was arrested in 545, and taken to Constantinople. There he did agree to condemn *The Three Chapters,* in 548. But then the Pope retracted the condemnation and refused to sign an edict by Justinian in 551 which condemned *The Three Chapters.* The Pope had to flee. Justinian proposed a Council, which was not to be truly universal but attended by only a few bishops from the west. The Pope did condemn the errors of Theodore of Mopsuestia and Theodoret of Cyrus, but let Ibas alone. Justinian was not content, so the Council condemned Vigilius until such time he should repent. Of course a Council acting without a Pope has no validity at all. Yet, Vigilius broke under pressure, and did condemn *The Three Chapters.*

Vigilius is not an admirable character. But his shifting statements on *The Three Chapters* did not involve doctrinal error. As we said, Theodore of Mopsuestia was guilty of error and did not retract. The other two could be condemned for their errors, or could be absolved since they had retracted. So no matter what the Pope said about them, it would be doctrinally correct.

3) POPE HONORIUS

In the seventh century, Sergius, Patriarch of Constantinople, was also trying to reconcile the heretical Monophysites. Sergius spoke of "one energy" or "one mode of operation in Christ." This was ambiguous because it could mean either (a) there was never a conflict between the human and the divine will in Jesus, or (b) there was no human will at all in Jesus. The second meaning would be heretical, but the first would be fully true.

Pope Honorius seemed not to fully grasp the maneuverings of Sergius. Hence, in 634 he wrote two letters to Sergius that were not heretical, but were ambiguous. Not long after, Pope John IV, in 641, wrote a letter to Emperor Constantius III defending Honorius from a charge of heresy. He said Honorius just meant that Jesus "never had two contrary wills."

But the Council of Constantinople in 681 A.D. wanted to go farther. It voted to call Pope Honorius a heretic. However, as in the case of Pope Vigilius, a Council acting without the Pope has no doctrinal force. Pope Agatho was on the verge of giving formal approval to that conciliar false teaching. But God provided. Pope Agatho died before the conclusion of the council. His successor, Pope Leo II, followed the guidance of Divine Providence and stated the matter precisely: "Pope Honorius . . . failed to add luster to this Apostolic Church by teaching the Apostolic tradition, but on the contrary, *permitted* the spotless [faith] to be defiled."

So Pope Honorius was not charged with heresy—he was not guilty of that. He was charged, rightly, with carelessness by letting true doctrine become ambiguous.

Appendix 2

CHARGES OF ERRORS IN SCRIPTURE

1) DID VATICAN II ALLOW US TO SAY SCRIPTURE CONTAINS ERRORS?

The Church has always insisted there is no error at all in Scripture. Thus Pius XII wrote (*Divino afflante Spiritu*), "In our age, the Vatican Council [I], to reject false teachings about inspiration, declared that these same books [of Scripture] must be considered 'as sacred and canonical' by the Church, 'not only because they contain revelation without error, but because, being written by the inspiration of the Holy Spirit, they have God as their author, and as such have been handed down to the Church.' But then, when certain Catholic authors, contrary to this *solemn definition* of Catholic doctrine . . . dared to restrict the truth of Holy Scripture to matters of faith and morals. . . . our Predecessor of Immortal memory, Leo XIII, in an Encyclical, *Providentissimus Deus* . . . rightly and properly refuted those errors."[260]

The statement is forceful. It is not enough to say the books of Scripture are sacred because the Church later approved works made merely by human labor; nor is it enough to say they contain revelation free of error. No, the basic reason is that "they have God as their author" and of course contain no error. Further, Pius XII called this teaching of Vatican I a "solemn definition." Then he complained that in spite of that definition, some Catholic writers "dared to restrict the truth of Holy Scripture to matters of faith and morals," and to consider scientific or historical matters, or *"obiter dicta"* (things said incidentally and in passing) as not guaranteed. This claim, said Pius XII, is wrong. We may not say there are errors in scientific or historical matters, or in things said incidentally and in passing. Such a claim goes against a solemn definition.

We need, then, to consider the implications of two things: (1) God is the author of Scripture, and (2) We cannot dismiss things on the claim that they are not part of the faith, but are just said in passing.

What does it mean to say God is the author? It means there are two authors of Scripture, God and the human author. God, since He is transcendent (above and beyond all our categories) can employ the human author as a free instrument, and do it in such a way that the human remains free, but yet the human writer will write down what God wants him to write, and write it without error of any kind. Does this mean that God will give the human author *new information by revelation* which he did not have otherwise? God can do that, and at times does, but inspiration as such is something different from revelation. It may or may not include the added data that God can reveal.

What of the literary style, or even grammatical habits a human has? Does God change them? He could, but inspiration is aimed at truth, not at style or even grammar. And so it happens that some lines in St. Paul, for example, are written in beautiful style, such as the chapter on love in *1 Cor.* 13, while other lines can be a bit clumsy in expression, as *Phil.* 2:1-2. But as we said, inspiration protects truth, not literary quality.

Pius XII complained that some scholars were trying to limit this freedom from error to religious matters, so that they admitted error in matters of science or history. Today, many not only claim errors of science and history, but even errors of religion, ruling out only things needed for salvation. They even say that Vatican II reversed previous teaching which includes, according to Pius XII, a "solemn definition" and lets us think there are religious errors in Scripture! Here is the text of Vatican II to which some appeal: "Since all that the inspired authors, or sacred writers assert should be regarded as asserted by the Holy Spirit, we must acknowledge that the books of Scripture, firmly, faithfully, and without error teach *that truth which God, for the sake of our salvation, wished to be confided to sacred Scripture.*"[261]

Some say the above italicized words are ambiguous.[262] That is, the clause could be either *restrictive* or *descriptive.* If restrictive, it would mean that *only* things needed for salvation would be free of error. If descriptive, it simply describes the Scriptures as for our salvation.

We admit that the words are ambiguous, *provided that we ignore the context*—which is something no scholar should ever do with any document.

1) If Vatican II had really wanted to make that clause clearly restrictive, there is an unambiguous Latin construction that would have made it clear called *qui quidem* with the subjunctive.[263] The Council did not use that structure.

2) Vatican II added a note to the sentence in italics, which refers us to the statements of Vatican I, Leo XIII, and Pius XII, all of whom insisted that there is no error, not even scientific or historical error, in Scripture.[264]

3) Pius XII, as we saw, said the statement of Vatican I that there is no error at all in Scripture was a "solemn definition."

So can we suppose the Church reversed a solemn definition in language that is ambiguous if we ignore the context, but clearly meaning the same as the past if we consider the context? And that it added a note referring us back to the very statements it would supposedly

contradict? If there ever was a case of strained pleading, the objectors are giving it here. Of course, they
think they can prove errors in Scripture, and mention
some alleged errors, chiefly *Job* 14:13ff. We will examine those later in this Appendix (in l.c.).

Before going ahead we had better deal with a possible objection: How can the Church declare Scripture
inerrant, when the Church needs Scripture as a basis
for its own claims? Is there a vicious circle?

The reply is basically the same as that which we saw
early in this book. The claims of the Church to teach
with providential protection are established, *before we
look on Scripture as inspired,* and so, *before we depend
on the Church to declare Scripture inerrant.* Only the six
simple facts were needed to prove the teaching mission
of the Church; these we established without appealing
to the help of the Church at all. They were such easy
things to show. There was a man called Jesus, who
claimed to be a messenger from God, who proved it by
miracles done in special frameworks. He had an inner
circle of followers to whom He spoke more, whom He
told to continue His teaching; and He promised that
God would protect that teaching. We established these
by showing that the writers of the Gospels lived early
enough to have the facts, that they had ample chance to
get them, that their concern for their own eternity
would make them tell things honestly. We saw special
new evidence of even meticulous care on the part of St.
Luke.

So there is no vicious circle. Now we can go ahead to
check claims of error in three areas: science, history,
and religion.

a) CLAIMS OF ERRORS IN SCIENCE

The basic answer, which is sufficient in itself, is very
simple for one who understands the approach by way of
genres (Chapter 8 and Appendix I.6). Scripture does

not *assert* scientific data. Nor do people today, for that matter, *assert* that the sun rises in the east. They know it does not really rise; rather, that the earth is revolving on its axis and going around the sun. We are just using popular speech in saying the sun rises in the east. Even if we did not know the scientific facts, we still would be just using normal expressions of the day. Similarly Pope Leo XIII wrote, "There is no error when the sacred writer, speaking of physical things, 'follows what appears to the senses' as St. Thomas says."[265]

b) CLAIMS OF ERRORS IN HISTORY

These too are easily answered. Many of them need only an application of the approach via literary genres. For example, some say that in *Daniel* 1:1 we read that King Nebuchadnezzar besieged Jerusalem in the third year of King Jehoiakim, which seems to be 607 B.C. But, from the Chronicle of King Nebuchadnezzar, we know that the siege must have been three years later.

Before having recourse to genres, we must notice that the chronology of the kings of Judah presents problems. Some would suggest that Jehoiakim became king in 608 B.C. according to Palestinian reckoning, but the Babylonian system, used by Daniel who resided there, would make 605 the third year of Jehoiakim.[266]

Further, we must notice with Leo XIII that scholars seem strangely confident that all secular chronicles are accurate, and would rather doubt the Biblical records.[267]

Also, some things about ancient kings that seemed insoluble in the past have been resolved with new discoveries. Thus the book of Daniel calls Belshazzar the last king of Babylon, while the Babylonian records say it was Nabunaid. However a recently found tablet tells us that Nabunaid gave his son royal power, went to Arabia, and never really reassumed the throne.[268] So a future discovery may unravel this question about

Daniel 1:1. However, we do not really need any of the above at all. We ask in what genre the book of Daniel is written. All admit that there are two genres. One of them is apocalyptic, evidenced in the strange visions. The other is still being discussed. It is known that at least by the fifth century B.C. a genre of edifying narrative, with a didactic purpose, became popular, as seen in the Ahikar story. This genre somewhat resembles a romance or historical novel. It is an edifying story in which there is some fact, especially in the setting, but is a free fictional handling of many things, especially those not needed for the purpose of the work. In such a setting, the dates and names are unimportant. Yes, the writer may have put down what he happened to think about dates, but he did not mean to *assert* these were accurate, for accuracy was not needed for his purpose.

Another example of an historical problem. For example, in *Mark* 2:26 we read that David entered the house of God, "under Abiathar the high priest" and ate the bread of the presence. But *1 Sam* 21:1 says it was not under Abiathar, but under his father Abimelech.

The solution is very easy. The Greek has: *epi Abiathar archiereos.* Now Greek *epi* with the genitive of the person easily takes a generic meaning, i.e., "in the days of . . . ."[268] So the phrase really means, "in the times of Abiathar." Both were alive at the time. The reason for using Abiathar's name rather than Abimelech is that he was much more prominent and better known to readers of the Old Testament than his father, in view of his close association with David, under whom he became chief priest along with Zadok.

One further example: In *Matthew* 27:9 we read that a prophecy of Jeremiah was fulfilled in the fate of Judas. Yet some say the quote is from *Zech.* 11:12 ff. We reply that the note in the non-conservative *New American Bible* explains well, "Matthew's free citation of *Jer.* 18:2 f; 19:1 f; 32:6-15 and *Zech.* 11:13 shows that he regards Judas' death as a divine judgment." So we gather that Matthew really put together passages from both Jeremiah and Zechariah. The rabbis used to do such things, and when they did, they put the name of the best-known author on the combination.[270]

We already saw, in Chapter 10, the answer to still another historical problem, the agreement of Paul and Acts on the Council of Jerusalem. There are more problems, all easily solved. At the end of Appendix II, we will explain the most prominently raised difficulties.[271]

c) CLAIMS OF RELIGIOUS ERRORS IN SCRIPTURE

Many today are claiming that there are numerous errors in Scripture, even religious errors. For example, Thomas A. Hoffman, in *Inspiration, Normativeness, Canonicity and the Unique Sacred Character of the Bible* dismisses the term inerrancy: "The term inerrancy is dropped in this paper as having no positive theological contribution to make."[272] He adds that to try to refute all charges of error is "basically patching holes on a sinking ship." Bruce Vawter even says the terms "infallible" and "inerrant" are even "anti-biblical."[273] Because these claims are so very important, before taking up some specific examples, it will be worthwhile to examine the underpinning, as it were, of the claims.

Confusion is injected at once, by the common assertion that the Word of God is "human and time-conditioned."[274] This statement is true but potentially misleading. The Bible is human in that there is a human as well as a divine Author, the Holy Spirit.[275] The Holy Spirit uses the human author in such a way that the human author retains his own literary style, but yet he writes without any error what the Holy Spirit wills that he write. It can be called time-conditioned in that the kinds of expressions used by the human author will be affected by the culture of his own time.

There is a certain parallel in the case of official documents of the Church. On the one hand, Paul VI, in *Mysterium fidei* insisted, "The rule of speaking, which the Church with long labor over the centuries, not without the protection of the Holy Spirit, has arrived at and has confirmed by the authority of Councils . . . must be preserved as holy, nor should anyone at his own wish or on pretext of new knowledge presume to change it."[276] Yet it is to be admitted that there is a sort of time conditioning, such as we just described, and so language may be capable of improvement. Hence the Doctrinal Congregation, by order of Paul VI, on June 24, 1973, told us, "With regard to this historical condition. . . . it sometimes happens that some dogmatic truth is first expressed incompletely (but not falsely), and at a later date . . . receives a fuller and more perfect expression." Yet, "it must be stated that the dogmatic formulas of the Church's Magisterium were from the very beginning suitable for communicating revealed truth, and that as they are, they remain forever suitable . . . to those who interpret them correctly. . . ."[277] In the same spirit, Vatican II, in its *Decree on Ecumenism,* wrote, "If the influence of events or times has brought deficiencies in conduct, in ecclesiastical discipline, or even in the expression of doctrine—which is to be carefully distinguished from the deposit itself of faith—these things ought to be suitably rectified at the proper time."[278]

Today some try to distinguish three stages in the meaning of Scripture: the sense originally intended by the inspired author, the changed sense it may acquire when a book of Scripture is put into the canon, and the various senses the Church may give the same text.

As to the second stage, the meaning given by insertion into the canon, we turn to what is called canonical criticism. This method goes back to James Sanders, in

Torah and Canon, in 1972.[279] According to T. J. Keegan, "Canonical critics agree . . . that it is the reader who produces the meaning of the text, but insist as one of their fundamental presuppositions, that it is only the believing community that is capable of reading and interpreting the Bible."[280] But this does not simply mean that the Church can authentically interpret the Bible, and give us its true meaning in a final statement. No, canonical critics think every work of literature has many meanings.[281] So the Church—as in stage three mentioned above—is said to give many different interpretations, which need not necessarily agree with each other.

This is the same as saying that the Church does not tell us the real meaning of Scripture, and that various Church statements may contradict each other. Of course this is not the case. The Church, under divine protection promised to Her by the Divine Messenger we saw in the first part of this book, can and does interpret Scripture correctly. Vatican II, in its *Constitution on Divine Revelation*, declared, "The task of authoritatively interpreting the word of God, whether written or handed on [Scripture or Tradition] has been entrusted *exclusively* to the living Magisterium of the Church, whose authority is exercised in the name of Jesus Christ."[282] Note the word *exclusively*—Scripture scholars have no authority at all. Their work is described thus: "It is the task of Scripture scholars to work according to these rules for the deeper understanding and presentation of the sense of Sacred Scripture, so that by as it were *preparatory* study, the judgment of the Church may mature."[283] The sentence just before our quotation explained "these rules": "Since Sacred Scripture must be read and interpreted according to the same Spirit by whom it was written, no less attention must be devoted to the content and unity of the whole of Scripture, taking into account the Tradi-

tion of the entire Church and the analogy of faith."[284]
Scholars today often ignore this teaching of Vatican II.
They note that each Evangelist has his own special
scope and intention—which is true—but they go on to
assert that one Evangelist can even contradict another
(we will see below a strong instance of a claim that
Mark and Luke contradict each other). Of course this
cannot be true, since, as Vatican II insists, it is one and
the same Holy Spirit who is the author of all parts of
Scripture. The Council adds that the scholars must look
to "the analogy of faith," that is they must never interpret a text in such a way that the meaning would
clash, even by implication, with any official teaching of
the Church.

We admit that Church statements at times may use
what is called an "accommodated sense" of Scripture.
That is, a text is applied to something, in a fitting way,
even though the sense proposed was not the one intended by the inspired author. St. Paul himself, in view
of his rabbinic training, often enough does this sort of
thing. But the Church does not always do this. By
careful study we can find out whether or not the
Church is giving us an accommodated sense of Scripture. For example, the Council of Trent wrote: "If anyone says that by the words, 'Do this in memory of me'
Christ did not make the Apostles priests, or did not or-
dain that they and other priests should offer His body
and blood, let him be anathema."[285] The context, of opposing Lutheran errors, makes clear that in this instance Trent was defining the sense of *Luke* 22:19 and
1 Cor. 11:24.

A methodology closely related to canonical criticism
is reader-response criticism. Both concepts maintain
"that it is the reader who produces the meaning of the
text."[286] But reader-response criticism does not insist on
the role of the community in interpreting, and supposes
that the text can have "an infinite variety of mean-

ings."[287] So we see total subjectivity—far from the truth as explained by Vatican II.

A word about the deep roots of this subjectivity is useful. The ideas of Paul Ricoeur have been very influential.[288] He holds that once a manuscript leaves its author's hands, it takes on a life of its own, and can take on a large number of different meanings. This of course reminds us of Historicism, which we dealt with in Chapter 6, and of Existentialism, which maintains that every person and event is unique.[289] Hence, endless subjectivism. Hence also, the unfortunate ideas of Bultmann, who made the Gospels mean the same as the German Existentialist Heidegger's interpretation of them.[290]

2) CLAIMS OF A DENIAL OF AFTERLIFE IN THE OLD TESTAMENT

Many today think that *Job* 14:13-22 denies an afterlife.[291] Further, "It is generally held by scholars that no hope of individual survival after death is expressed in the Old Testament before some of its latest passages."[292] Of course, it is one thing not to express it, another thing to deny it. But Vatican II, as we also saw above, taught, "Since Sacred Scripture must be read and interpreted according to the same Spirit by whom it was written, no less attention must be devoted to the content and unity of the whole of Scripture."[293]

So, if the Holy Spirit is author of *all* of Scripture, He obviously will not say one thing in one place and contradict it in another. Therefore we know with absolute certainty that Job could not contradict later Scripture, which affirms the afterlife; and we can show that this is true even though some think the very attempt to prove the Holy Spirit did not contradict Himself here is an "unmitigated disaster."

To begin, we must notice that they have forgotten a very important point. Namely, conditions in the afterlife were very different during Old Testament times before the Redemption, than they are now. That is, the just who died before the death of Christ were not admitted to the vision of God, they were detained in the Limbo of the Fathers, and entered Heaven only after Christ had actually died. The *Dictionnaire de Théologie Catholique* calls this teaching "the common view of the Fathers,"[294] and rightly, for we find it in—to name just the chief examples: *Shepherd of Hermas, Parable* 9:16.5; St. Justin, *Dialogue with Trypho* 72; St. Irenaeus, *Against Heresies* 3:20.4; Clement of Alexandria, *Stromata* 6:6; St. Athanasius, *Ad Epictetum* 6; Origen, *On Romans* 5:1; St. Hilary, *On Psalm* 118:11; St. John Damascene, *De fide orthodoxa* 3:29; and St. Bede the Venerable, *On 1 Peter* 3:19. St. Thomas Aquinas teaches the same in *Summa, Supplement* 69:7.c, and an unknown author of an ancient homily, which we read in the Roman Breviary for Holy Saturday, beautifully dramatizes the meeting of Christ and Adam in this Limbo.

Further, it is unlikely, even before investigating, that the Hebrews would have no knowledge of the afterlife. Job is probably to be dated between 7th and 5th centuries B.C., but before that, in the 8th century, *Isaiah* 14:9-11 represents the shades in Sheol taunting the fallen rulers of Babylon, and *Isaiah* 26:19 says, "Your dead shall live, and my body shall rise again; awake and sing, you that dwell in the dust. Your dew is the dew of light; and the land of the shades shall fall." Even the *Jerome Biblical Commentary* says on *Isaiah* 26:19, ". . . there is an explicit hope in the resurrection of individuals."[295] The Protestant *Interpreter's Dictionary of the Bible* in an article on immortality says, "The idea of a possible return to life gained wider and wider acceptance. The Israelites could not remain unaffected by the Canaanite belief in the death and resurrection of a divinity who symbolized the life of nature. The faithful linked themselves with the idea of death and resurrection within the cult."[296] M. Dahood, in *Psalms, Anchor Bible,* notes that the late Bronze Age Canaanites (c.1500-1200 B.C.), among whom the Hebrews lived, knew of immortality.[297] Dahood also argues from many psalm texts, as seen in the light of new discoveries in Ugaritic.[298] Further, the Hebrews had lived in Egypt for several centuries, where a vivid belief in an afterlife was general. So it is really hard to believe that the Hebrews would never have picked up the idea from those neighbors of centuries, Egyptians and Canaanites.

Further, should we take their words about Sheol as meaning annihilation? Jesus Himself silenced the Sadducees, who denied a resurrection, by reasoning that God said to Moses: *"I am the God of Abraham, and God of Isaac, and the God of Jacob. He is not the God of the dead, but of the living. You therefore do greatly err."* (*Mk.* 12:26)

So it is not hard at all to believe that Job could believe in an afterlife. In fact, it is possible to see such a hope explicitly present in *Job* 19:25-27. RSV reads, "For I know that My Redeemer lives, and at last he will stand upon the earth; and after my skin has been thus destroyed, then from my flesh I shall see God." NAB has, "I know that my Vindicator lives, and that he will at last stand forth upon the dust; whom I myself shall see: my own eyes, not another's, shall behold him, and from my flesh I shall see God."

The Douay-Rheims reads, "For I know that my Redeemer liveth, and in the last day I shall rise out of the earth. And I shall be clothed again with my skin, and in my flesh I shall see my God. Whom I myself shall see, and my eyes shall behold, and not another: this my hope is laid up in my bosom."

Could these lines mean someone will come to rescue him *in this life* and restore him? Hardly, for in *Job*

7:6-7 he says, "My days have passed more swiftly than the web is cut by the weaver, and are consumed without any hope."

However, even without the help of those debated lines, we can show that it is quite possible to take *Job* 14:13-22 in a sense that does *not* deny an afterlife.

Chapter 14, verse 13 says, "Who will grant that you hide me in Sheol [and] hide me until your wrath turns aside, and appoint for me a set time and remember me?" In verses 10-12 just before this, Job had said that in contrast to a tree which may die and shoot up again, man does not return. In other words, he does not return to *this life*. No one has ever come out of the grave and rejoined family and friends.

But then, since Job is deeply afflicted in a trial from God, in verse 13 he indulges in a *fanciful wish,* saying he would like to hide, without dying in Sheol, the underworld, until God's wrath has passed. Now this is, as we said, fanciful. Job knows no one goes to Sheol and returns to rejoin his own *in a continuation of the present life.*

But, we must not forget the *genre* of Job. It is poetry, very high poetry. Now poets in any culture are noted for indulging in fanciful things. So Job does this. Marvin Pope, in the *Anchor Bible* commentary on this passage, takes this attitude: "If only God would grant him asylum in the netherworld, safe from the wrath that now besets him, and then appoint a time for a new and sympathetic hearing, he would be willing to wait or even to endure the present evil."[299] Then Pope points out that we have a parallel to this fanciful thought elsewhere: "*Isa.* XXVI 20 calls ironically on the people of Judah to hide in their chambers till Yahweh's wrath be past, and *Amos* IX 2ff. pictures the wicked as trying vainly to hide in Sheol, Heaven, Mount Carmel, [or] the bottom of the sea."

Let us examine verses 14-17. These are best taken as

a continuation of the fancy of verse 13: "If a man dies, will he live [again]? All the days of my service I would wait until my change would come. You would call, and would answer you [and] you would want the work of your hands. Then you would number my steps, you would not keep watch over my sin. My transgression would be sealed up in a bag, and you would sew up my iniquity." The first question, taken alone, goes back to the idea of verses 10-12, that is, no one rejoins the present life. But then he resumes the fancy of verse 13, of hiding until God would give him a new hearing and cover his iniquity.

Verses 18-22 say, "But a mountain falling loses its strength, and the rock is moved from its place. The waters wear away the stones, the torrents wash away the soil of the earth [and] you destroy the hope of man. You overpower him forever and he passes; you change his countenance and send him away. His sons come to honor and he knows it not. They become despised, and he perceives it not. His flesh on him has pain, and his soul mourns over him."

After indulging in the fancy of hiding, Job in effect says, "No, I cannot hide. God always wins. Not even mountains or hardest rocks can stand against God. Man dies, and returns not *to this present life.*" But Job does not say anything against a future life, especially a *glorious* future life in the vision of God, of which he does not know—unless we take Chapter 19:25-27, which we saw above, as meaning strictly that he "will see God" in that vision.

But rather, Job talks of the future life *as he knew it,* and as Jews thought of it. Job and his people thought of life as a drab survival—*which is what it really was before the death of Christ.* It was a dim limbo of the fathers, in which they had no means of knowing what transpired on earth, whether their children prospered or suffered. By way of the beatific vision of God a person can know what goes on on earth. But without that vision he cannot. And that vision was not to be had in the days of Job, not until Jesus had died. So, Job says that the dead man feels only his own pain. *The fact that he feels pain shows his continued existence. So there is an afterlife.*

So we ask now: Is this interpretation of Job hopelessly strained? Not at all, it is one that takes into account (1) *the genre of Job* and *(2) the actual conditions of afterlife* in the days of Job—which many should know about, but seem to ignore. Pope, in *Anchor Bible,* saw the truth about the fancy Job thinks of, without seeming to know of the different conditions of afterlife. So we do have excellent support. For certain, no one can claim he is *forced* to charge contradiction in Scripture, because at very least, we have shown a plausible alternative.

Further, as we said, since the one Spirit wrote all parts of Scripture, we know He cannot and does not contradict Himself. In fact, the Holy Spirit may be teaching afterlife and even beatific vision in *Job* 19:25-27, as we saw above.

So no one can call our work an "unmitigated disaster."

Some also claim some texts in Sirach/Ecclesiasticus deny an afterlife. Let us explore this. *Sirach* 14:16-17 says, "Give and take and enjoy yourself, for it is not possible in Sheol to seek luxury. All flesh grows old as a garment. For the decree of ages is: You must surely die." The answer to this curious verse is very easy. Ecclesiasticus was probably written around 200-175 B.C., certainly long before Christ. But as we saw, the just who died in that period were not admitted to the vision of God until the death of Christ. So the abode of the dead was the dull Limbo of the fathers, where "it is not possible to seek luxury."

Again, Sirach/Ecclesiasticus 17:27-28 (vs. 22-23 in

NAB) says, "who will praise the most high in Sheol?... For from the dead as from those who are not, praise perishes. One who is alive and well will praise the Lord."

M. Dahood, in his *Anchor Bible,* comments on *Ps.* 6:6, which has a similar thought: "The psalmist suffers not because of the inability to remember Yahweh in Sheol [Hell], but from being unable to share in the praise of Yahweh which characterizes Israel's worship." He has in mind the grand liturgical praise of God. But there was no such thing in the dull limbo of the fathers. We can add that *Isaiah* 38:18 also has similar language: "For Sheol will not thank you [nor] death praise you." The verb for praise, *hallel,* in Hebrew is precisely the same verb used in *1 Chron.* 16:4 and *2 Chron.* 5:13 and 31:2 for the *liturgical* praise of God. That of course would not take place in Hell.

Finally, Sirach/Ecclesiasticus 38:21 reads: "Do not forget, for there is no return road, and you will not help this one [the deceased] and you will harm yourself." This means there is no use trying to bring the dead one *back to this life,* to rejoin us. And it says nothing about his survival in the future life, nor does it speak of a glorious resurrection at the end of time.

For added emphasis, let us add some texts from Qoheleth/Ecclesiastes on the same question of survival. These can be solved by using the points we made above, but additional things are desirable here too. So we will first explain the added considerations.

We saw in Chapters 19-20 of this book that in divine matters, we can meet with two contrary revealed truths, or two seemingly conflicting sets of statements. We know each is true, but we may not know how to reconcile them. Sound method is essential here, for we must faithfully hold to both truths, once we are sure they are both revealed (checking our work carefully in these cases is essential). We must *avoid forcing the interpreta-*

tion of one to meet the demand of the other. Instead, we wait, in faith, for the true solution to appear in the future.

Now Qoheleth of Ecclesiastes was in such a situation: (1) He knew that the good and wicked often fare the same way in this life; (2) He also knew that God judges justly. We can easily reconcile these things by the doctrine of future rewards and punishments. He seems not to have known of this clearly. But he faithfully made both kinds of statements.

The problem was further complicated for him by the general, and true, belief that the afterlife was a drab thing, not much more than survival. We saw above that this belief was *correct for that age.*

So if we carefully study all statements of Qoheleth/Ecclesiastes in the light of the points just given, we will find that all comes out well. Here are the chief samples of both kinds of statements.

So marked is the contrast of the two sets that, chiefly in the past, some scholars have thought there must be two authors for Ecclesiastes [Qoheleth].

First set:

Ecclesiastes [Qoheleth] 2:14: "The eyes of a wise man are in his head: the fool walks in darkness. I myself perceived: the same thing comes to all of them." In other words, all die and return to dust.

Ecc. 3:19: "For what happens to man is the same as happens to beasts. As one dies, the other dies."

3:20: "All are from dust and will return to dust." Of course, both man and beast die and return to the same thing, to dust. In this sense, their fate is the same.

3:21: "Who knows whether the spirit of the sons of man goes up and the spirit of the beasts goes down?"

This is a heavily debated line. NAB renders it "life-breath" instead of *spirit.* Is there any concept of a soul *expressed* here? Ecclesiastes makes a distinction of man's breath or spirit going up, that of the beast down. For certain, this 3:21 does not positively deny survival. It merely brings out the fact that men and beasts both return to dust.

9:5-6: "The dead know nothing. They have no more reward . . . their love and their hate and their envy have perished. Nor do they have any more forever a portion in all that is done under the sun." He says the dead do not know what goes on on earth. Of course not, in the limbo of the fathers there was no way of knowing. Nor do they have a share in the *present life,* "in the work that is done under the sun."

Second set:

3:17: "I said in my heart: God shall judge both the just and the wicked." But Ecclesiastes knew it often does not seem to work out fairly in this life. So, he implies there must be a judgment beyond this life.

8:12: "If a sinner does evil a hundred times, and prolongs his life, yet I know surely that it will be well with those who fear God."

This verse seems to imply retribution after death, for in *Ecc.* 8:14, he adds, "There are just men to whom it happens according to the deeds of the wicked; and there are wicked men to whom it happens according to the deeds of the just."

The author could not see these injustices rectified in this life, so objectively, there is an impliction that there must be a retribution beyond this life.

9:10: "For there is no work, or reason, or knowledge, or wisdom in Sheol to which you are going."

12:14: "For God will bring every deed into judgement, every hidden thing, whether good or evil."

Again, a clear implication of retribution after death, for the author knows justice is not always done in this life.

We conclude: Qoheleth or Ecclesiastes faithfully

reported both ideas, from the two sets of statements. Yet as we saw in detail, the two sets can fit together readily. He did not know clearly how to reconcile both sets of ideas, but we do. Objectively, *all* he said was true.

3) CLASH OF LUKE AND MARK OVER THE IMAGE OF MARY?

Many today think that Luke's picture of Mary is contradicted by Mark. Thus Wilfred Harrington says flatly, "For Mark it [3:31-35] is a continuation of vv. 20-21 . . . his own did not receive him."[301] And he seems to include Mary. Harrington even says that the passage "may be seen to distinguish those who stood outside the sphere of salvation, and those who are within it."[302] Outside of salvation stands His Mother!

Behind this charge lies *Mark* 3:21 and 31. In 3:21 we find, "And when his friends had heard of it, they went out to lay hold on him. For they said: He is beside himself." Jesus was so occupied on speaking to the crowds that He didn't take the time to eat. His friends thought He was mad and went out to get Him.

Who are Jesus' friends? Harrington and others think they are those mentioned nine verses later. *Mark* 3:31 says, "And his mother and his brethren came; and standing without, sent unto him, calling him."

There are two ways to answer this charge, each sufficient in itself. One way is by the teachings of the Church, and the other by Scriptural analysis.

a) REFUTATION BY TEACHINGS OF THE CHURCH

There are at least four teachings of the Church that prevent such a view from being true:

1) Vatican II taught, as we saw above, "Since Sacred Scripture must be read and interpreted according to the same Spirit by whom it was written, no less attention

must be devoted to the content and unity of the whole of Scripture."[303] So, though there can be different perspectives in the Gospels, there can be no contradiction. To say Mark contradicted Luke is to say the Holy Spirit contradicted Himself.

2) Vatican II also taught *Mary's total dedication to Jesus from the very start:* "The Father of mercies willed that the *acceptance* by the planned-for Mother should precede the Incarnation, so that thus, just as a woman contributed to death, so also a woman should contribute to life ... And so Mary, the daughter of Adam, by *consenting* to the divine word, became the Mother of Jesus, and *embracing the salvific will of God* with full heart, held back by no sin, *totally dedicated herself* as the handmaid of the Lord *to the person and work of her Son,* by the grace of Almighty God, serving the mystery of the Redemption with Him and under Him. Rightly then do the Holy Fathers judge that Mary was *not merely passively employed* by God, but was cooperating in *free faith and obedience* in human salvation."[304]

These words refer to the time of the Annunciation when the Incarnation took place. God then asked her to *consent* and she *embraced the saving will,* and she *totally dedicated herself* to the person and work of her Son. Nor was this just a passive use of her, since she joined freely. Clearly then, she was already dedicated to Jesus from the start. Hence it is utterly false to suppose she did not believe in Him.

3) The Church has taught over and over again, and Vatican II has repeated, that Jesus was conceived virginally, without a human father.[305] Of course Mary could not help knowing that. Could she help believing in so marvelous a Son?

4) Vatican II also taught, "At the beginning [of His public life] when moved by pity at the wedding in Cana of Galilee, she by her intercession obtained the begin-

ning of the miracles of Jesus the Messiah."[306] Clearly then, she believed in Him more than others at the start of His public life.

b) REFUTATION BY SCRIPTURAL EXEGESIS

Here we will focus on two passages: *Mark* 3:21 and 31; and the Annunciation scene.

The Douay-Rheims version of the bible says Jesus' friends went out to lay hold on Him. RSV translates *Mark* 3:21 by saying that "his *friends*" went out to seize Him. NAB makes it "his family." The Greek is *hoi par' autou,* which is vague. It means those around Him— friends, relatives, household, so we are not fully sure who they were. Next RSV says they came to "seize" Him. NAB says, "take charge of" Him. Again, the Greek is not precise, for it can mean anything from "to persuade Him to take it easy" to "to take Him by force."

After that vague verse 21, we have nine verses telling how scribes charged that He was casting out devils by the devil. Jesus said that was the unforgivable sin against the Holy Spirit. After that long interlude we find that, "His mother and his brothers came" and wanted to speak to Him.

Are the two groups, those in verse 21, and those in verse 31, the same? They could be, though it is not fully certain. But let us suppose, for the sake of argument, that they were the same. Would it follow that His Mother did not believe in Him if some other relatives did not believe? Hardly—she could have gone along with them precisely to try to restrain them. Further, many seem to forget that even a very ordinary mother is apt to stick up for her son even when everyone else is *against* him and thinks him guilty. So, would she turn against him even when most people were *for* him? Of course not. We have already seen, with the help of Vatican II, that she was totally dedicated to Him from the day of the Annunciation.

c) THE ANNUNCIATION SCENE

Next we turn to the scene of the Annunciation. Before studying it, we must note that many think Luke really had little information from which to comprise his first two chapters, so he built up a few scant bits of data by making his account parallel to Old Testament incidents.[307]

They are wrong in this assumption. Even John L. McKenzie, hardly a conservative scholar, wrote in the *National Catholic Reporter*, ". . . one wonders how a Gentile convert (or a Gentile proselyte) could have acquired so quickly the mastery of the Greek Old Testament shown in the use of the Old Testament in Luke's infancy narratives. If Luke the physician had been able to study medicine with such success, he would have discovered a cure for cancer. . . .Luke must have had a source for his Old Testament texts and allusions; and it is hard to think of such a collection of texts without a narrative for them to illustrate, a pre-Lucan infancy narrative is suggested, I beg to submit."[308]

Again, R. H. Fuller, one of the chief form critics, wrote in the *Catholic Biblical Quarterly*, "It is ironic that just at a time when the limitations of the historical-critical method are being discovered in Protestantism, Roman Catholic scholars should be bent on pursuing that method so relentlessly." That was in 1978. By 1980, the same R. H. Fuller considered the method they followed so relentlessly to be "bankrupt."[310]

Still further, when Luke announced in his opening lines that he would write with care and precision, using earlier sources, he meant it. We saw new evidence in Chapter 9 that he did just that. So could he, right after such an announcement, relate a largely fanciful picture of the birth and infancy?

But, far more importantly, Vatican II speaks of the infancy narratives as fully factual, even though, shortly before (§55) it showed extreme reserve on *Genesis* 3:15 and *Isaiah* 7:14. After the full analysis of the implications of the Annunciation which we cited above, the Council continues in the next section: "This union of the Mother with the Son in the work of salvation is evident from the time of the virginal conception of Christ even to His death. In the first place, it is evident when Mary, arising in haste to visit Elizabeth, is greeted by her as blessed because of her faith . . . [it is evident] at His birth, when the Mother of God joyfully showed her firstborn Son—who did not diminish, but consecrated her virginal integrity—to the shepherds and the Magi."[311] We notice that the Council accepts even such details as shepherds and Magi from the infancy narratives of Matthew and Luke.

We notice too, in passing, that the Council reaffirms the virginal conception, which is quite a problem for some who think that if Jesus had no human father, Mary really would *not* have been able not to believe in Him, and would have told Him of His own nature, so that he could not have been ignorant of His divinity, as so many assert.

So, with the assurance of Vatican II that the Annunciation was real and that in it she did conceive virginally and did dedicate herself totally to her Son, we will examine Luke's narrative.

First, as we saw in Chapter 22, the Targums take the prophecy of Jacob in *Genesis* 49:10 as Messianic, as foretelling that the Jews would have their own rulers until the Messiah would come. But not long before the day of the Annunciation, Jews failed to have their own rulers at all, with the advent of Herod, of Idumean and Arabian descent. There were Messianic expectations at the time; and when the Magi came to Herod, his theologians readily reported that the Messiah was to come from Bethlehem (*Matthew* 2:4-6, referring to *Micah* 5:2).

In *Luke* 1:32, the angel says that her Son will be called "Son of the most High." A devout Jew could be called a son of God, but the angel added, ". . . the Lord God will give to him the throne of David his father; and he shall reign in the house of Jacob for ever. And of his kingdom there shall be no end." This clearly means the Messiah, for as Levey writes, most Jews believed the Messiah would live forever.[314] So the promise of the everlasting reign means the son will be the Messiah.

Then *Luke* 1:35 continues, "The Holy Ghost shall come upon you, and the power of the most High shall overshadow you. And therefore also the Holy one which shall be born of you shall be called the Son of God." Now "overshadow" was the term used for the Divine Presence filling the tabernacle in the desert (*Ex.* 40:34-35. Cf. the cloud filling the temple in Jerusalem when just consecrated 1 *Kgs.* 8:10). So, *precisely because* the Divine Presence would fill her, *"therefore" for that reason* He would be called Son of God. But that would be unique; no one else was called Son of God for that reason. Hence, Mary would know even His divinity, besides His Messiahship.

Three papal statements come to mind. Pope St. Leo the Great, in the middle of the 5th century, said in a homily on the nativity, "The royal virgin of the line of David is chosen who, since she was to be made pregnant with the Sacred offspring, first conceived the divine and human Child in her mind, before doing so in her body. And so that she would not be struck with unusual emotions, in ignorance of the heavenly plan, she learned what was to be done in her by the Holy Spirit from the conversation with the angel."[315] Pope Leo XIII, in his *Parta humano generi* wrote, "O how sweet, then, how pleasing did the greeting of the angel come to the Blessed Virgin, who then, when Gabriel greeted her, sensed that she had conceived the Word of

God of the Holy Spirit."[316]

Finally, Pope Paul VI, in his Christmas allocution of Dec. 28, 1966, complained of studies which "try to diminish the historical value of the Gospels themselves, especially those that refer to the birth of Jesus and His infancy. We mention this devaluation briefly, so that you may know how to defend with study and faith the consoling certainty that these pages are not inventions of people's fancy, but that they speak the truth. 'The Apostles,' writes one who understands these things, Cardinal Bea [a noted Scripture scholar], 'had a true historical interest. We do not mean a historical interest in the sense of Greek and Roman historiography, that is, of a logically and chronologically arranged account that is an end in itself, but of concern with past events as such and an intention to report and faithfully hand down things done and said in the past.' A confirmation of this is the very concept of 'witness,' 'testimony,' and 'testify,' which in varied forms appears more than 150 times in the New Testament. The authority of the Council has not pronounced differently on this: 'The Sacred Authors wrote ... always in such a way that they reported on Jesus with sincerity and truth.'" [citing Vatican II, on *Divine Revelation* §19].[317]

Appendix 3

AREAS OF CONTENTION

"There are none so blind as those who will not see." So runs the old saying. We think of it in Scripture studies, when the development of new techniques— chiefly the approach by literary genres, and Form and Redaction Criticism—has made us able to solve so many difficulties that seemed impossible early in this century, yet today is precisely the time when many scholars are claiming they cannot solve problems, and are saying there are errors in Scripture. Yet so many of the problems are positively easy to solve. The answer to some of them has been known for a long time.

My book, *Free From All Error* (Prow Press, 1985), gives answers to many of the most serious charges that require a long answer. In this chapter we will give examples of easy problems, that can be handled briefly.

1) JOSEPH A. FITZMYER, S.J.

In his "Life of Paul" in *Jerome Biblical Commentary,* Fitzmyer writes, in speaking of the three retellings of the story of Paul's conversion in Acts, "Although there are variants about certain details in the three accounts (whether the companions stood by speechless or fell to the ground; whether they heard the voice or not—and although Jesus addresses Paul 'in the "Hebrew" language' he quotes a Greek proverb, the essential message conveyed to Paul is the same. . . . The variants may be due to the different sources of Luke's information."[318]

So Fitzmyer sees three contradictions, and says perhaps Luke used different sources, which disagreed.

We know Luke used sources, and if any writer were to repeat two sources which did not agree, we would know by that very fact that he did not *assert* (see our remarks on asserting and genre in Appendices I.6 and II) that either of them was fully accurate. It would be as if he said, "Here is what I found. Two things do not agree. I cannot tell you which is which."[319]

However, there is no need at all to resort to that measure, since the solution has been known for a long time.

In *Acts* 9:7 we read that the men with Paul "stood speechless, hearing the voice, but seeing no one." Yet in 22:9, "Those who were with me saw the light but did not hear the voice." This seems like a contradiction but it is not. Elementary Greek students know that the Greek verb *akouein, to hear,* can mean to pick up a sound, or to pick it up and also understand it.

Even the English *listen* has a spread of meanings: to use the ears, or to obey. And in *Matthew* 13:13 we find, in the quotation from Isaias: "Hearing they hear not." Similarly in *John* 12:28-29, Jesus in public speaks to the Father and, "Then a voice came from heaven, 'I have glorified it [His name] and I will glorify it again.' The crowd standing by heard it, and said that it had thundered." It seems they heard the voice, but did not understand what it said.

Next, in *Acts* 9:7, the men with Paul "*stood* amazed," whereas in *Acts* 26:14: "We had all *fallen* down on the ground." To solve this question, one needs not even elementary Greek, just a little common-sense thought. Imagine being there, seeing the light from the sky, hearing something without knowing what was said. It would not be strange to be literally taken off one's feet. But then, what would the normal person do? As soon as possible he would scramble to his feet and stand there looking shocked.

The third point is this: in *Acts* 26:14, "I heard a

voice saying to me in the Hebrew language, 'Saul, Saul, why do you persecute me? It hurts to kick against the goads.'" Fitzmyer worries that the voice spoke in Hebrew (which might stand for Aramaic), whereas the saying about the goad is known in Greek, but not in Semitic. Again, the answer is simple. Some sayings cannot be translated into another language, especially if they involve a play on words. But others can. Clearly, this one could be understood in many languages. It means merely that "The call of Christ from now on will constrain you, and you, mulish fellow, will find it hard to keep on resisting."

2) R. BULTMANN

Bultmann is the chief pioneer in applying Form Criticism to the New Testament. In his *New Testament and Mythology* he wrote, " . . . some of its features [the New Testament] are actually contradictory. For example, the death of Christ is sometimes a sacrifice and sometimes a cosmic event. Sometimes His person is interpreted as the Messiah and sometimes as the Second Adam. The *kenosis* [emptying] of the pre-existent Son (*Phil.* 2:6 ff) is incompatible with the miracle narratives as proofs of His messianic claims. The virgin birth is inconsistent with the assertion of His pre-existence. The doctrine of the creation is incompatible with the conception of the 'rulers of this world' (*1 Cor.* 2:6 ff). . . . "[320]

The lack of understanding is shocking. First, if the death of Christ is a sacrifice, which it is, that does not make it any less a cosmic event, a turning point in history. Again, to be the Messiah foretold by the prophets does not prevent His being also the Second Adam, as St. Paul calls Him, that is, the new head of the human race, who reverses the damage done by the First Adam.

Further, if the Second Person of the Holy Trinity—

who pre-exists, who has always been—wishes to take on human nature, He can surely do so. His eternal existence does not hinder that at all. As to the doctrine that God created the world, He can still permit evil spirits to have a hand in doing their evil to the extent that they might be called "rulers of this world" in *1 Cor.* 2:6. (Actually, the line in *1 Cor.* is unclear. It could easily refer to the Roman and Jewish authorities who condemned Jesus to death.) St. Paul says they would not have done so had they known who He really was. About the *kenosis*—this is St. Paul's expression in *Phil.* 2:7: "He emptied himself, taking the form of a servant." Paul is probably copying a liturgical hymn here, but no matter whether he or someone else wrote it, the meaning need not be at all what Bultmann supposes. In fact, what he supposes is utterly impossible. Bultmann seems to imply that if Jesus *gave up His divinity* He could not have worked miracles. First, God cannot stop being God: it is total nonsense to even suggest such a thing. Further, if we were to suppose He could, for the sake of argument, we must assume that others than God can work miracles. Prophets in the name of God often do that. Even evil spirits by powers natural to them can do some marvels. So there are multiple errors in the greatest of form critics.

3) W. PANNENBERG

In his book, *Jesus—God and Man,* he writes, "In its content, the legend of Jesus' virgin birth stands in irreconcilable contradiction to the Christology of the incarnation of the pre-existent Son of God found in Paul and John."[321] This is much the same as part of the nonsense we have just seen in Bultmann. The pre-existent, the eternal Son of God, the Second Person of the Blessed Trinity, if He wanted—and He did—to take on human nature, could surely do so by way of a virgin birth. There is no shadow of conflict in the two things at all.

4) JOHN L. McKENZIE

In his *A Theology of the Old Testament,* McKenzie makes some very remarkable statements. First, he says that there is an inconsistency between the fact that the Old Testament prohibited images of God, and yet used many anthropomorphisms, speaking of God with human traits.[322] He sees a further problem in the location of God symbolically where the Ark reposed. But, he adds, the Old Testament "neither sought nor achieved theoretical consistency."

We comment: The Ten Commandments prohibit images of God, but images are one thing (people prone to idolatry might adore them); anthropomorphisms are another. In the latter, we speak of God as having anger, as coming to see the tower of Babel, etc. These are just ways adapted to the human understanding of a primitive people, ways of trying to make divine realities clear to them. There is no possibility of adoring anthropomorphisms. Even today we have difficulty expressing the concept contained in the anger of God. He has no emotions, being a pure spirit. The phrase means that He disapproves of something, and will act, will punish, as a man in anger would do.

Next, Yahweh has no image, but His presence is thought to be specially at hand over the Ark of the Covenant. There is no problem. A spirit is present wherever he *acts,* for a spirit does not occupy space as we do. So all this means is that where the Ark was, God was specially pleased to act. So there is no conflict with being imageless.

McKenzie also has a misunderstanding about words of Ezekiel. He contrasts the proverb then current (18:2) about the fathers eating sour grapes, and the children's teeth being on edge, with the response of Ezekiel that each is responsible only for his own sins.[323] McKenzie thinks the response of Ezekiel is "unrealistic." We all are in a way involved in collective guilt; he says, "We do suffer for the sins of others."

McKenzie misses a distinction. Ezekiel denies that God *directly punishes* a son for his father's sins, or vice versa. He would not deny that there are *indirect results* of the sins of one on the other. First there is an objective moral order and the unity of the Communion of Saints such that when one does well, it is beneficial to all; when one sins, the others are not punished, but just lack the added benefit they might have had. Secondly, there is no such thing as a victimless crime. If a man is depraved in character, that has repercussions in society in general, at least by way of bad instead of good example. Peer pressure in example is very powerful. Or in a family, the bad ways of a parent may give bad example to the children. Some children react away from copying such behavior; others do copy it. But in no case are these things a *direct* punishment (Ezekiel rejected that) even though they are an *indirect effect* or consequence, not a penalty.

McKenzie is also disturbed about the fact that the book of Jonas implies God's compassion for the Assyrians, noted for terrorism. He thinks that this runs counter to the belief in God's election of Israel and the covenant.[323]

We comment: It is true that in the eyes of the Jews, and others too, the Assyrians were the worst of people because of deliberate terrorism in war. But there is no clash between the teaching of Jonas and the covenant. Jonas shows that since God takes care of even Assyrians, He must love *all* men. But the covenant shows a *special favor* over and above this general love. So there is no conflict at all.

There is another problem: McKenzie thinks that Amos, Micheas and Jeremias foretold the destruction of the temple, while the prophet Haggai pleaded for collection of funds to build a temple.[324] He wonders if we could speak of the same prophetic spirit in all these prophets.

Strange unperceptiveness! The first three prophets he lists foretold the coming destruction of the temple as a punishment for sin. After the punishment and the exile were over, God wanted the temple rebuilt. No clash at all.

Still another worry,[325] says McKenzie, appears from the fact that *Ezechiel* 26:7-14 promised Nebuchadnezzar victory over Tyre. He or a scribe had to retract this later (*Ezechiel* 29:17-20).

But the victory did come, as even the *New American Bible* admits in a note on *Ezechiel* 29:18: "The fulfillment of Ezekiel's prophecy against Tyre (chapters 26-28) was a thirteen-year siege of the city by Nebuchadnezzar (587-574 B.C.). Tyre seems to have been taken, but its resources were exhausted and the booty was small. Therefore Ezekiel now prophesies that Nebuchadnezzar will collect his wages as God's instrument in the punishment of Tyre by plundering Egypt."[326]

As to the fact that *Ezechiel* 29:18 says flatly, "neither he [the king] nor his army received any wages from Tyre"—this is just familiar Semitic exaggeration. It was small, but there was some booty, as the NAB said. (Some think Tyre gave tribute instead of surrender).

Critics rather generally agree, says McKenzie, that *Amos* 9:8-15 are an addition made to the original collection of words of Amos. He thinks this quite likely, "especially since 9b is a direct contradiction of 9a."[327]

In the NAB verse 9 reads, "For see, I have given the command to sift the house of Israel among all the nations, as one sifts with a sieve, letting no pebble fall to the ground." Verse 10 adds: "By the sword shall all sinners among my people die." *Jerome Biblical Commentary* says about verse 9: "An ambiguous verse, it is difficult to know whether it is a threat or a promise." If it is ambiguous, one can hardly claim a plain contradiction as McKenzie does! The verse probably means a threat of exile in which all sinners will be punished, but a remnant (a persistent Old Testament theme) that a few faithful ones left over will not go into exile—or they will go, but finally be restored.

We take one more example from McKenzie. He thinks that Isaiah in Chapters 36 and 37 sounds like the false prophets at the royal court in the ninth century who said all was well. Neither Isaiah nor the false prophets rebuke the sins of kings and people. Isaiah just promises deliverance. "The verification of this oracle by the events presents a historical problem which biblical theology cannot solve."[328]

Chapters 36-37 of Isaiah tell of the threat to Jerusalem by Sennacherib of Assyria in 701 B.C. McKenzie wonders why there is only a promise of deliverance, and no threats against Hezekiah. The answer is so easy. That king had made great religious reforms and was a devout king. We find his reforms described in detail in *2 Chronicles* 29-31. The start of Chapter 37 of Isaiah tells how Hezekiah put on sackcloth, and prayed when he learned of the threat. So the Old Testament depicts him as receiving the reward due to his piety. Even Assyrian inscriptions agree substantially that Sennacherib did not capture Jerusalem—though those texts love to boast—but was satisfied instead with a tribute (*2 Kings* 18:13-16).

5) THE FACTUALITY OF THE INFANCY GOSPELS

Here we are not tying the discussion to any one writer, since so many are inclined to question, in varying degrees, the factual character of *Matt.* 1-2 and *Luke* 1-2.[330] However, the material belongs in Appendix III, since, with only one exception, we can find the needed answers rather easily.

Basic to the discussion is the question of the genre of these chapters. Many think it is midrash—others do not. But there is much disagreement on how to define the genre of midrash.[331] There is a tendency to think midrash is a rather loose genre, with a core of history, but with developments and additions made on the basis of the Old Testament. However, to say the genre of the Infancy Gospels is midrash is not the same as to say they contain no historical facts; again, authors differ.

So we will review the chief specific claims against factuality of these chapters.

First, it has been remarked that in Matthew the angel speaks to Joseph; in Luke, the angel speaks to Mary. Of course, if we can fit together the two accounts—and we will do that—there is no real problem. Each Gospel, probably drawing on different sources, reports part of the events.

Second, some say the accounts cannot be reconciled since in Luke, it seems that the Holy Family has residence in Bethlehem. *Luke* 2:11 speaks of the Magi as entering the *house,* whereas in Matthew, Jesus is born in a stable. However, the difficulty is only apparent. After Jesus was born in the stable, it is not at all possible to think Joseph would continue to stay there during the early days of the life of Jesus. No, most naturally, he would find a house as soon as possible. So the Magi found them there. The fact that Herod ordered a slaughter of infants up to two years of age clearly implies that some time had elapsed.

More basic is the question of fitting together the accounts of Matthew and Luke as a whole. First there are some basic facts that are found in both: Jesus was born in Bethlehem, in the reign of Herod, of Mary, a virgin engaged to Joseph who was of the house of David. An angel announces His coming birth, which is to be through the Holy Spirit. The name Jesus is imposed before His birth, and He is identified as Savior; The

Holy Family finally settles in Nazareth.

The center of the problem is about the fact that Luke makes no mention of a visit of Magi, or a flight into Egypt, followed by a return to Nazareth. Matthew on the other hand does have these events, but does not mention a presentation in the Temple, or a "census." *Luke* 2:39 says: "And when they had completed all these things according to the law of the Lord, they returned to Galilee, to their town of Nazareth." So Luke goes directly from the presentation in the temple to a return to Nazareth.

First, we notice that Luke and Matthew probably had different sources. Second, Luke does not say "right away" or any such thing. Further, it is widely thought that Luke may telescope two events, e.g., some think there were two council meetings in Jerusalem. Joseph Fitzmyer, speaking of Acts, says "many of Luke's accounts are known to be telescoped résumés."[332] We admit such a possibility readily. So there is no problem in admitting that Luke, for his own reasons, or because of the nature of his sources, may have telescoped events here, i.e., may have decided not to mention the flight into Egypt.

However, it is not difficult to see the sequence of events, combining the accounts of both Matthew and Luke: Mary and Joseph come from Nazareth to Bethlehem for the enrollment. They find no place suitable for the birth of Jesus, and hence, temporarily go to a stable. However, as soon as possible, naturally, Joseph would find a house to use. It is there that the Magi find them. However, some time has already elapsed since the birth of Jesus, during which He is circumcised on the eighth day, and presented in the temple. Some time after that, the Magi arrive, and are warned in a dream to go back by another way. Joseph is warned to flee to Egypt and he does so; later he returns to Nazareth. So there is no difficulty in finding a way to fit the events together.

The only considerable difficulty is about the "census" at the time of the birth of Jesus. No record is found outside the Gospel of a census at the time supposed for the birth of Jesus, which is commonly dated about 6-4 B.C. The suggestion is even made that the mention of the census is only a "literary device" to connect Jesus to Bethlehem, city of David.

But there really is a solution, found in some remarkable new research by E. L. Martin, in *The Birth of Christ Recalculated.*[333] It has received very favorable comments and reviews from Classicists, Biblical archeologists, and astronomers. For example, *Greece and Rome, The Journal of the Classical Association* (Oxford University Press, April, 1981) said, "New light has been thrown on the date of the nativity.... Martin tackles the problems convincingly." Professor Jack Finegan, noted writer on biblical archaeology, said, "Your arguments are very persuasive." The *Los Angeles Times* of Dec. 10, 1980 reported, "at least 10 planetariums in the United States, Germany and Greece are revising their shows this Christmas season to correspond with the dating theories of Ernest Martin.... Scores of others are considering a shift." Among these is the noted Griffith Observatory.

Astronomers are especially interested because the whole question of the date of the birth of Christ turns on an astronomical point. Flavius Josephus, the ancient Jewish historian, reports that Herod died soon after a lunar eclipse.[334] Of course, astronomers can tell us when such eclipses would be seen in Palestine around the time of the birth of Christ. They give us these dates: March 23, 5 B.C.; Sept. 15, 5 B.C.; March 13, 4 B.C.; and Jan. 10, 1 B.C. Calculations of the birth of Christ have usually been based on the eclipses of 5 and 4 B.C. Martin, however, shows by multiple arguments that the eclipse in question must have been on Jan. 10, 1 B.C.[335] One reason is that the events Josephus says came between the eclipse and the Passover (also mentioned by Josephus) simply could not fit within the days available on the eclipses of March 13, 4 B.C. and March 23, 5 B.C. Other grave difficulties rule out Sept. 15, 5 B.C. But the eclipse of January 10, 1 B.C. fits readily and accords with several other facts, which we will now enumerate.

But first, we follow up: If it was the eclipse of 1 B.C., then the difficulty about the census vanishes. For we know that there was an enrollment—Luke's *apographe* is broad enough to cover that easily—to take an oath of allegiance to Augustus before he received the prestigious title of Father of his Country in 2 B.C. A Greek inscription has been found in Paphlagonia (N. Asia Minor) which tells us that in 3 B.C. all the people in the land took an oath of loyalty to Augustus.[336] Further, the Armenian historian Moses of Khorene reports that in 3 B.C. such an oath was taken there.[337] Also, the 4th century A.D. historian Orosius reports that in 3 B.C. "all the peoples of the great nations took oath in this one name of Caesar."[338] So the lost "census" has been found, and turns out to be a different kind of enrollment, independently attested by several ancient sources, as taking place in 3 B.C. Jesus then would have been born in 3 B.C.

Tertullian in his *Adversus Iudaeos* also tells us that Jesus was born in the 41st year of the empire of Augustus.[339] Some have been puzzled over this method of dating. But there were several ways of dating the power of Augustus. Tertullian seems to date it from 43 B.C., the time when Augustus, along with Anthony and Lepidus, received supreme power by a special grant as the Second Triumvirate. This is a less usual way of counting, but it gives us the right date, 3 B.C. We can see Tertullian means that year because in the same passage he adds that Augustus had power 28 years after the death of Cleopatra, who died in 30 B.C., which would give 2 B.C. as the birth of Jesus. Further, Tertullian says Augustus lived 15 years after the birth of Christ. Augustus died in 14 A.D. So, if Tertullian subtracted 15 from 14 A.D. (neglecting the fact that there would have been two years 1—B.C. and A.D.), he would reach 2 B.C. So we get 3 or 2 B.C. as the date of the birth of Christ.

Also, Classicists have had great difficulty with the events of an obscure decade, 6 B.C. to 4 A.D.[340] The chief problem is that we know Augustus received his 15th acclamation for a major victory, achieved by one of his generals, around this time. If we pick 4 B.C. for the War of Varus in Palestine, which came after the death of Herod, we cannot find a victory to warrant the acclamation, which came in 1 A.D. But if we make the birth of Christ 3 B.C., then the war would be running at about the needed time, and finished in 1 A.D.

One difficulty remains: Luke says Quirinius was in charge at the time of the enrollment. But we know the governors of Judea during the period, and Quirinius is not listed. Again a very plausible solution is at hand. Quirinius fought an important war against the Homonadenses, in Cilicla, north of Judea. The probable date of the war is about 5-3 B.C.[341] Now if the regular governor of Judea, whoever he may have been, knew in advance—everyone did—of the coming great honor to Augustus, probably early in 2 B.C., he would likely have gone to Rome for obvious reasons. He would then need someone to mind the store for him in his absence. Quirinius, a very competent general, was at hand, as we have seen. So he conducted the enrollment for the regular governor. Luke uses the word *hegemoneuein* for the role of Quirinius. It is not the noun *governor,* but a verb which can mean *to be governor,* but is really a generic word, capable of meaning a different kind of leader. And of course, Quirinius, in our reconstruction, would really be acting governor.

The honor to Augustus was a very great one. Suetonius tells us that there was first "a universal movement" by the people to give him that honor.[342] The people sent a deputation to him at Antium. He at first declined. Then a crowd again offered it to him outside the Theater. Finally the Senate followed suit. Augustus was deeply moved: "Weeping, Augustus answered—I quote his exact words as I did for Messala—Fathers of the Senate, finally I have achieved my highest amibition."[343] With a "universal movement" of the people starting the process, the coming of the honor must have been widely known long in advance, long enough to induce the governor of Judaea to come to Rome to take part in the festivities, and, of course, to strengthen his own situation.

The honor was so great that the next emperor, Tiberius, declined to accept it.[344]

We see, then, that there are no real obstacles to taking the Infancy Gospels as at least basically factual.

We can recall too the way Vatican II spoke of these events, as we explained in Appendix II. 2.c.

We recall too the evidence we saw in Chapter 9 of new research showing the meticulous care Luke took in translating Hebrew documents. The evidence we summarized runs the same in these two chapters of Luke as it does in the rest of his Gospel.[345]

NOTES

CHAPTER ONE: For Openers

   1. Cf. Francis J. Lescoe, *Existentialism With or Without God,* Alba House, N.Y. 1974, pp. 25-76, esp. 55-62.

   2. In KM 19 & 211.

   3. DS 3009.

CHAPTER TWO: Causes of Teenage Doubt

   4. T.V. Moore, *Heroic Sanctity and Insanity,* Grune & Stratton, N.Y., 1959, p. 102.

CHAPTER THREE: Wonders Never Cease

5. KM 5.
6. KM 197.
7. KM 199, italics added.
8. Ibid.
9. Alexis Carrel, *Man the Unknown*, N.Y., 1935 and *The Voyage to Lourdes*, N.Y., 1950.
10. Cf. P. Flood, ed., *New Problems in Medical Ethics*, Newman, Westminster, 1953, pp. 187-88.
11. Cf. Ruth Cranston, *The Miracle of Lourdes*, McGraw-Hill, N.Y. 1955, and Dr. F. de Grandmaison de Bruno, *Twenty Cures at Lourdes Medically Discussed*, tr. H. Bevenotand & L. Izard, Herder, St. Louis, 1912; and L. Elliott, "A Pilgrimage to Lourdes," in *Reader's Digest*, April, 1982, pp. 65-69.
12. Cf. Bruno Sammaciccia, *The Eucharistic Miracle of Lanciano, Italy*, tr. A. E. Burakowski, F. J. Kuba, Stella Maris Books, Ft. Worth, Tex.
13. Cf. *A Handbook on Guadalupe*, Marytown Press, Kenosha, Wis. 1974; *The Dark Virgin* (a documentary anthology) ed. C. Demarest and C. Taylor, Cole Taylor Inc., Freeport, Maine and N.Y., 1956; Simone Watson, *Cult of Our Lady of Guadalupe, a Historical Study*, Liturgical Press, Collegeville and Hildebrando Garya, *Madonna of the Americas*, Liturgical Press, Collegeville, 1954. For the latest studies, see Jody B. Smith, *The Image of Guadalupe*, Doubleday, N.Y., 1983.

CHAPTER FOUR: Is There a God?

14. Data from *Scientific American*, special issue of Sept., 1979, esp. pp. 45-46, 55 and 113.
15. J. W. O'Malley, "Reform, Historical Consciousness, and Vatican II's Aggiornamento" in *Theological Studies* 32 (1971) pp. 597-98, cf. Avery Dulles, *The Survival of Dogma*, Doubleday, N.Y., 1971, p. 164.

CHAPTER SIX: The Heart of the Matter

16. Herodotus 7.152.
17. Thucydides 1.22.
18. Ibid 5.26.
19. Cf. M. L. W. Laistner, *The Greater Roman Historians*, in *Sather Classical Lectures* 21, University of California, Berkeley, 1947, p. 129.

20. Tacitus, Annals 1.7.
21. Cf. Wm. G. Most, "A Biblical Theology of Redemption in a Covenant Framework" in Catholic Biblical Quarterly, 29 (1967) pp. 1-19.
22. The movement began with G. Vico in his *Scienza nuova* (3d ed. 1744), which held that to truly know something it is necessary in some sense to have made it. Prominent others were J. G. Droysen, W. Dilthey, E. Troeltsch, Fr. Meinecke. Especially influential has been R. G. Collingwood, in *The Idea of History,* Oxford, 1946. Historicism found an ally in the notions of Paul Ricoeur and H. G. Gadamer, who held that when a text leaves the author's hands, it has an independent life of its own, and can take on many meanings—what the original author meant cannot be determined, and it is not necessary to know. Existentialism (cf. note 1 above) also contributed.
23. Cf. R. J. Trotter, "The Truth, the Whole Truth and Nothing But . . ." in *Science News* 108 (1975) pp. 269-70.
24. Cf. *Jerome Biblical Commentary,* ed. R. Brown, J. Fitzmyer, R. Murphy, Prentice Hall, Englewood Cliffs, N.J., 1968, II, pp. 580-85.
25. Papyrus is a tall aquatic sedge, from which a type of paper was made in ancient times. In the dry climate of Egypt, papyri could keep for centuries, even without care.

CHAPTER SEVEN: A Faithful Text?

26. Plato, *Laws* 676-77; *Phaedrus* 247-49; *Phaedo* 79ff and 114.
26a. Aristotle, *On the Heavens,* 1.10.279 B.
27. Diogenes Laertius, *Zeno,* 7.137.
28. Aristotle, *Politics* 7.10.
29. Mircea Eliade, *The Myth of the Eternal Return,* tr. W. R. Trask, Princeton, 1954, pp. 104, 143.
30. Ibid. p. 143.
31. St. Ignatius of Antioch, *Epistle to Rome* 1-6.
32. For more on genres, see Appendix II.6 below. For more on Form Criticism see Appendix II.7.
33. N. Perrin, *Rediscovering the Teaching of Jesus,* Harper & Row, N.Y., 1967. p. 16.

CHAPTER EIGHT: What Did The Author Want To Say?

34. Cf. *Jerome Biblical Commentary* II, p. 783.

35. Citations from these are given in W. Most, *The Consciousness of Christ,* Christendom, Front Royal, 1980, p. 227, n. 58.
36. For a fuller treatment, cf. *The Consciousness of Christ,* pp. 174-228, 8-38.

CHAPTER NINE: Greek Doctor Writes Gospel!

37. Wm. G. Most, "Did St. Luke Imitate the Septuagint?" in *Journal for Study of the New Testament,* July, 1982, pp. 30-41.
38. Cf. Klaus Beyer, *Semitische Syntax im Neuen Testament,* Göttingen, 1962. I. p. 67.
39. My version.
40. On Targums cf. Chapter 22 below.
41. M. Johannessohn, "Das biblische *kai egeneto* und seine Geschichte" in *Zeitschrift für Vergleichenden Sprachforschung,* 1926, pp. 161-212, esp. 184-85, 190.

CHAPTER TEN: Did Luke Write Luke?

42. Irenaeus 5.33.4.
43. Eusebius 3.39. Martin Hengel, Professor of New Testament at the University of Tubingen, highly respected even by liberals. *Studies in the Gospel of Mark* (tr. John Bowden, Fortress, Philadelphia, 1985) insistently defends the tradition that Mark followed St. Peter and wrote from his preaching.
44. The word "sayings" in Greek is *logia.* It can have the narrow meaning of *sayings,* but can also be broadened to mean *deeds* as well, in view of Hebrew *dabar* and Aramaic *milah,* both of which have both meanings.
45. Some claim that the plays on words in Greek, which are not possible in Hebrew, prove that it could not be a translation. But the Latin translator of *Hosea* 13:14 injected a familiar play on words not found in the Hebrew original or in the Greek Septuagint: *Ero mors tua, O mors, morsus tuus inferne.*
46. Eusebius 3.39.
47. Cited in Patrick Henry, *New Directions in New Testament Study,* Westminster, Phila. 1979, pp. 33-34. Cf. also Hengel, *op. cit.,* pp. 47-50.
48. For the Latin text, cf. Kurt Aland, *Synopsis Quattuor Evangeliorum,* ed. 8, Württemburg, Stuttgart, 1967, pp. 532-33.
49. St. Irenaeus, *Adv. Haereses* 3.1.1.
50. Letter to Florinus, cited in Eusebius 5.20.

51. Tertullian, *Against Marcion* 4.2.2.
52. Origen, *Comm. in Matth.* 1 and *Homilia in Lucam* 1—in Aland, pp. 540-41.
53. Martin Hengel, *op. cit.,* p. 107, defends the reliability of Papias.
54. Much information can be conveyed in a single interior touch, called a locution. See note 86 below.
55. St. Augustine, *City of God* 22.5.
56. Cited in Eusebius 4.3.1-2.
57. Clement I, *Epist. to Corinth* 5.

CHAPTER ELEVEN: A Man Sent From God
58. Tacitus, *Annals* 15.44.

CHAPTER TWELVE: Signs and Wonders To Believe
59. Tacitus, *Histories* 4.81.
60. Cf. note 11 above, esp. the item from *Reader's Digest.*
61. Cf. St. Thomas, *De potentia* 6.5. ad 5; *In Ioannem* 9.3.8; and *Summa* II-II. 178.2 and St. Augustine, *City of God* 10.16. If some, like the court magicians of Pharaoh (Exodus 7:8-13) are permitted to do marvels (probably by the powers natural to fallen angels) a means is also provided to tell the true from the false, as we see in the passage cited in Exodus.
62. This passage refers to the Jews of the day who were all called to the Messianic kingdom (Church), yet few were entering.

CHAPTER THIRTEEN: The Inner Circle
63. *Many* probably reflects Hebrew *rabbim, the all who are many.* Aramaic *sgy'yn* at least at times had the same sense: cf. E. C. Maloney, *Semitic Interference in Marcan Syntax,* Scholars Press, Chico, CA, 1981 p. 140. St. Paul commonly uses *polloi* (which means *many* in secular Greek, and is used in *Matt.* 22:14) to mean *all,* like *rabbim,* e.g., *Rom.* 5:19. St. Matthew obviously could do the same.

CHAPTER FOURTEEN: Behold, I Am With You All Days
64. Some doubt that 1 and 2 Timothy are by St. Paul himself. They are specially moved by the degree of organization in the Church already to be seen there. It sounds like circular reasoning: this cannot be authentic, because it reflects conditions for which we have no evidence at the time. So they deny the evi-

dence to get no evidence. Actually, the earliest letter of St. Paul, *1 Thess.* 5:12 says: "Respect those who labor among you and *are over you* in the Lord and admonish you in the Lord." So Paul had established authorities that early (about 51 A.D.). In fact, *Acts* 14:23 reports that on his very first missionary trip—before coming to Thessalonica—Paul had established authorities: "When they had appointed elders [presbyters] for them in every church, with prayer and fasting, they committed them to the Lord." Still earlier, *Acts* 11:30 reports that Christians at Antioch sent a collection to Jerusalem because of a famine: "they did so, sending it to the elders [presbyters] by the hand of Barnabas and Saul." Even the New American Bible, in its note on *Acts* 14:23 says: "In each church they installed presbyters: the communities are given their own religious leaders. Seemingly (cf. *Jas.* 5:14) a part of their task is the performance of liturgical rites, especially the liturgy of the Eucharist; cf. *Acts* 2:42." In *Titus* 1:5 Paul just tells Titus to do what he has been doing since *Acts* 14:23, and *1 Thess.* 5:12. Further, the first Epistle of Pope Clement I, written around 95 A.D., says in 44: "Our apostles knew through our Lord Jesus Christ that there would be strife over the name of bishop. For this reason, having received complete foreknowledge, they established those we have mentioned, and afterwards added a provision that if they should fall asleep [die] other approved men should succeed in their ministry." (We must note that the terms *presbyter* and *episcopos* at an early period were more generic than specific: it takes time in any field to get a general agreement to limit the meaning of words that in themselves can be used more broadly. Thus in *Acts* 20:17 and 28 we find the two terms used interchangeably.)

65. I Clement 5.
66. Ibid. 44.
67. W. F. Albright and C. S. Mann, *Matthew,* in *Anchor Bible* 26, Doubleday, Garden City, 1971. p. 198.
68. The first General Council, held at Nicea, 325 A.D., defined the divinity of Jesus.

CHAPTER FIFTEEN: Küngly Objections
69. Hans Küng, *On Being a Christian,* tr. E. Quinn, Doubleday, Garden City, 1976, pp. 285, 286. Italics his.
70. Ibid. p. 285.

71. Ibid. p. 199.
72. Ibid. p. 278.
73. Ibid. p. 323.
74. Ibid. p. 285.
75. Ibid. p. 323.
76. Richard McBrien, *Catholicism,* Winston Press, Minneapolis, 1981, pp. 570-77.
77. Ibid. pp. 598-99 (no. 3) and p. 770 (no. 18).
78. DS 1601, cf. 1864.
79. DS 1703.
80. DS 1752, 1773.
81. DS 1716 and 1801.
82. Cf. McBrien, Op. Cit., pp. 526-32.
83. Wm. G. Most, *The Consciousness of Christ,* Christendom Press, Front Royal, 1980.
84. Ibid. Chapter 7.
85. Cf. A. Poulain, *The Graces of Interior Prayer,* tr. L. L. Yorke Smith, London, Routledge and Kegan Paul, 1950, pp. 304-06.
86. St. Teresa of Avila, *Life* 25, 1 Obras Completas, B.A.C. Madrid, 1951. 1. p. 741: When God speaks in this way, "the soul has no remedy, even though it displeases me, I have to listen, and to pay such full attention to understand that which God wishes us to understand that it makes no difference if we want or not. For He who can do everything wills that we under-stand, and we have to do what He wills." Cf. also *Interior Castle* 6.3.7. *Obras,* II, p. 426: "These words do not pass from the memory after a very long time—and some of them never pass."
87. Certitude can fade (ibid): "When time has passed since heard, and the workings and the certainty it had that it was God has passed, doubt can come."
88. Pierre Teilhard de Chardin, *The Future of Man,* tr. N. Denny, Harper & Row, 1964, p. 184.
89. Arthur B. Klyber, C.SS.R., *Once a Jew,* Chicago, 1973.
90. Cf. *Acts* 20:17 and 28.

CHAPTER SIXTEEN: You Are Peter

91. Clement I, *Epistle to Corinth* 5.
92. Ibid. 1.
93. Ibid. 59.
94. St. Irenaeus, *Against Heresies* 3.3.2.

95. DB 112. Cf. DS 3056.

96. Cf. J. Harduin, *Conciliorum Collectio*, Paris, 1715 II. 305-06.

97. Cf. J. D. Mansi, *Collectio Conciliorum* 11. 665, Florent. et Venet. 1759-98.

98. DS 861.

99. DS 1307.

100. DS 3073-75.

101. Vatican II, *On the Church* § 25.

102. Ibid.

103. Ibid. 22.

104. Albright & Mann, *Anchor Bible* 26, pp. 195.

105. Ibid. p. 196.

106. Ibid. pp. 197-98.

107. R. Brown, *John, Anchor Bible*, Doubleday, Garden City, 1970, 26 A p. 1113.

CHAPTER SEVENTEEN: Protestant Scripture Alone

108. Vatican II, *On Ecumenism* § 11.

109. Ibid. § 6.

110. Vatican II, *On Divine Revelation* § 10.

111. G. Maier, *The End of the Historical-Critical Method*, tr. E. W. Leverenz & R. F. Norden, Concordia, St. Louis, 1974, pp. 61 & 63.

112. On authenticity, see note 64 above.

CHAPTER EIGHTEEN: Faith Alone: Luther's Discovery?

113. Letter 501, to Melanchthon, Aug. 1, 1521, in *Luther's Correspondence*. Lutheran Publication Society, Phila. 1918. II, p. 50.

114. DS 1561-65.

115. *Interpreter's Dictionary of the Bible, Supplementary Volume,* Abingdon, Nashville, 1976, p. 333.

116. Vatican II, *On Divine Revelation* § 5. Inner quote from Vatican I: DS 3008.

117. DS 374, 377.

118. The Church has condemned the idea of total corruption: DS 1568. St. Paul speaks of us as a "new creation," which, being totally remade, can hardly be totally corrupt: *2 Cor.* 5:17; *Gal.* 6:15. Cf. also *Eph.* 2:10; 2:15; 4:24; *Col.* 3:10; *2 Cor.* 4:6.

119. *Brief Statement of the Doctrinal Position of the Missouri Synod.* Concordia, St. Louis, 1932, § 14.

120. Cf. J. Hardon, *Christianity in Conflict,* Newman, Westminster, 1959, p. 194.

CHAPTER NINETEEN: Help for Ecumenism: On Predestination
121. DS 397.
122. DS 623.
123. For a full presentation, Cf. W. Most, *New Answers to Old Questions,* St. Paul Publications, London, 1971.
124. St. Augustine, *Epistle* 194.5.19.
125. Cf. Shepherd of Hermas, Mandates 4.3.1-6. Even so, grace is very powerful, and natural fear at the end might bring a change of heart, so one should not despair.
126. Cf. note 119 above.

CHAPTER TWENTY: Do We Contribute To Our Salvation?
127. Cf. W. Most, *New Answers,* pp. 335-88.
128. DS 1554.
129. Cf. note 124 above.

CHAPTER TWENTY-ONE: False Angels
130. St. John of the Cross, *Ascent of Mt. Carmel* 3.39.1, tr. E. Allison Peers, Newman, Westminster, 1946, I. p. 321.
131. St. Francis de Sales, *Introduction to the Devout Life* 4.13.
132. St. Teresa, *Interior Castle* 6.9, Peers II. p. 319.
133. "Speak to each one individually after the manner of God . . . not all wounds are healed by the same remedy."—*Introduction to the Devout Life,* Part I, chap. 3.

CHAPTER TWENTY-TWO: The Jewish Messiah
134. Vatican II, *On Non Christian Religions* § 4, alluding to *Eph.* 2:14-16.
135. Cited in A. Klyber, *Once a Jew,* pp. 144-45.
136. DS 3009.
137. Translated from the Hebrew by the author.
138. Vatican II, *On the Church* § 55.
139. Translated by the author from the Aramaic text in: Alejandro Diez Macho, *Targum Palestiniense Neofiti,* Consejo Superior de Investigaciones Clentificas, Madrid, 1968. Cf. Genesis Rabbah 20.5, which also sees this verse as Messianic.
140. Jerome Biblical Commentary II, p. 359. Cf. also W. Most, *Free*

From All Error, Prow Press, Libertyville, 1985, pp. 25-30.

141. Samson H. Levey, *The Messiah: An Aramaic Interpretation,* Hebrew Union College, Cincinnati, 1974, p. 13. Cf. p. 135.

142. Cf. for example, St. Justin Martyr, *Dialogue with Trypho* 100; St. Irenaeus, *Against Heresies* 3.22.4; 5.19.1 and *Proof of the Apostolic Preaching* 33; Tertullian, *On the Flesh of Christ* 17; St. Cyril of Jerusalem, *Catechesis* 12.15; St. Jerome, *Epistle* 22.21; St. Ambrose, *Epistle* 63.33, and *On Luke* 4.7; St. Augustine, *Sermon on Psalm* 149.2 and *On the Christian Combat* 22.24 and *On Holy Virginity* 6.6.

143. RSV as modified by the author.

144. Translated by the author from *Targum Neofiti.*

145. Levey p. 8.

146. Levey pp. 108, 114.

147. Levey p. 46.

148. Levey p. 45.

149. I. W. Slotki, *Soncino Books of the Bible: Isaiah,* Soncino Press, London, 1957, p. 44.

150. Levey p. 45.

151. J. F. Stenning, *The Targum of Isaiah,* Oxford, 1949, p. 32.

152. In *Hamlet.* By the Queen, Act III, Scene II.

153. Cf. Levey, pp. 45-46.

154. Translated by the author from the Aramaic in: Brian Walton, *Biblia Sacra Polyglotta,* Akademische Druck, Graz, Austria, 1964, III.

155. Cf. Levey p. 67.

156. Cf. Levey p. 152, n. 10.

157. H. J. Schoeps, *Paul,* tr. H. Knight, Westminster, Phila. 1961, p. 129.

158. Translated by the author from *Biblia Sacra Polyglotta.*

159. Cf. Levey p. 93.

160. Ibid.

CHAPTER TWENTY-THREE: Other Sheep I Have

161. DS 2866.

162. DS 3871 citing DS 3821.

163. Vatican II, *On the Church* § 16.

164. Vatican II, *On Missions* § 7.

165. DS 802.

166. Clement I, *Epistle* 7.

167. St. Justin Martyr, *Apology* I. 46.
168. St. Justin Martyr, *Apology* II. 10.
169. Hermas, *Shepherd,* Visions 2.4.1.
170. Pseudo-Clement, *Epistle* 14.2.
171. St. Irenaeus, *Against Heresies*, 4.28.2.
172. Clement of Alexandria, *Stromata* 7.17.
173. Origen, *Against Celsus* 4.7.
174. Arnobius, *Against the Nations* 2.63.
175. Hegemonius, *Acta Archelai* 28.
176. St. Augustine, *Epistle* 102.12.
177. St. Augustine, *Retractations* 1.13.3.
178. St. Gregory Nazianzus, *Orations* 18.6.
179. St. John Chrystostom, *On Romans*, Book II, Homily 5.
180. Pope St. Leo the Great, *Sermo* 23.4.
181. Pope St. Gregory the Great, *Homilies on Ezechiel* 2.3.16.
182. Vatican II, *On the Church* §49.

CHAPTER TWENTY-FOUR: We Have Here No Lasting City

183. Tacitus, *Annals* 6.6.
184. Plato, *Theatetus* 176-77.
185. My version.
186. St. Augustine, *Confessions* 1.1.
187. St. Cyril of Jerusalem, *Catechesis* 17.14.
188. DS 1000.
189. St. Thomas, *Summa*, Suppl. 92.1.
190. J. P. Arendzen, *Purgatory and Heaven*, TAN, Rockford, Ill.,
    1972, p. 60.
191. In *Lay Witness*, April, 1982, p. 7.

APPENDIX ONE: Claims of Errors in Church Teaching

192. In my book, *Free From All Error* (Prow, Libertyville, 1985), I
     give many answers to claims of error and show how the new
     techniques can be used to answer charges of error.
193. *On the Church* §25.
194. Ibid.
195. *Humani generis*, Aug. 12, 1950. AAS 42.568. DS 3885.
196. *On the Church* §25.
197. Cf. Jeffrey A. Mirus, "Galileo and the Magisterium, a Second
     Look" in *Faith and Reason* 3.2 (summer 1977) pp. 65-69, esp.
     p. 68.

198. Cf. L. Geymonat, *Galileo Galilei: A Biography and Inquiry,* tr. S. Drake, McGraw-Hill, p. 114 citing the Favaro edition of the works of Galileo, XIII, p. 182.

199. Cf. Kevin G. Long, "Galileo on Trial," in *Faith and Reason* 6.3 (Fall, 1980) pp. 230-37, esp. p. 235.

200. DS 870-75.

201. Introduction to DS 870.

202. Cited from *The Pope Speaks,* Fall, 1955, pp. 210-11. Cf. AAS 47.678.

203. *Contra errores Graecorum* 36. § 1125.

204. DS 1442.

205. Cf. Wilfrid Harrington, *The New Guide to Reading and Studying The Bible,* Enlarged Edition, Glazier, Wilmington, 1984, p. 32. Cf. also the claims of Avery Dulles in Appendix I. 8.

206. John E. Steinmueller, *The Sword of the Spirit,* Stella Maris, Waco, 1977, pp. 7-8, note 1.

207. EB 549.

208. The fact that Jesus compared Himself to Jonah (*Matt.* 12:39-41; 16:4; *Lk.* 11:29-32) does not prove Jonah is historical. Anyone can allude to a literary work, even *Alice in Wonderland,* to illustrate a point, without taking it as real. St. Paul did similarly in *1 Cor.* 10:4. *Jude* 9 does the same.

209. EB 161.

210. EB 558.

211. DS 3898.

212. It is interesting to compare the interpretation given by Pope John Paul II, in his audience of Nov. 7, 1979 of the formation of Eve. It is a way of expressing the unity of the human race: "Perhaps, therefore, the analogy of sleep indicates here not so much a passing from consciousness to subconsciousness, as a specific return to non-being . . . that is, to the moment preceding the creation, in order that, through God's creative initiative, solitary 'man' may emerge from it again in his double unity as male and female." Cited from: John Paul II, *Original Unity of Man and Woman, Catechesis on the Book of Genesis,* St. Paul Editions, Boston, 1981.

213. EB 551, citing EB 109-111.

214. *On Revelations* § 12.

215. Cf. note 206 above.

216. *Jerome Biblical Commentary,* Ed. R. Brown, J. Fitzmyer, R.

Murphy, Prentice-Hall, Englewood Cliffs, N.J., 1968, I. p. 5.

217. EB 181.

218. John A. T. Robinson, *Redating the New Testament*, Westminster, Philadelphia, 1976.

219. J. Munck, *The Acts of the Apostles, Anchor Bible*, Doubleday, Garden City, 1967, pp. xlvii-liv. For answers to other objections against *Acts of Apostles*, see *Free From All Error*, Chapter 18.

220. For a detailed critique of Form Criticism, cf. W. Most, *The Consciousness of Christ*, Christendom, Front Royal, 1980, pp. 174-228.

221. In CBQ 26.3, 1964, pp. 300.

222. Cf. the *1964 Instruction*, in CBQ 26.3 (July 1964) p. 302: "The fact that the Evangelists report the words and deeds of the Lord in different sequences, and that they express His statements in varied ways, not verbatim, but in keeping the sense does not at all affect the truth of the narrative."

223. Cf. M. de Tuya, *Evangelio de San Mateo*, in *Biblia Comentada*, 3d ed. Biblioteca de Autores Cristianos, Madrid 1977, Va, p. 173.

224. Cf. chapter 8 on genre.

225. Joseph Fitzmyer, *A Christological Catechism. New Testament Answers*, Paulist, N.Y., 1982, p. 128.

226. Translated from Latin text in *Catholic Biblical Quarterly*, 26 (1964) p. 302.

227. *Ibid*. p. 301. Italics added.

228. Cf. John P. Meier, *Matthew*, Glazier, Wilmington, 1985. p. 180. Most of the early Fathers also thought Peter understood divinity.

229. Cf. W. F. Albright and C. S. Mann, *Matthew*, in *Anchor Bible*, Doubleday, N.Y., 1971, pp. 194-95, 181.

230. In "The Figure of Peter in Matthew's Gospel as a Theological Problem" in *Journal of Biblical Literature* 98 (1979) p. 74, note 25.

231. They do not attribute ignorance to a Divine Person; they mean an item did not register on the human mind of Jesus.

232. Cf. W. Most, *The Consciousness of Christ*, Christendom, Front Royal, , 1980. pp. 134-45.

233. *Op. cit*. p. 46.

234. CBQ 26.3, pp. 301. (Italics mine).

235. Cf. note 87 above and *Interior Castle* 6.3; and *Life* 25, and Poulain, p. 305.
236. R. H. Fuller, *The Foundations of New Testament Christology*, Charles Scribner's Sons, N.Y., 1965, p. 109.
237. W. Wrede, *The Messianic Secret*, tr. J. C. C. Greig, James Clarke Co., Cambridge and London, 1971, 3rd ed. pp. 50-51. For further analysis of Wrede, see W. Most, *The Consciousness of Christ*, pp. 202-05.
238. Reginald Fuller, "What is Happening in New Testament Studies" in *St. Luke's Journal of Theology* 23 (1980) p. 96.
239. Cf. Most, *The Consciousness of Christ*, p. 223 and notes 57 & 58.
240. *1964 Instruction*, in CBQ 26.3, p. 300.
241. DS 3009. See also Chapter 22 above, where we saw many concrete cases of clear Old Testament prophecies.
242. In *Catholic Theological Society of America Proceedings*, 1976, pp. 240-41.
243. On Ecumenism § 11.
244. Vatican II is obviously right on this point: just as individuals need to worship God for their own needs, so too the state. But some would add this: since this is a positive (not a negative) obligation, there is opening for an excuse. They think history has shown the state incapable of deciding what religion God wills.
245. "Was Vatican II Evolutionary?" in *Theological Studies* 36 (1975) pp. 493-502.
246. *Church in Modern World* §37.
247. Cf. "Guide to Renewal for Teachers of Sacred Doctrine" in *Catholic Educational Review*, April 1968, pp. 217-29.
248. *On Religious Freedom* §2.
249. Cf. DS 3866.
250. Gregory XVI, *Mirari vos*, Aug. 15, 1832.
251. DS 2866. Cf. Vatican II, On the Church §16.
252. Tertullian, *To Scapula* 2.2.
253. Pius IX, *Quanta cura*, Dec. 8, 1864.
254. Pius XII, *Ci riesce*, Dec. 6, 1953.
255. For a survey of the scientific evidence against evolution, cf. R. L. Wysong, *The Creation-Evolution Controversy*, Inquiry Press, Midland, Mich., 1976, and Gary E. Parker, *Creation, The Facts of Life*. C. L. P. Publishers, San Diego, 1980 (Parker is a

former evolutionist).

256. *De Genesi ad Litteram* 6.12.20.

257. *Homily on Genesis* 22.21. Cf. note 212 above.

258. DS 3896.

259. Cf. "Is Man a Subtle Accident?" in *Newsweek*, Nov. 3, 1980, pp. 95-96, and "Research News: Evolutionary Theory Under Fire" in *Science*, Nov. 21, 1980, pp. 883-87.

APPENDIX TWO: Charges of Errors In Scripture

260. *Divino afflante Spiritu*, Sept. 30, 1943: EB 538, citing Vatican I: EB 77.

261. *On Revelation* §11.

262. In *Divino afflante Spiritu*, EB 538.

263. Cf. e.g., W. G. Hale and C. D. Buck, *A Latin Grammar*, Mentzer, Bush, N.Y., 1903, §522; and B. L. Gildersleeve and G. Lodge, *Latin Grammar*, Heath. Boston, 1894. §627.

264. A note by Vatican II on the *Constitution on Divine Revelation* §11 refers to: S. Augustine, *De Gen. ad litt.* 2.9.20; *Epist.* 82.3; St. Thomas Aquinas *De veritate* 12.2; Council of Trent, Sess. 4: DS 1501; Leo XIII, *Providentissimus Deus*: EB 121, 124.126-27; Pius XII, *Divino afflante Spiritu*: EB 539.

265. EB 539, citing St. Thomas, *Summa* 1.70.1 ad 3.

266. Cf. K. A. Kitchen, *Ancient Orient and Old Testament*, InterVarsity Press, Downers Grove, Ill. 1966, pp. 76-77.

267. EB 123.

268. Cf. J. Finegan, *Light from the Ancient Past*, Princeton Univ. Press, 2nd. ed., 1969, p. 228.

269. Cf. H. W. Smyth, *A Greek Grammar for Colleges*, American Book Co., N.Y., 1920 § 1689; and Thucydides 7.86; and Aeschines 3.178. J. Jeremias in *New Testament Theology* (Scribner's Sons, N.Y., 1971 tr. J. Bowden) p. 47 notes: "Semitic languages have no regular word for 'time' in a durative sense, and use the phrase 'the days of x' as an expedient for describing a life-time, reign, or period of activity."

270. Cf. De Tuya, *op. cit.* p. 441.

271. W. Most, *The Consciousness of Christ*, pp. 39-92.

272. In *Catholic Biblical Quarterly* 44 (1982) pp. 451, note 17 and p. 452.

273. Bruce Vawter, *Job & Jonah. Questioning the Hidden God*, Paulist, N.Y., 1983, p. 11.

274. Wilfrid Harrington, *The New Guide to Reading and Studying the Bible*, Glazier, Wilmington, 1984, revised edition, pp. 23-24.

275. Cf. W. Most, *Free From All Error*, Prow, Libertyville, 1985, pp. 1-7.

276. Paul VI, *Mysterium Fidei*, AAS 57 (1965) p. 758.

277. *Mysterium Ecclesiae*, Doctrinal Congregation, June 24, 1973, translation from NC News Service Documentary.

278. Vatican II, *On Ecumenism* §6.

279. Cf. also J. A. Sanders, *Canon and Community*, Philadelphia, Fortress, 1984 and B. Childs, *Introduction to the Old Testament as Scripture*, Philadelphia, Fortress, 1979.

280. T. J. Keegan, *Interpreting the Bible. A Popular Introduction to Biblical Hermeneutics*, Paulist, N.Y., 1985, pp. 133-34.

281. Ibid. p. 133.

282. Vatican II, Constitution on Revelation §10, italics added.

283. Ibid. §12.

284. Ibid. §12.

285. DS 1752. Pius XII, *Divino afflante Spiritu (Enchiridion Biblicum* §565) says the Church has fixed the sense of few texts. But the analogy of faith (note 284 above) guides us to true sense of many more.

286. Keegan, *op. cit.*, p. 133.

287. Ibid. p. 83.

288. Cf. Paul Ricoeur, *Interpretation Theory: Discourse and the Surplus of Meaning*. Texas Univ. Press, Fort Worth, 1976 and H. G. Gadamer, *Truth and Meaning*, Seabury, N.Y., 1975.

289. For a lucid presentation of Existentialism, see Francis J. Lescoe, *Existentialism With or Without God*, Alba House, Staten Island, 1973.

290. On Bultmann and Heidegger, cf. W. Most, *The Consciousness of Christ*, Christendom, Front Royal, 1980, esp. pp. 175-228.

291. Cf. for example John C. Gibson, *Job*, Westminster, Philadelphia, 1985, pp. 120-21.

292. Cf. *Jerome Biblical Commentary* II, p. 765. §167.

293. *On Revelation* §12.

294. *Dictionnaire de théologie cathlique*, Paris, 1903-64, I.114.

295. I. p. 277.

296. *Interpreter's Dictionary of the Bible*, II p. 689.

297. M. Dahood, *Psalms III* in *Anchor Bible*, 1970, p. xlii and n. 33.

298. Ibid. I. p. xxxvi; II. xxvi-xxvii; III. xli-lii.

299. Marvin H. Pope, *Job*, in *Anchor Bible*, 1965, p. 102.

300. In *Anchor Bible, Psalms* I. p. 38. Dahood there renders *Ps*. 6.6 thus: "For no one in Death remembers you, in Sheol, who praises you?"

301. Wilfrid Harrington, *Mark*, Glazier, Wilmington, 1979, p. 47.

302. Ibid. p. 48.

303. *On Revelation* §12.

304. *On the Church* §56.

305. Vatican II, *On the Church* §57.

306. *On the Church* §58.

307. For examples of those who do and do not reject the historicity of the incident, see note 330 below.

308. *National Catholic Reporter*, Dec. 2, 1977, p. 10.

309. *Catholic Biblical Quarterly* 40.1 (1978) p. 120.

310. Cf. note 238 above.

311. *On the Church* §§56-57.

312. There was no need to reaffirm, since the virginity of Mary has always been taught, beginning with the oldest creeds, e.g., DS 10-30.

313. For further developments on Mary's knowledge, Cf. Wm. G. Most "Maria conservabat omnia verba haec" in *Miles Immaculatae* (Rome) 21 (1985) pp. 135-69. Reprinted in *Faith & Reason* 11 (1985) pp. 51-76.

314. Levey, *op. cit.* p. 108.

315. Leo I, *Sermo de Nativitate*.

316. Leo XIII, *Parta humano generi*, Sept. 8, 1901.

317. Paul VI, Allocution of Dec. 28, 1966, in *Insegnamenti di Paolo VI* IV, pp. 678, 79, Vatican Press, 1966.

APPENDIX THREE: Areas of Contention

318. *Jerome Biblical Commentary*, II, p. 218.

319. Cf. Free From All Error, pp. 87-91.

320. In KM, p. 11.

321. W. Pannenberg, *Jesus-God and Man*. tr. L. Wilkins and D. Priebe, Westminster, Philadelphia. 2nd ed. 1977, p. 143.

322. John L. McKenzie, *A Theology of the Old Testament*, Image Books, N.Y., 1976, p. 52.

323. Ibid. pp. 120-21.

324. Ibid. p. 128.

324a. Ibid. p. 126.

325. Ibid. p. 104

326. Josephus, *Against Apion* 1.156; *Antiquities* 10.228.

327. McKenzie, pp. 105-06.

328. Ibid. p. 112.

329. Cf. J. B. Pritchard, ed., *Ancient Near Eastern Texts*, rev. ed. Princeton, 1955, p. 287ff.

330. Examples of those who strongly defend historicity: J. Daniélou, *The Infancy Narratives* tr. R. Sheed, Herder & Herder N.Y., 1968; R. Laurentin, *The Truth of Christmas Beyond the Myths,* Desclée et Desclée de Brouwer, Paris, 1982. Examples of those who in varied degrees reject historicity: J. Fitzmyer, *Luke,* in *Anchor Bible* 28, Doubleday, N.Y., 1981 esp. pp. 304-21, 392-93, 402-05; F. C. Grant, "Matthew, Gospel of" in *Interpreter's Dictionary of the Bible*, Abingdon, N.Y., 1962, III. p. 306.

331. Cf. A. Wright, *The Literary Genre Midrash,* Alba House, Staten Island, 1967.

332. In *Jerome Biblical Commentary* II, p. 237 §4.

333. E. L. Martin, *The Birth of Christ Recalculated*, 2nd ed. Foundation for Biblical Research, Pasadena, 1980.

334. Flavius Josephus, *Antiquities*, 17.§§167-92.

335. Martin, *op. cit.*, pp. 28-56.

336. Cited in N. Lewis, & M Reinhold, *Roman Civilization. Sourcebook* II, Harper & Row, N.Y., 1966, pp. 34-35.

337. Cited in Martin, *op. cit.*, p. 96.

338. Paulus Orosius, *Histories* 6.22 and 7.2-3.

339. Tertullian, *Adversus Iudaeos* 8. In *Adversus Marcionem* 4.19 Tertullian says census (plural) were taken by governor Saturninus. Many scholars date Saturninus 9-6 BC. chiefly because they cannot figure out the dating in *Adversus Iudaeos*, cited above. But Martin, *op. cit.*, p. 74, dates him 4-2 B.C. appealing (on p. 100) to Josephus, *Antiquities* 17.57.

340. Cf. R. Syme, "The Crisis of 2 B.C.," in *Verlag der Bayerischen Akademie der Wissenschaften*, Beck, Munich, 1974. Other problems solved by Martin's solution are explained in Martin, pp. 76-86.

341. Dates proposed by Fitzmyer, *op. cit.*, p. 402, in accord with the views of Martin, pp. 100-102.

342. Suetonius, *Augustus* §58.

343. Ibid.

344. Tacitus, *Annals*, 1.72.
345. Specific data on the locations in which Luke uses the special Semitism, *apodotic kai*, can be seen in W. Most, "Did St. Luke Imitate the Septuagint" in *Journal For The Study of the New Testament*" 15, 1982. pp. 30-41.

If you have enjoyed this book, consider making your next selection from among the following . . .

Revelations of St. Bridget. St. Bridget of Sweden........ 2.00
Magnificent Prayers. St. Bridget of Sweden............. 1.00
The Happiness of Heaven. Fr. J. Boudreau 6.00
St. Catherine Labouré of the Mirac. Medal. Dirvin...... 7.50
The Glories of Mary. (pocket ed.). St. Alphonsus Liguori 5.00
The Love of Mary. Roberto......................... 5.00
Begone Satan. Fr. Vogl............................. 1.50
The Prophets and Our Times. Fr. R. G. Culleton 6.00
St. Therese, The Little Flower. John Beevers 3.50
The Life & Glories of St. Joseph. Edward Thompson.... 9.00
An Explanation of the Baltimore Catechism. Fr. Kinkead 8.50
Humility of Heart. Fr. Cajetan da Bergamo 4.50
The Curé D'Ars. Abbé Francis Trochu 15.00
Love, Peace, and Joy. St. Gertrude/Prévot 4.00
St. Joseph of Copertino. Fr. Angelo Pastrovicchi........ 3.00
Mary, The Second Eve. Cardinal Newman 1.50
The Faith of Our Fathers. Cardinal Gibbons 9.00
Manual of Practical Devotion to St. Joseph. Fr. Patrignani 9.00
The Wonder of Guadalupe. Francis Johnston........... 5.00
The Way of Divine Love. Sister Josefa Menendez.......12.00
The Way of Divine Love. (pocket, unabr.). Menendez... 5.00
St. Pius V—His Life, Times, Miracles. Anderson 2.00
Mystical City of God—Abridged. Ven. Mary of Agreda..15.00
Beyond Space—A Book About the Angels. Fr. Parente .. 4.50
Dialogue of St. Catherine of Siena. Algar Thorold 6.00
Catholic Answer to Jehovah's Witnesses. D'Angelo...... 5.50
Twelve Promises of the Sacred Heart (100 cards). 4.00
St. Aloysius Gonzaga. Fr. Meschler................... 7.00
Evidence of Satan in the Modern World. Cristiani........5.50
Child's Bible History. Most Rev. F. J. Knecht 2.00
Bible History of the Old & New Testaments. Schuster ... 8.00
Apologetics. Msgr. Paul Glenn 6.00
Baltimore Catechism No. 3. Fr. Kinkead............. 5.00
The Blessed Eucharist. Fr. Michael Mueller............ 9.00
Thirty Favorite Novenas. Booklet.................... .40
Devotion to the Infant Jesus of Prague. Booklet .... .40
Fundamentals of Catholic Dogma. Ludwig Ott 15.00
The Agony of Jesus. Padre Pio 1.00
St. Gertrude the Great. Anonymous .... .75
St. Joan of Arc. John Beevers 6.00
Life of the Blessed Virgin Mary. Anne C. Emmerich 10.00
Convert's Catechism of Catholic Doctrine. Fr. Geiermann 2.00

Prices guaranteed through June 30, 1987.

Prices guaranteed through June 30, 1987.

At your bookdealer or direct from the publisher.

Prices guaranteed through June 30, 1987.